SCOTLAND IN MODERN TIMES

SCOTLAND IN MODERN TIMES

An outline of Economic and Social
Development since the Union of 1707

W. H. MARWICK

Lecturer in Economic History at the University of Edinburgh

FRANK CASS AND CO. LTD.
1964

First published in 1964 by
Frank Cass and Co. Ltd., 10 Woburn Walk,
London, W.C. 1

Printed by Thomas Nelson (Printers) Ltd.
London and Edinburgh

CONTENTS

LIST OF MAPS

FOREWORD

THIS work does not profess to be a definitive history of the economic and social development of modern Scotland, nor does it attempt an analysis in terms of modern economic theory. Its aim is the humbler one of providing a mainly factual outline of the results of study, mainly within the last forty years, of these aspects of Scottish history, hitherto scattered through many specialised books and articles. It makes no pretension to original research, except on minor points relating to the Victorian era, additional to those contained in my earlier book. Acknowledgments are made of the main sources used, both in the bibliography and in notes at appropriate points ; a complete list would involve the citation of innumerable articles, reports, newspapers, etc. Much of the material is based on lectures delivered for the past ten years to the Second Ordinary Course in Economic History in the University of Edinburgh.

I also wish to thank the Geography Department of the University of Edinburgh for their kind help in the preparation of the maps.

W. H. MARWICK.

UNIVERSITY OF EDINBURGH,
September 1962.

INTRODUCTION

SCOTLAND remained largely medieval in economic structure until the mid-eighteenth century. The Reformation, however important in the religious and ecclesiastical spheres, had little effect on the way of life of the ordinary man, and such changes as occurred in land ownership seem to have made little difference in agricultural conditions. The Union of Crowns affected trade and industry, on the whole prejudicially, but these were too undeveloped to affect the general economic situation vitally.

The economic consequences of the Union of Parliaments have been and still are hotly debated. To some it appears to have given Scotland every virtue but sobriety (which we are told no Act of Parliament can ensure) ; to others it is the root of all evils from which Scotland has subsequently suffered. Certainly it now seems that the picture of utter backwardness in 1707, which the literary charm of H. G. Graham has impressed on many readers, is exaggerated, and depends too much on the partial evidence of propagandist documents and travellers' tales, often superficial and supercilious. Recent research, pioneered by Dr. G. P. Insh, and developed by such scholars as Professor Nef, Mr. Lythe and the Clows, indicates distinct commercial and industrial advance in the seventeenth century, even if mainly of what Mumford calls the eotechnic phase. The undoubtedly parlous condition of the early eighteenth century must in large part be attributed not to original primitiveness but to the setback given by the years of famine in the 1690's, the " disaster of Darien " and the Williamite War.

The " Industrial Revolution " is a term now rather blown upon, but seems appropriate to Scotland, in so far as that, within a generation or two, the way of life of the mass of the people was transformed. Concrete illustration may be found in a comparison of the two Statistical Accounts of the 1790's and the 1840's, or in such works as " Senex's " rambling reminiscences of Old Glasgow, and Cockburn's more polished presentation of the transition in Edinburgh.

The Union of 1707 was due primarily to considerations of international politics, and was accepted by the majority of Scots mainly as a means of securing the Protestant Succession. The Jacobite revolts were in effect sideshows in the Second Hundred Years' War with France. At the same time, it is true that economic issues were prominent in the terms of the Treaty, and some of its provisions were designed to mollify Scottish sentiment by concessions in trade and finance. The residue of the Equivalent, at last fructifying in the fostering of industry by the Board of Trustees, and the opening of the American colonies to Scottish merchants, were the two chief tangible gains.

The relationship between English and Scottish economic development has indeed been close, but not a one-way traffic. Even in the seventeenth century, despite friction and barriers raised by growing Mercantilism, trade across the Border expanded. Scots had already trodden the Johnsonian road to seek advancement in London ; Nigel had many exemplars in real life in his quest of fortune in the south. William Paterson in his connexion with the foundation of the Bank of England (even if Clapham deems his share exaggerated) and of the " Company of Scotland " is but the most conspicuous ; while John Holland the London merchant played an important part in founding the Bank of Scotland, and the ubiquitous Bevis Bulmer was active in mining enterprise in both countries. In the eighteenth century James Watt developed his inventions in Birmingham with the financial assistance of Boulton ; he trained Murdoch ; Macadam's roadmaking and Rennie's bridge-building were largely in the south. Conversely Roebuck of Sheffield was a pioneer of chemicals and founder of Carron ; the Welsh Robert Owen made New Lanark the model factory of the new textiles, while Galloway Scots developed the cotton trade in Manchester ; the Houldsworths of Derbyshire origin transferred their energies from cotton to ironfounding, and eventually for generations to the ironworks at Coltness, one-time seat of Sir James Steuart, doyen of Scots economists.

The Scots have always combined ardent nationalism with cosmopolitanism, and the reciprocal influence of Scotland and other countries has been of economic and cultural value to both. France in the Middle Ages, the Netherlands in the Age of Transition, Germany in the nineteenth century, the Scandinavian countries intermittently throughout, probably U.S.A. in the twentieth, are outstanding. From the economic standpoint the influence of the Dutch is noteworthy, in natural science, agriculture, architecture and law. Veere in Walcheren, once a great trading centre, now shrunk to a fishing port, still preserves tangible evidence of the Scots Staple in the Conciergerie of the Scots merchants. Leiden, once the haunt of the Scottish wandering scholar and Covenanting refugee, inspired the emergence of the Scottish Universities as pioneers of medical education.

Conversely, Scots have influenced economic development in Europe and other continents. The financial devices of John Law had for good or ill great effects on eighteenth-century France. Sweden received considerable immigration of Scots, industrialists and merchants as well as soldiers. Veterans of Gustav Adolf's campaigns have left Scots names among the landed gentry ; Carnegie, Chalmers, Dickson and Keiller are names witnessing to the Scottish share in the growth of Göteborg as a port and industrial centre. The participation of Scots in the expansion of the British Empire will be amply illustrated in the subsequent narrative.

1

Scotland in the Early Eighteenth Century

(c. 1707-60)

THE economic development of Scotland in the early eighteenth century must be viewed in the framework of the Second Hundred Years' War, the Jacobite revolts, the growth of constitutional monarchy and of the Cabinet system. The contrast between the backwardness and impoverishment of this period and the rapid growth in prosperity during the latter half of the century has perhaps been over-emphasised. Its history has also been written overmuch in terms of the effects, for good or ill, of the Treaty of Union, to the neglect of other factors which would probably have operated irrespective of the Union or of its particular terms. These however must not be ignored, and it may be convenient at the outset to make some reference to them.

Of a total of 25 clauses in the Treaty, 16 are wholly or partly economic in content ; clauses IV and V relate specifically to freedom of trade and shipping ; clauses VI to XIV deal, some in great detail, with matters of taxation ; clause XV establishes the Equivalent ; clauses XVII and XVIII refer to currency, weights and measures ; clauses XX and XXI preserve vested interests in heritable offices and rights of royal burghs. In summary, the main economic provisions are : the establishment of a customs union, the opening of the colonial trade ; the unification of coinage and (with temporary exceptions) of taxation, and the awarding of financial compensation in the form of the Equivalent.

Whatever may have been the intention of these provisions, the short-term effects, as far as they can be segregated, may be

summarised as follows : The burden of taxation, even with
the temporary alleviation, was severe, in view of the impoverished state of Scotland relatively to England. The total Scots
revenue, mainly farmed out, at the time of the Union attained
a total of only £160,000 ; the taxes on salt and malt were
particularly resented, and felt as detrimental to important
Scottish enterprises. An impetus was given to smuggling, and
the " Free Trader ", as evidenced by Scott's novels, became a
popular hero. Competition by English producers was injuri-
ous to the woollen manufacture, which the Restoration
Government had sought to foster. On the credit side may be
put the opening of the American market, though it was not
till a generation later that this became of real importance ;
the effect, also somewhat belated, of the administration of the
Equivalent by the Board of Trustees ; and more immediately
the extension of the cattle trade, with its reaction on agricultural improvement. The economic case for the Union was
elaborated a century later (1800) by J. Bruce in the Report
which he prepared for the Government with a view to com-
mending to the Irish the similarly incorporating Union of
1801. Adam Smith's verdict, in his occasional references in
the *Wealth of Nations* is generally favourable to the Union, and
his dictum on the social consequences is of interest : " The
middling and inferior ranks gained a complete deliverance
from the power of an aristocracy which had always before
oppressed them."

The land in more than one sense was still the basis of
livelihood for the great majority of Scots, and therefore first
claims attention. Probably no feature of Scottish life has been
more neglected by writers on the seventeenth century than the
land system, and it is therefore a matter of inference how
long-standing were the conditions of which we find evidence
in the early eighteenth. A variety of estate papers and other
contemporary records have been preserved, and studied by
modern scholars, but generalisations based on these random
samples must be tentative. The most accessible have happily
a wide geographical distribution, including Aberdeenshire,
Kincardineshire, Perthshire, Dumfriesshire and Berwickshire.

The general picture is one of backwardness. The technical
improvements of the late medieval period, especially on the

monastic lands, described by Franklin,[1] seem not to have survived the change to lay ownership. At least two-thirds of the area was uncultivated, much of it marsh or bog. As in early days the hill slopes were preferred to low-lying ground. The famine years of the 1690's were virtually repeated more briefly in 1709, 1740 and 1782. Technique in particular remained primitive : the wooden plough, the harrow " more fit to raise laughter than soil " (Lord Kames), the flail for threshing, the stone quern for grinding, the lack of wheeled transport and of " made " roads, on which it could move. The distribution of the land into infield and outfield, of unknown antiquity, still prevailed, and Adam Smith gives the classic definition of it : " the lands which were kept constantly well manured and in good condition seldom exceeded a third or a fourth part of the whole farm. The rest were never manured, but a certain portion was in turn cultivated and exhausted." [2] The common crops were bere (barley) and oats ; draining, fallowing and rotation of crops were little practised.

The geography of much of Scotland made it suited to stock rearing rather than to arable farming ; hence the infrequency of the " village community ". The rearing of flocks and herds was handicapped by the lack of feeding stuffs, so that killing and salting in autumn for winter use was common. Pigeons provided almost the only all-the-year fresh meat ; the keeping of a dovecot was a privilege cherished by the laird and resented by his tenants ; some specimens have survived the mansions to which they were attached. The destruction of the primeval forest and the inclemency of the climate left much of Scotland without timber ; but the oft-quoted gibes of Sir Anthony Weldon, that " Judas would have been hard put to it to find a tree whereon to hang himself ", and of Dr. Johnson, that " a tree in Scotland was as rare as a horse in Venice " are obvious exaggerations, as, e.g., the resort of English ironmasters to Scotland for wood smelting bears out. The attention devoted to flower and herb gardens by some of the landed class, as described by Elizabeth Haldane,[3] shows that the skill

[1] T. B. Franklin, *A History of Scottish Farming* (1952), ch. iii–vi
[2] A. Smith, *Wealth of Nations*, Book I, ch. xl
[3] E. S. Haldane, *The Scotland of our Fathers* (1933), ch. xii, pt. iii

in horticulture, which made the Scots gardener famous and sought after, was already manifest.

As regards conditions of land tenure, the feuing system, whose late fifteenth-century origin on the church lands has been demonstrated by Professor Hannay, had apparently proceeded apace, and was instrumental in the alienation of much of the Common Lands of the burghs. Entail (" tailzie ") was also frequent, and restricted the effective development of the resources of the soil and the sale of unprofitable ground, thus increasing liability to debt. Investment in mortgage (" wadset ") was a favourite use of surplus capital. The obscure institution of " kindly tenancy "—probably customary tenure, originally for the kin of the proprietor—was virtually obsolete. The collection of teinds in kind, in accordance with the settlement of 1633, was an encumbrance, especially in view of the diffusion of ownership of teinds.[1]

The enigma of " enclosure " remains unsolved. It is generally accepted that there was no such widespread movement as in sixteenth- and eighteenth-century England, and that the word was commonly used in Scotland in the purely physical sense of the erection of a fence or dyke. The Highland Clearances have a character of their own, and will be dealt with later. Controversy centres on the meaning and effects of the two Acts of 1695 " anent Runrig and Commonties ". The former (No. 36, July 5) " statutes and ordains that wherever lands of different heritors ly runrig it shall be leisom [lawful] to either party to apply to the Sheriffs . . . [or other magistrates] . . . to the effect that these lands may be divided according to their respective interests ". We have inadequate evidence as to how far this provision for voluntary rearrangement by judicial process was adopted in practice, but probably it was not much utilised till later in the next century.

More dubious is the bearing of Act 69, (July 17) which " for preventing the discords that arise about Commonties, and for the more easie and expedient deciding thereof, statutes and ordains that all Commonties, except [those] of the King and Royal Burrowes [Burghs], may be divided at the instance of any having interest, by summonds raised against all persons

[1] A. Birnie, *Short History of the Scottish Teinds* ; A. A. Cormack, *Teinds and Agriculture* (1930)

concerned before the Lords of Session, who are hereby empowered . . . to value and divide the same according to the value of the rights and interests of the several parties concerned ". Some writers, like Mr. Thomas Johnston,[1] have assumed that " commonties " implies land in common ownership of a local community, and inferred that the Act empowered the break-up of communal life and property for sectional interests ; others interpret " commontie " in the narrower sense of land held in joint possession by several owners, and hold that whatever " common ownership " by the tribe or clan may have existed in antiquity, had long given way to feudal institutions. The one known example of resistance to " enclosures " is that mentioned incidentally by Wodrow, when about 1725 rioting occurred in parts of Galloway, where the boom in cattle rearing had led to monopolisation of land for pasture.[2]

Relevant to this aspect of land holding is the point already made regarding the infrequency of the " nucleated village " in Scotland. More common is the scattered hamlet or " toun " or clachan, the inhabitants of a parish being separated, e.g. some in the kirk-toun (Kirkton) around the church ; others beside the mill in the mill-toun (Milton), and so forth ; a layout still visible in some rural areas, and traceable in such now urbanised localities as Duddingston. Joint tenants commonly lived in a group, sometimes in the Mains or home farm.

" Tack " is the usual Scots term for a lease, and might refer to fishing or milling rights as well as to agricultural holdings. The term " tacksman ", especially in the Highlands, is sometimes reserved for the superior class of tenants, often kin to the proprietor, who acted as middlemen, or (more euphemistically) as organisers, and sublet their holdings. Varied terms are found for these sub-tenants, partly related to the size of their holdings ; we hear of husbandmen, with an average of some fifty acres, and " possessors " as well as of landless labourers, sometimes styled " grassmen ". Obscure names for units of land—ploughland, merkland, horseland, gavoch—are cited ; it has been plausibly argued that in some cases the acreage was

---

[1] T. Johnston, *History of the Working Classes in Scotland* (1920), 159–60
[2] Johnston, op. cit. 183–8

" nominal " rather than actual, being calculated with regard to average output rather than to extent. The frequency of joint tenancy is notable. Payment was still commonly in kind, a " ferme " especially of oatmeal and malt, with occasional " kains " of e.g. poultry, and an incidental " girsome " or heriot on succeeding to a lease. Dues might be exacted for the upkeep of a school or a smithy. " Mail " was the term for a money rent. Certain services might be obligatory—master work on the home farm, peat casting, carriage of goods, ditching and dyking.[1]

The livelihood of the masses was insecure because of recurrent shortages of food supply ; as in the Orient in recent times, a local deficit was not readily made good by a surplus elsewhere. While the starvation of the Famine years did not recur, there were several failures of harvest, most acute in 1740 and 1782. There was however in some areas normally a surplus for sale in the towns or for export, especially in East Lothian, Aberdeenshire and the Orkneys. At the best of times the food supply was probably in many cases inadequate by nutritional standards, but as the recent survey of the Scottish dietary by Dr. Passmore[2] has brought out, it was of better dietetic quality than that of the nineteenth-century urban worker, especially after the general introduction of the kailyard and the potato, consisting largely of oats, milk, eggs and broth.

Scottish housing standards were traditionally low. The dwellings in the rural areas were flimsy structures—clay hovels or " biggins ", comprising at best a " but and ben " with stone or mud floors, thatched roofs, often lacking chimneys, and providing accommodation under one roof for beasts and men. Burns's birthplace at Alloway, one of the few survivors, is a relatively late and superior example. In the towns there was much congestion and discomfort shared by all classes in the high tenements. Lack of sanitation and drainage were notorious, despite civic efforts at improvement ; " gardyloo " is but the most familiar example of primitive crudity in the disposal of refuse. Diseases such as ague, rheumatism and smallpox were endemic ; epidemics of typhus and other

---

[1] An example is given in *The Court Book of the Barony of Urie 1604–1747* (ed. A. G. Barron, 1892).

[2] A. H. Kitchin and R. Passmore, *The Scotsman's Food* (1949)

pestilences recurred. The high rate of infantile mortality in all social classes is noted by Adam Smith and illustrated by the fate of the families of Queen Anne and of the Traills, the Orkney merchants whose papers have been edited by Dr. Hugh Marwick ; [1] probably those fit to survive were of corresponding vigour.

Church records reveal the failure of Church discipline to maintain high moral standards ; Burns is again but the best-known example of those who incurred ecclesiastical penalties, even if his achievements as a Don Juan have been exaggerated by Catherine Carswell and James Barke. The saturnalia of Penny Weddings, rural fairs, perhaps even sometimes of public celebrations of the sacrament, provide further evidence of sub-Christian customs ; chapbooks such as those of Dugal Graham were as popular reading as Holy Writ ; in the witch cult, as interpreted by Dr. Margaret Murray, practices of primitive paganism survived.

With considerable exceptions, the Scottish economy may thus be described as self-contained and localised. Much production of food, clothing and shelter was still " domestic ", in the more literal sense of being effected by members of the family within the home. There was however an increased resort to travelling weavers and tailors, who might spend some days or weeks in a household ; while packmen carried wares through the countryside.

Weekly markets in the burghs for the disposal of agricultural produce from the locality continued, and a wide range of commodities was made available at the annual fairs, originally a monopoly of the royal burghs, but extended in various cases by charter to local lords. In some cases specialised fairs were held at different dates. Some evolved into cattle trysts, and in agricultural centres developed the feeing fair, at which farm workers hired themselves for a year. As their commercial importance declined, the period of the Fair, as in Glasgow and Kirkwall, became rather one of entertainment, and the name survives for Glasgow trades holiday.

Over against this static presentation of early eighteenth-century economy must be set the commercial and financial developments which ultimately undermined it. Among the

[1] H. Marwick, *Merchant Lairds of Long Ago*, pt. i (1936)

former, priority must be given to the cattle trade, especially with England. It had already, in Archibald Haldane's [1] words, passed through " the transition from lawless cattle driving to lawful cattle droving ", and though hampered by English jealousy and restrictions attained some volume in the late seventeenth century ; 30,000 head are said to have been sold to England in 1705. It was however thanks largely to the Union that it grew in prosperity, and became " a marked feature of the Scottish economy ". Incidentally, the uncertainties of the Union negotiations enabled a leading dealer, Patrick Heron (1672–1761) to make a coup by cornering stock and selling them at a high price when import prohibition was removed, and so to establish the fortunes of a noted Galloway family. His grandson Patrick (1737–1803) was a partner in the Ayr Bank, and as Whig candidate for the county had the support of Burns. The historic Rob Roy was originally a cattle dealer.

The trade, so admirably depicted by Dr. Haldane in his *Drove Roads*,[1] came to centre in the great " trysts ", held first at Crieff, established in 1672, afterwards at Falkirk, founded about 1710, where in 1792 some 60,000 Highland cattle changed hands. Cattle were driven on foot, sometimes through fords, from their original breeding-places in the Highlands and Islands and Galloway, and from the tryst to England, where many were at first fattened in East Anglia before going to the London markets ; Scots beef was favoured by naval contractors. With improved home feeding, beasts were fattened at home, and prices rose high, especially in the Napoleonic Wars. The system survived till near the end of the nineteenth century, but droving was gradually superseded by railway transport, while cattle gave place to sheep as the chief Highland stock.

The fisheries [2] were a long-standing source of livelihood, and dried fish had for centuries been a leading Scottish export. During the seventeenth century grandiose schemes for its expansion were fostered by government, e.g. the Royal Fisheries Company (1670), described by Professor J. R. Elder ; but with little success, due partly to Dutch competition. The

---

[1] A. R. B. Haldane, *The Drove Roads of Scotland* (1952), p. 2
[2] P. F. Anson, *Scots Fisherfolk* (1950)

technique of curing was improved towards the end of the century ; the name of John Spreull, a Greenock merchant, is commemorated in that connexion as well as for his sufferings as a Covenanting prisoner on the Bass Rock, and the " Glasgow magistrate " (cured herring) became a popular delicacy. The salt long provided by evaporation of water on the Forth and Ayrshire coast proved less suited for this purpose, and the brine of Cheshire was developed about the same time. From this cause, together with the increase of taxation after the Union, the Scottish salt-making industry declined, and the fisheries were depressed. The cost of barrels and staves, usually made of imported material in England, was another handicap. This was one cause of the decline of the Fife ports during the eighteenth century. Attempts at encouragement were made by the grant of bounties from 1718 to 1829 and the establishment of semi-official bodies, the Society of Free British Fisheries (1760–72) and the British Society to Extend Fisheries (1786), which operated chiefly through the improvement of harbours. The fisheries however remained mainly the sphere of family ownership or small-scale partnerships ; women played a prominent part in making nets, preparing bait and marketing the catch. Some 3,000 to 4,000 boats [1] on the average went to sea annually, mainly in the West, though, perhaps due to a shifting of shoals, the share of the Clyde diminished. A temporary market was afforded by the West India sugar plantations ; in T. G. Snoddy's epigram, " the negroes lost their herrings when they won their freedom ".[2]

A particular branch was the whaling fleet, not strictly " fishing ". A noted company was the East Lothian and Merse Whale Fishery Company, with five vessels and 199 shares, held mainly by local landowners, which had fully half a century's career before dissolving in debt (1804). Whale fat was particularly in demand for soapmaking.

That the expansion of the market is a main cause of industrial progress is a familiar dictum of Adam Smith, and the corollary, that commercial development antecedes and fosters manufacture is also illustrated by Scots experience. Trade indeed probably declined in eastern ports, though the

[1] D. Bremner, *Industries of Scotland*, pp. 515–16.
[2] T. G. Snoddy, *Round about Greenock* (1937), p. 8

import of flax from Holland and the Baltic grew ; the old staple at Veere however fell into decay as the medieval organisation became obsolete. North Berwick had a brief heyday associated with the family of Falls, originally corn-dealers, who dabbled in herring-curing and in the whaling just mentioned ; the last of the family went bankrupt in 1788. Relations between Orkney and Norway continued, mainly in the exchange of grain for timber, while Scots settlers developed the " klippfisch " trade at Kristiansund.

The Union permitted the admission of Scots to the service of the East India Company, and the privilege of private trading allowed some to acquire the position of " nabob ", reflected in Scott's *Surgeon's Daughter*. The most eminent was perhaps James Macrae (1677–1744), Governor of Madras, who utilised his wealth in the approved style by acquiring estates in Ayrshire. Holders of East India stock include such names as those of George Dempster and Sir Laurence Dundas.

It was the trade with the American colonies, however, which " was of basic importance in Scottish economic development ".[1] The research scholar who uses this phrase adds that " its profits provided development capital "—a contribution to the obscure and debated topic of the source of investment in later industrialisation. The jealousy of the Bristol merchants, who sought in the 'twenties legal restriction on Scottish enter-prise, was at first an obstacle ; it was only in the early 'forties that the trade attained real magnitude. It was aided by a shift of the favoured route to more northerly ports, those of the Mersey and Clyde, at the expense of those of the Severn and Channel, as the former proved shorter and quicker, and during the French wars, apparently safer from privateers. Operating costs were kept low ; at first the skipper acted as supercargo, selling and buying goods in the colonies on com-mission ; but he was soon superseded by resident agents or factors, of whom Patrick Colquhoun became the best known ; some of these gained the reputation of " shrewd hard business men, veritable Shylocks." [2] At the same time they are

---

[1] D. I. Fagerstrom, *The American Revolutionary Movement in Scottish Opinion* (Ph.D. Thesis, 1951), ch. II

[2] A. M. Schlesinger, *Colonial Merchants and the American Revolution* (1917), p. 35

accused of giving excessive credits, and unduly encouraging the monoculture of tobacco.

The provision of suitable goods for export (one point on which the " Darien " Company had fallen down) stimulated the manufacture of linen, hats, ropes, leather goods and farm implements. About forty firms are said to have engaged in the trade, but much of it was concentrated in the " Big Six " or " Tobacco Lords "—the Cuninghams, Cochranes, Speirs, Glassfords, Dunlops and Buchanans and their partners.

Much the most important commodity was tobacco. Hence it was a peculiar subject of friction with the English merchants, who accused the Scots of undercutting through evasion of duties. More rigid enforcement of payment was attained. Imports to Scotland rose from ½ million lb. in 1710 to a peak of 46 million lb. in 1775 ; this constituted about 50 per cent of British imports, and 80 per cent of Scottish imports from America. A large proportion, said to have amounted in value to about a half of Scottish exports, was re-exported, especially to France, where the " Régie " of *fermiers-généraux*, who held a monopoly, made contracts with Scottish dealers, first William Alexander and Sons of Edinburgh, ruined in 1773, and subsequently Sir Robert Herries, a partner in the private bank of Sir William Forbes.

The American revolt temporarily reduced import to a minimum, ruined some of the merchants and caused others to divert their energies and capital to the nascent industries ; but apparently a rapid recovery was made after the peace settlement. Meantime small and rather unsuccessful attempts at home cultivation were made in the Borders.[1]

The import of sugar was developed by retired army officers, Colonel William McDowell and Major James Milliken, in the 1720's. Some twenty firms were engaged by 1800, among whom Connals of Glasgow were outstanding. The bulk came from Jamaica (as the Glasgow street of that name recalls), where some estates were in Scottish hands ; Burns's narrow escape from exile there is well known.[2]

[1] J. O. Mitchell, *Old Glasgow Firms* ; G. Stewart, *Curiosities of Glasgow Citizenship*
[2] L. A. G. Strong, *The Story of Sugar* ; S. G. Checkland in *Scottish Journal of Political Economy*, June 1957

Vessels for the colonial trade were at first chartered from English ports such as Whitehaven, but a stimulus was soon given to local building and owning. In 1735, 15 boats left the Clyde for Virginia, 8 for the West Indies, 10 for European and 20 for Scottish and Irish ports. The Clyde tonnage in 1772 was estimated at about 60,000.

Of the Clyde ports, Glasgow, a royal burgh since 1636, to Defoe " a most beautiful little town " on whose banks salmon were fished, and the population of which numbered 12,500, began with a quay at the Broomielaw, and raised its quota of ships from 13 to 46 in five years after the Union. It was handicapped by the shallowness of the Clyde for navigation, and sought a remedy by acquiring land at Newark, just above Greenock, where Port-Glasgow was established as a Burgh of Barony dependent on it ; here goods were transhipped into barges or dispatched by road, and the chief customs house for the Clyde was situated for a century from 1710. Greenock was developed contemporaneously through the local lairds the Shaws, who provided it with a harbour (c. 1700–10), made it a free port and gave it a charter of self-government (1751). Dumbarton on the opposite side of the Clyde, an ancient royal burgh, a trading and naval base, stood up for its privileges against these upstarts, but came to an agreement with Glasgow in 1700. In 1760 Glasgow and Greenock were reckoned together as constituting the first Scottish port ; Leith came second with 79 vessels, Irvine was a close third with 77.

An important factor in the advance of industry was governmental action. One main agency was an offspring of the Treaty of Union. The residue of the Equivalent and certain accruing revenues were designed to be expended on the promotion of industry. This was not put into effect until 1727 when, on the recommendation of the Convention of Burghs, Acts were passed to regulate the linen manufacture, and to establish a " Board of Trustees for Manufactures " to administer the sum now available (about £6,000). A first distribution was made to the herring fisheries, linen and woollen industries, while " Spinning Schools " were established. The Board existed until 1844 ; three years later remaining funds were diverted to art education.[1]

---

[1] N. Munro, *Royal Bank of Scotland* ; I. F. Dean, *Scottish Spinning Schools*

The second agency was a by-product of the Jacobite revolts. In 1716 an Annexed (or Forfeited) Estates Commission was set up to administer the estates of which participants in the '15 were dispossessed. After payment of debts the surplus was to be devoted to ecclesiastical, educational and industrial purposes. Thirteen Commissioners were appointed, at £1,000 per annum ; the seven English included Sir Richard Steele the essayist ; the six Scots, Patrick Haldane of Gleneagles, (1686–1769) noted for his chequered career as Professor of History and Provost of St. Andrews and King's solicitor, and the unpopularity which lost him a seat on the Bench (1722). His alleged liability to corruption, and obstructive litigation and disputes with the Court of Session over jurisdiction, hampered the early efforts of the Commission. In 1717 it was empowered to sell estates by auction. Several, including those of Winton and Panmure, were acquired by the York Buildings Company, originally established to supply water to the Strand area of London, and developed as a speculative enterprise by Billingsley, a solicitor. It thus became one of the greatest landowners in Scotland, but outran its capacity in attempting industrial enterprises, and was eventually relieved by an Act of 1763 which enabled forfeited estates to be bought back by heirs.

Meantime a further Act of 1752 had entrusted the estates forfeited in the '45 to a new body of Commissioners, 28 in number, unsalaried, and including the chief law officers and leading nobles. This body " brought to the task devotion and whole-heartedness " and made a " brilliant success of management ". It granted £3,000 a year for nine years to the Board of Trustees, and ultimately took over much of its responsibilities. It fostered by grants linen manufacturing, fisheries, highways and bridges, enclosing and planting. In 1784, by the Disannexing Act, the estates were restored and the Commission wound up. Its surplus funds were devoted to the building of the Register House in Edinburgh, and the construction of the Forth and Clyde Canal.[1]

A further stimulus was given by the initiative of "improving"

---

[1] A. H. Millar (ed.), *Forfeited Estate Papers* (1909) ; D. Murray, *The York Buildings Company* (1883) ; a summary of their activities is given by J. E. Handley in *Scottish Farming in the 18th Century* (1953), 236–43.

landlords. Among these, names which recur are those of Sir William Pulteney, George Dempster and Sir William Douglas. Pulteney (1729–1805), born a Johnstone of Wester-hall, Dumfriesshire, took his wife's name on marrying the heiress of the Earl of Bath (Walpole's rival) ; he left £2 million. He was a patron of Telford, a Commissioner for the Caledonian Canal, and a leader in the British Fisheries Society ; his name is commemorated in Pulteneytown, a suburb of Wick, and in that of his godson, the social reformer Dr. W. P. Alison.

Dempster (1732–1818), laird by inheritance of Dunnichen in Angus, and by purchase of Skibo in Sutherland, promoted fisheries and roadmaking, devised a process to freeze salmon for transport, was a founder of Dundee Banking Company (1763), built on his Angus estate the model village of Letham and granted it a model constitution, and was associated with Dale in the ill-starred attempt to carry on a cotton mill (Spinningdale) on his northern estate.

Sir William Douglas (1745–1809), son of a Galloway farmer, engaged in the Virginia trade, and made half a million, in part, it is said, through privateering and in trading with the Red Indians. He laid out his gains in the purchase of estates in his native shire, where he founded the burghs of Newton-Stewart and Castle-Douglas, and established cotton mills.

The Edinburgh Society for Encouraging Arts, Science, Manufactures and Agriculture, formed in imitation of one in Dublin, during its generation of existence (1735–53) raised funds by voluntary subscription, and applied them to giving premiums for industrial enterprises.

The contribution of the Scottish banking system to economic progress is generally recognised, as is that of the contemporary English country banks to industrial development there. The differences between the two systems may have been exaggerated, and certainly there has been no special study of the Scottish system by an expert economist. Its history has been written with considerable fullness of detail, but by practical bankers or by historians not specially versed in financial theory. It is at any rate clear that no Scottish bank ever attained the central and commanding position of the Bank of England, as followed almost inevitably from the loss of a separate government in 1707.

The foundation of the Bank of Scotland preceded the Union, and followed hard on that of the Bank of England, and like it represented collaboration between English and Scottish interests. The original directorate included seven Edinburgh and five London directors, among whom John Holland was most active. It received a 21 years' monopoly, was at first chiefly concerned with bill discounting, but soon issued notes and took deposits, on which it later allowed interest. It had to suspend payments temporarily in 1704. Probably because of suspicion of the Jacobite sympathies of some directors (which its historian, Dr. Charles Malcolm,[1] deems unwarranted) its monopoly was not renewed when the charter was due for revision in 1716. In 1727 the bank adopted the " optional clause ", whereby creditors were given the alternative of delaying reimbursement for six months in return for payment of interest.

Its main rival, the Royal Bank of Scotland, had a somewhat involved origin. Holders of the Scottish national debt had been guaranteed reimbursement from the Equivalent, which proved inadequate for the purpose. They meantime received debentures, and in 1719 formed the Equivalent Society to protect their claims, which in 1724 was constituted as a company, and in 1727 received a charter, authorising it (much on the model of the original shareholders of the Bank of England and National Debt) to undertake banking. Lord Islay, later Duke of Argyll, and virtual ruler of Scotland, became Governor, and thanks to his influence the Bank soon attained prominence and prosperity, and acted as banker to the Board of Trustees and the Forfeited Estates Commission. It is recognised as the pioneer of the famous " cash credit system " by which advances were made on personal security, thus allowing men without capital of their own to launch enterprises ; it is held thus to have contributed to industrial advance, and also to witness to the high standard of integrity and ability which made such confidence feasible.[2]

Among the London private banks of the period was that formed about 1720 by Andrew Drummond, who thereby was enabled to purchase the forfeited estate of his brother Lord

[1] C. A. Malcolm, *The Bank of Scotland* (1946)
[2] N. Munro, *Royal Bank of Scotland* (1928)

Strathallan ; Drummond's Bank was acquired by the Royal Bank in 1924.

The third of the great chartered banks was the British Linen Company,[1] whose earlier history belongs to the linen trade. It went over almost exclusively to banking in the 1760's, though not formally chartered as a bank until 1849. By transforming its local agencies it became the pioneer of branch banking.

At this point may be noted the first legislative regulation of Scottish banking by the Act of 1765, which prohibited the " Optional Clause " and the issue of notes below the value of one pound ; issues of smaller denominations had been frequent, chiefly because of the scarcity of currency. The One Pound Note thus became a peculiarly characteristic and popular feature of the Scottish system.

Private banking, as in England, emerged from the transactions of goldsmiths such as George Heriot, bankers to James VI & I, and merchants, especially grain dealers, like the elder Law of Lauriston and Sir William Dick, Lord Provost of Edinburgh. The most famous example is John Coutts (1699–1751) who abandoned corn dealing for banking in the 1720's, established a London agency and eventually transferred his headquarters there ; the family fortune ultimately descended to Baroness Burdett-Coutts, the Victorian philanthropist and peeress by special creation. The Edinburgh firm passed into the hands of Sir William Forbes (1739–1806) who took as partner (1773) James Hunter (afterwards Sir James Hunter-Blair) ; and Forbes, Hunter & Co. became the best-known Edinburgh bank, commemorated in Forbes's *Memoirs of a Banking House* (1859). Other noted Edinburgh private bankers were Mansfield & Co., originally drapers, William Alexander & Son, heavily involved in tobacco dealing, and Thomas Kinnear, also acting as an insurance broker. These banks sometimes exercised the right of " free " note issue, but usually acted as agents for and intermediaries of the chartered banks, on whose directorates they were sometimes represented. Some were precariously based, and failures were common in times of crisis such as 1773.

Country banking is said to have commenced with a

[1] C. A. Malcolm, *The British Linen Bank* (1950)

short-lived company in Aberdeen (1749), resuscitated later. Glasgow, thanks to the expansion of the colonial trade, soon took the lead, with the Ship Bank (1750), fostered by the Bank of Scotland, and the Arms Bank (1751) similarly a protégé of the Royal. Each was largely owned by colonial merchants, and the Ship was long managed by the notorious arch-exemplar of Scots thriftiness, the reputed miser Robert Carrick (1737–1821). With the typical Glasgow resentment of Edinburgh control, both soon declared their independence, and the efforts of the Old and New Banks, discarding their rivalry to unite against the upstarts, to undermine them by organising " runs ", were frustrated by the pertinacity and ingenious, sometimes ludicrous expedients of the newcomers. They were joined in 1761 by the Thistle Bank, largely associated with the West India trade. Local concerns in Dundee, Perth and other rising industrial centres followed. The best known and most ill-fated was the Ayr Bank, formed in November 1769 under very aristocratic patronage, with a capital of £150,000 ; its 136 shareholders included the Dukes of Queensberry and Buccleuch, and Patrick Heron of the Galloway cattle-rearing family. It made large advances, often on inadequate security, which helped to further the agricultural improvements of the period. The crisis of 1771 gave it a severe shock, and it was eventually liquidated in August 1773. Losses were estimated at over £600,000.

The importance of transport and communications for the advance of trade is obvious, and has been fully demonstrated by such historians as Professor Lilian Knowles. An Act of 1669 had asserted the duty of Statute labour, and authorised " stenting " by heritors, to be enforced by Sheriffs and J.P.'s, but this had been largely inoperative. As elsewhere, the device of Turnpikes was adopted as a supplement, and Trusts were established by local Acts after the Union. Parts of the Highlands were furnished, chiefly for military reasons, with a good complement of roads, about 200 miles, and forty bridges, under the supervision of General Wade, between 1728 and 1737 ; his work was continued after the '45 for about twenty years by Major Caulfield.

By the middle of the century such local gentry as George Drummond of Blair and the Earl of Loudon had taken the initiative in stimulating local activity, and in the second part " the use of the wheel (hitherto often impracticable) had become general and revolutionised economic life." [1]

For the West Highlands sea transport was of major importance, and in 1744 the " Islay Packet" was established by heritors to provide regular service to Inveraray. A coastal voyage to London was often preferable to a land journey, and this was facilitated by a company originating in Berwick, which from 1791 ran a regular service between Leith and London.

MANUFACTURING INDUSTRY

The medieval organisation of handicraft production in the gilds, often styled " incorporations ", survived. These were constituted by Seals of Cause, granted by the Superior, and in some royal burghs were united in a Convenery, through which they were represented on the Burgh Council. Their effective control of their trades was however diminishing, as surviving records indicate. They did indeed make efforts to enforce their monopoly of the practice of a craft, as in the notorious, if unverified, case of James Watt ; [2] but licenses came to be granted to non-members, legal exemption was granted in some cases, e.g. ex-servicemen of the Seven Years' War ; and their jurisdiction over areas outwith the burgh boundary was successfully challenged. One aspect of the rising *laissez-faire* outlook was the " right to work " (*droit de travailler*), i.e. to engage in any craft, emphasised by Adam Smith. Like the London Companies the Incorporations tended to become exclusive bodies, restricting apprenticeship and admission, increasingly divorced from active participation in their trade, and concerned mainly with the administration and enjoyment of their properties, as illustrated by the story of the Tailors of Canongate and others published by the Old Edinburgh Club. Their privileges survived to 1847.

Meanwhile there grew, especially in rural areas, the (unhappily so-called) " Domestic System ", familiar to readers

---

[1] H. G. Lebon in *Sc. Geographical Magazine* (1946)
[2] Cf. article in *Glasgow Herald*, 26 Dec. 1911, which seeks to refute the " legend ".

of *The Annals of a Parish* and the later chronicles of *Thrums*. As in England the textile trades afford the main example ; they were frequently practised as a spare-time occupation. " Customer " weavers retained a large degree of independence, and were often peripatetic. To market the product there arose a class of middlemen, sometimes called " Scotch drapers ", such as John Forrester of Stirling, and James Finlay, progenitor of a noted clan of industrialists. The beginnings of industrial capitalism are found among these as well as among master craftsmen.

The linen industry, as in Ireland, being non-competitive with English manufacture, was the specially favoured child of government. It was the recipient of one of the first annual grants from the Board of Trustees, and this was augmented later by the Forfeited Estates Commission. One expedient was the establishment of Spinning Schools to train women in the art ; import of flax from Holland and the Baltic was fostered, while encouragement was also given to home cultivation. Skilled technicians were encouraged to immigrate, including the weavers whose place of origin is commemorated in Picardy Place in Edinburgh. Bounties on export were given for nearly a century, and exemption from craft rules granted in 1755.

The introduction of the spinning wheel is obscure ; that of the loom has been romanticised in the stories of the clandestine methods attributed to Mrs. Henry Fletcher of Saltoun, sister-in-law of the Nationalist, described in fictional guise by Dot Allan. The inkle loom for weaving narrow strips or tape is said to have been introduced to Glasgow by Alexander Harvie about 1730. Other improvements in technique included the scutching machine. Probably however the chief technical agent in the transformation of the manufacture was the advance in bleaching ; this was one aspect of the " chemical revolution " to which the Clows have recently directed attention. Professor Francis Home's lectures (*c*. 1750) and subsequent treatise on " Experiments in Bleaching " gave the scientific basis for processes which were gradually substituted for reliance on the forces of nature, slow and uncertain in operation, and demanding considerable areas for the " fields ". The increased capital costs of the new processes encouraged concentration of manufacture, and contributed to give the master bleacher effective control over other stages in production. The most noted bleachers were the Christies, Quakers of Scottish descent, who came from County Down to Ormiston in East Lothian.

The linen industry developed several branches. The manufacture of linen thread is associated with Mrs. Miller of Balgarran, Ayrshire (*c.* 1725), " heroine " in her youth of one of the last witch trials. Of the finer types, Dunfermline from the start attained repute for damasks, manufactured by James Blake about 1720. Lawns and cambrics in the Glasgow area soon excelled the Dutch, and contributed about half the value, though only about one-fifth of the output of the industry. The coarser and more plentiful fabrics such as Osnaburgs were concentrated in Angus, where, e.g., a factory was set up by Provost John Wallace in the Abbot's House in Arbroath (1752). There was a fivefold increase of output between 1707 and 1760 ; manufacture was distributed throughout twenty-six counties. Considerable impetus was given by the British Linen Company, originating in an Edinburgh copartnery, and chartered in 1746 through the good offices of Lord Milton (son of Mrs. Henry Fletcher). It operated through local agencies all over Scotland as a wholesale merchant, advanced loans, imported flax, bought linen from domestic producers and sold it at home and abroad. The company however in the 'sixties virtually abandoned linen dealing for banking.

The growth of shipping, which provided a demand for the sailcloth of the Angus weavers, also stimulated the making of ropes and cordage, in which two notable and long-lived companies were engaged—the Edinburgh Roperie Company (1750) and Port Glasgow Rope and Duck Company, better known by its later name of the Gourock Ropeworks.

The other native textile, wool, remained depressed despite the efforts of the Board, especially at Galashiels. Much Border wool was sold for manufacture in Yorkshire. Rough serges, exported to Holland, were the chief native goods. The weaving of stockings flourished as a " domestic " industry in Aberdeenshire, attaining about 70,000 pairs per year.[1]

Among other industries which were very little affected by

---

[1] I. F. Grant in *Sc. Historical Review*, vol. xviii

the Industrial Revolution were upholstering, introduced by John Howden, " a famous fanatic " ; silverware, and nail-making, of which Pathhead (Kirkcaldy) and St. Ninians (Stirling) were the main centres. The manufacture of paper increased, especially in Midlothian, utilising the Water of Leith and the Esk ; and in Aberdeenshire, on the Don. A paper mill established at Penicuik in 1709 was acquired in 1779 by the first of the noted Cowan family. Other notable mills were those at Springfield (Polton) and Bogsmill (Colinton) where Bank of Scotland notes were made. The art of printing had been introduced into Scotland by Chapman and Myllar early in the sixteenth century, and technique was improved in this period by William Ged's stereotype (c. 1725) and Alex. Wilson of St. Andrews' typefounding (c. 1740). The brothers Foulis of Glasgow gained high repute for the fineness of their printing (c. 1740). The oldest surviving Edinburgh firm, Neill, was founded about 1750. The periodical press began with the *Glasgow Courant* of 1715, but only in 1764 did it acquire some permanence with the *Edinburgh Advertiser*. The *Scots Magazine* enjoyed the first of several incarnations from 1739 to 1754.

The ancient craft of the potter was pursued in imitation of the Dutch by the " Delft " factory in Glasgow from 1748 ; it obtained clay from, and sent wares to Virginia. Early estab-lishments in the East were at Prestonpans, Bo'ness (associated with Roebuck) and Portobello. The kindred craft of glass-making was practised in Glasgow, Leith and Alloa, largely in the making of bottles for West India rum and native ale. Window glass was made in Glasgow, as was table glass in the Verreville works, where Patrick Colquhoun was a partner.

Whisky distilling continued to be mainly a domestic art, practised chiefly in the Highlands, though Duncan Forbes had his Ferintosh malt whisky distillery, privileged by exemption from the duty imposed in 1707.

Beer becomes a factory product about the middle of the century, with the foundation of William Younger's brewery in the precincts of Holyrood Abbey (1750), after two centuries still in the ownership of his descendants ; [1] and that of the apparently unrelated George Younger at Alloa (c. 1760).

[1] D. Kerr, *The Younger Centuries* (1951)

3

Tennents began the manufacture of lager at Wellpark (Glasgow) in 1745, and the " true Quaker ale " brewed by George Miller, a scion of the Craigentinny family, had contemporary repute. The industry was handicapped by heavy taxation of both malt and beer, but evasion seems to have been frequent, and the output reached half a million barrels a year. There was a close connexion with agriculture, a " seasonal cycle ", the breweries utilising barley as raw material and returning the waste as winter feed for livestock.

Increased import of sugar from the West Indies fostered the development of refineries, especially in Greenock ; the famous firms of Walker, Fairrie and Macfie date from the last years of the century ; the first is now the only survivor. Soap- and candle-making both depended largely on the products of the whale, and manufacture of both centred in Leith. Though much of the tobacco imported was re-exported, some was processed for local consumption by several small firms, of whom the best known were Mitchells of Linlithgow (1723) who removed to Glasgow a century later, and John Cotton of Edinburgh (1770).

The building of boats and small vessels mainly for fishing continued in many east-coast ports. The foundations of the great shipbuilding of the Clyde were laid in 1711 by Scott of Greenock, whose descendants carried on for over two centuries.

Even in the seventeenth century sporadic efforts had been made to smelt iron in rather remote wooded localities ; the early eighteenth saw several such ventures, sponsored chiefly by Cumberland ironmasters. The Rawlinsons of the Back-barrow Company formed a copartnery with their fellow-Quaker Charles Ormston of Kelso to establish a works at Invergarry (1727) ; it survived only till 1736. More long-lived were the enterprises of the Newland Company at Bunawe (Argyll) (1753–1866) and the Duddon Company near Inveraray (1775–1813). The York Buildings Company had their usual ill-success in an experiment to smelt ore from Tomintoul at Abernethy in Strathspey (c. 1730).[1]

They developed coal-mining with better results on the forfeited Winton estates in the Tranent area (c. 1720), sold about 1780 to their tenant, Cadell of Cockenzie. The Bruces,

[1] A. Fell, *Early Iron Industry of Furness* (1908)

the Wemysses and other landowners maintained the practices of their forbears. Outstanding was John Erskine, who later established his claim to the forfeited Earldom of Mar. He constructed a dam and aqueduct to provide water power for pumping and hauling in his Alloa collieries, introduced a Newcomen engine (1764) and established welfare schemes for his colliers.

These remained generally in a state of serfdom, attributable to the labour legislation of the early seventeenth century, especially Acts of 1606 and 1641, which had virtually bound them to an employer for life, a condition which tended to become hereditary through the acceptance of " arles " for infant children. Their wages improved during the eighteenth century, and were higher than those of free agricultural labourers, and there are instances of insubordination and " ca' canny ". Women were much employed, especially in carrying coals from the pitface to the surface. With the extension of mining in the west, regulations were relaxed. An Act of 1775 provided for gradual emancipation and this was fully achieved by the Act of 1799, though long-term, usually annual, contracts of service remained common.

There was as yet little industrial demand for coal, save in the declining salt manufacture and for lime burning ; export was mainly to Ireland and Holland. Technical advance was made by the utilisation of the Newcomen engine for pumping, of a windlass or horsegin for hauling coal to the surface, of wooden rails, underground or surface, for transport. The " railway " to Port Seton constructed by the York Buildings Company in 1722 acquired adventitious notice through crossing the site of the battle of Prestonpans.

The small Scottish deposits of silver and copper were occasionally worked. Lead-mining,[1] developed by the Hopes after their acquisition of the Leadhills estate in the early seventeenth century, continued under lease, mainly for export to Holland. The administration of " Venetian " James Stirling, sometime Snell Scholar, Professor of Mathematics at Venice and Jacobite émigré, restored its financial soundness and made it a model of benevolent employment, with welfare

[1] Allardyce, *Scotland and Scotsmen in 18th Century* (1888), ii, 307–26 ; J. M. Porteous, *God's Treasure House in Scotland* (1876)

schemes similar to those of Erskine of Mar (*c.* 1735–70). In the adjacent mines at Wanlockhead, at Fort William and at Ardnamurchan, less-lasting enterprises were initiated. The beginnings of the Aberdeen granite industry are assigned to the 1720's ; similar quarrying was undertaken in some parts of Argyll, where slate had been quarried at Easdale since about 1630.

The " conspicuous waste and ostentatious leisure " of the eighteenth century were catered for by the mineral spa, of which Bath and Tunbridge Wells are the best known. Small-scale Scottish imitation was attempted at Moffat about 1750, and at St. Ronans (Innerleithen) about the end of the century.

Before passing to the period of " revolutionary " change, a little may be said about the institutional framework of eighteenth-century Scottish life. The burghs, of which 66 were reckoned as Royal and about 300 as Burghs of Barony, were governed by Councils, which were, in terms of the 1469 Act (more observed in practice than most Scots legislation), quite unrepresentative. Many had adopted a scheme of membership based on James VI's Decreit Arbitral for Edinburgh, which alleviated the strife of merchants and craftsmen by prescribing a proportion of 17 merchants to 8 craftsmen. By whatever method, Councils were in effect filled by co-option. The controversy between royal and other burghs, especially as to the former's claim to monopolies of trade, continued. Rather contradictory enactments were passed by the Estates during their last brief period of activity in the 1690's ; the decision of the Court of Session in the Stromness case (1751) eventually freed trade from exclusive privilege. The burghal monopoly was also encroached on by special grants to land-owners of the right to hold markets and fairs. According to W. M. Mackenzie,[1] the burghs " existed by and for the merchants ", and as " the national intruded on the burgh economy " the special privileges of the latter were unavoidably curtailed.

As the Burgh Commission Report of 1835 brought out, the government of most burghs was not only oligarchic but sometimes inefficient, and even corrupt. The most serious indication and effect of this is the " dilapidation " of the Common

[1] W. M. Mackenzie, *The Scottish Burghs* (1949)

Good. By lease or still more by feu, much of the common lands passed out of the control of the burgh and became *de facto* private property. The Blythswood estate in Glasgow is a notable example. Petty customs were still levied and constituted the other main item of revenue. The precarious financial position of some burghs resulted in indebtedness, sometimes incurred through laudable expenditure on public works and civic improvements. The Convention of Burghs continued to meet, and was " the principal body in Scotland which represented trading and industrial interests ", which on occasion it pressed on Parliament, as in the setting up of the Board of Trustees.

In the rural areas the Commissioners of Supply, set up in 1667, were still mainly concerned with the raising of the " cess " or land tax. Justices of the Peace, first appointed in 1609, received a reinforcement of powers and duties after the Union, but were less active and influential than those in the South ; they might take joint action regarding such matters as enclosures and roads, and by the Acts of 1617 and 1661 were responsible for fixation of wages ; evidence of utilisation of their powers throughout the century is extant. Such local government services as existed, notably education and poor relief, were largely administered by kirk sessions.

As regards central government, in terms of the Union and subsequent enactments of the Scots Parliament before its demise, the Scottish peers were represented in the House of Lords by sixteen of their number, elected at the commencement of each Parliament ; while Scotland had 45 seats in the House of Commons—30 from the shires, 15 from the royal burghs, grouped for the purpose, Edinburgh alone having a representative to itself. In practice, members were usually elected by Commissioners from each burgh concerned ; thus bribery and intimidation were facilitated. The county franchise had been determined in 1681 and was purely feudal, depending on the holding of a " superiority " from the Crown. This was evaded by the temporary creation of " parchment barons " with fictitious qualifications. Legislative prohibition was so successfully circumvented that of a total of some 4,000 voters in 1790, one-third are said to have had fictitious qualifications.

Parliament in those days, meeting only for short periods, passed little legislation, and much was in the form of Private Acts, authorising the establishment of Turnpike Trusts, Police Commissions, Enclosures, etc. All its Acts were Acts of Great Britain, though some might apply only to Scotland. The Cabinet system was gradually emerging ; the Scots members were usually attached to the governing faction of the day. Scottish interests were nominally attended to by a Secretary for Scotland between 1707 and 1726, and 1731 and 1746 ; after the abolition of the office, they were left to whatever member of government might make it his business, notably " King Harry IX " Dundas who exercised dictatorial powers during the French Revolutionary period.

Governmental policy in respect of economic matters in Scotland as elsewhere was dominated by the Mercantilist outlook, exhibited in the fostering and regulating of industry and the imposition of controls on labour as well as by the elaborate network of " indirect " taxation. These features however being common to Great Britain call for little notice here.

Scottish writers on economics, apart from agricultural " improvers ", in the pre-revolutionary period include Andrew Fletcher of Saltoun, Patrick Lindsay, Lord Provost of Edinburgh, who in 1733 published anonymously *The Interest of Scotland Considered*, and Sir James Stuart (-Denham) (1713–80), sometime Jacobite exile, and laird of Coltness (later site of a noted ironworks), who made a premature attempt at systematisation in his *Political Economy* (2 v. 1767), almost immediately superseded by Adam Smith. Of the *Wealth of Nations* (1776), it need here be said only that its author is the " theorist of the domestic system ", writing before industrial capitalism has developed. While he is not primarily concerned with Scotland, and indeed seems anti-national in sentiment, his illustrations are often drawn from the rising commercial Glasgow and developing agricultural countryside of his own environment, and there is something indefinably but unmistakably Scots in his attitude ; " he seemed to think there was a Scotsman in every man ".

2

The Period of Revolution
(c. 1760-1830)

THE term " Industrial Revolution " has been much blown
upon of late, but seems appropriate to Scotland, inasmuch as
the life and work of the mass of the people was largely transformed within a generation or two. The censure directed by
the authors of *Capitalism and the Historians* against writers who
have held the revolution responsible for all the evils of contemporary society certainly does not apply to Scottish scholars,
who have if anything been inclined to blacken unduly pre-
industrial conditions. A more legitimate warning, emphasised
by Clapham, is against the excessive emphasis on the textile,
mining and metallurgical industries, which bore the brunt of
the changes in technique and organisation ; other industries,
relatively little affected meantime directly by these changes,
continued to flourish and expand, notably the building industry ; but in view of their relative stability, little further need
be said about them until we reach the Victorian age. Another
particular correction of the traditional view is suggested by the
Clows, who have demonstrated the important but hitherto
neglected contribution of chemical as well as physical science,
and that of the industries based upon it.

AGRICULTURE

First we may deal with the revolution in agriculture, for which
ample evidence is afforded in the first Statistical Account, in
the series of County " General Views of Agriculture ", in
collections of estate papers and other documents which have
been preserved and edited, and in the works of numerous
contemporary writers ; Andrew Wight's *Present State of*

Husbandry in Scotland (1778–84), based on surveys which he made for the Commissioners of Annexed Estates, is noteworthy.

The failure of the '45 probably helped to precipitate, as did the defeat of the South in the American Civil War, the downfall of an agrarian economy. The traditional community life was undermined, and there was a growing commercialisation, rather grandiloquently defined as a transition from status to contract. There was no large-scale enclosure movement comparable to that of England.

The main changes in technique and organisation were similar to those in England, and were to some extent adopted in imitation. There was enclosure in the narrow sense of the erection of fences or hedges, to demarcate and protect arable land, as farms were consolidated with the gradual abandonment of runrig. To some extent the earlier grouping of farm buildings in a " toun " gave place to isolated dwellings ; many farm steadings still existing date from the late eighteenth or early nineteenth century. Much drainage and reclamation of waste and bog took place ; Lord Kames's achievements at Blair Drummond are well known ; Lochs Spynie (Moray) and Forfar were among former waterlogged areas now brought into cultivation. Lime and other artificial aids were utilised to improve the soil ; kilns (still sometimes mistaken, as in the days of the *Antiquary*, for Roman remains) were set up in the countryside ; Limekilns on the Forth maintains the memory. Potatoes were introduced about 1730 and cultivation spread rapidly a few decades later, especially in the Highlands. Clover, rye grass and turnips also became known. Ley farming, practised on the late medieval monastic estates, was revived ; regular fallowing and rotation were introduced ; one variant was the six-year cycle of the Carse of Gowrie. " By the end of the century the modern system of Scottish husbandry, alternating between grain crops and green crops, was general throughout Scotland " (Handley).[1]

Improvements in implements included some native devices. James Small designed a light " swing plough " in the 1760's, manufactured in Berwickshire. James and Andrew Meikle, father and son, farmers in East Lothian, were responsible respectively for inventing a fanner and a threshing mill.

[1] *Scottish Farming*, op. cit. p. 213

Market gardening was pursued in the Lothians, and for about a century the Port-Glasgow area supplied the western metropolis until gardens gave place to shipyards. The Millers of Craigentinny, originally royal gardeners at Holyrood and leaders of Edinburgh Quakerism for three generations, built up a large enterprise as seedsmen and nurserymen. Many landed gentry undertook large-scale afforestation, partly to embellish their estates, partly from recognition of the commercial value of timber. Its importance for naval purposes was emphasised by Patrick Matthew, a small proprietor in Perthshire, in his *Naval Timber* (1831), and in an appendix, as he later claimed, he incidentally anticipated Darwin in promulgating the Law of Natural Selection. Among large planters were the Earl and Countess of Haddington at Tyninghame ; the former published a volume on *Forest Trees* (1756 ; reprinted 1953).

A statistical report of 1814 gave the acreage under various crops as : oats, 1¼ million ; wheat, 140,000 ; barley, 280,000 ; turnips, 400,000 ; potatoes, 80,000 ; flax, 16,500.

Cattle rearing continued active in Galloway ; the Ayrshire breed was developed by Dunlop of Cunningham. The introduction of turnips " turned the black cattle of Scotland into beef " ; [1] local fattening was undertaken in Fife and Aberdeenshire. The output of milk increased four to sixfold.

New breeds of sheep were introduced, especially in the Highlands. Attention was given to the rearing of types producing wool suited to the growing manufacture ; the soft fine wool of the Cheviots was adapted to hosiery ; the coarse hairy wool of the Blackfaces to carpetmaking. Horse breeding was fostered in Clydesdale, where regular fairs were held. The pig population was estimated at half a million (1814).

Probably a necessary stimulus was afforded by the grant of longer leases, of which the Cockburns of Ormiston and Professor John Erskine of Carnock were pioneers. Nineteen years was a common term, but a duration of 25, 31 or 63 was also known. " Improving " conditions might be stipulated, e.g. " cropping clauses ". Duncan Forbes as factor for the Duke of Argyll set a precedent, of which Sir Walter Scott was later a follower. Excessive attempts at regulation are sometimes

[1] T. B. Franklin, *A History of Scottish Farming*, p. 150

deplored. Rentals increased phenomenally; the records of the Marchmont estate, Berwickshire, show a ninefold increase between 1740 and 1820. Elsewhere they rose three to five times on the average, especially during the Napoleonic wars; the extent of inflation must be borne in mind. One incidental effect was the rebuilding of many country churches by the affluent heritors at a time when ecclesiastical architecture was at a low level of taste.

Agricultural output expanded less rapidly but was at least doubled. While some " services " survived, the bulk of farm labour was supplied by the hired servant or " hind ", while rentals were largely paid in money.

Credit for agricultural improvement is mainly assigned to the lairds, who indeed alone were in a position to initiate it.[1] The Cockburns of Ormiston, the Fergussons of Kilkerran, the Grants of Monymusk, the Barclays of Urie have gained special repute. Their attitude is sometimes contrasted with that of the " absentee " Irish landlords, and held responsible for the very different course of agrarian economy in the two countries; contemporaries such as Arthur Young however witness to the activity of not a few resident Irish gentry. The necessary finance may have been derived in part from the profits of trade; advances were made by the rising banks, notably the ill-fated Douglas Heron & Co. of Ayr. Compensation for the abolition of heritable jurisdictions (1747) may have aided in some cases. Amendments of the law of entail also helped, particularly the Montgomery Act (1770) which allowed the lease of entailed land up to 31 years and the burdening of the estate with debts incurred in making improvements.

Generally speaking, the era saw the growth of capitalist farming for the market, as distinct from a mainly subsistence economy. Subsidiary " domestic " industry was often combined with farming, as on the Monymusk estate. The process was however a gradual one, and affected the remoter areas but little; it was opposed by a reluctant conservatism and sometimes received a setback from the excessive zeal of its promoters and their inappropriate imitations of English methods. Of these John Cockburn of Ormiston, and Maxwell of Arkland, Secretary of the Society of Improvers, ruined

[1] Sir J. Fergusson, *The Lowland Lairds* (1949)

themselves in the process.   The effects on population are disputed.   Consolidation of farms in some areas reduced the demand for labour, which increased elsewhere with the extension of cultivation.   A general rise in the standard of living is indisputable, and is marked in respect of housing, dress and food.

Private and governmental encouragement was given by the pioneer Society of Improvers (1723–45) and the long-lived Highland and Agricultural Society, established 1784 ; by the Board of Trustees and the Board of Agriculture.   The latter was instituted in 1793 at the instance of Sir John Sinclair,[1] under his own presidency ; it was abolished as a post-war economy in 1822.   It was responsible for the compilation of the Scottish County Agricultural Reports (1793–5) and the General Report on Scotland (1814).

Writing on agricultural matters was prolific.   An article in *History* (1950) conveniently reviews the most important, who are also dealt with in Professor Scott Watson's *Great Farmers* (1937) and Handley's *Scottish Farming in the Eighteenth Century* (1953).   A Chair of Agriculture was founded in Edinburgh in 1790 at the instance of Sir William Pulteney ; William Cullen, as Professor of Chemistry, had included lectures on agriculture in his course.   The pioneer author was James Donaldson, printer, Edinburgh, in his *Husbandry Anatomised* (1697).   The Jacobite general, Macintosh of Borlum (1662–1743), devoted his post-rebel years to agriculture, and wrote *Essays on Enclosing and Fallowing* (1729).   James Hamilton, schoolmaster, East Calder, appended to an edition of Vergil's *Georgics* an excursus dealing with his own experiments, especially on the chemistry of the soil (1742).

Among writers who dealt with both agriculture and industry three are outstanding.   Dr. James Anderson (1739–1808), a practical farmer and later editor of *The Bee*, was author of *Observations on National Industry* (1777) and *The Present State of the Hebrides* (1785).   He anticipated the " Ricardian Law of Rent ", supported the wool against the linen industry, looked favourably on the growth of population as conducive to eco-

---

[1] The definitive biography *Agricultural Sir John* (1962), by Rosalind Mitchison, gives a full account of Sinclair's many contributions to Scottish progress.

nomic progress, deprecated emigration and advocated fostering the home market rather than colonial trade. David Loch (*d.* 1780), merchant and shipowner, Leith, and Inspector-General of Woollen Manufactures and Fisheries, in his three-volume *Essays on the Trade Commerce and Manufacture of Scotland* (1778), expressed similar views on population and on the wool trade ; he advocates " buying Scottish ", and gives a detailed account of industrial activities throughout Scotland. John Naismith, author of *Thoughts on Various Objects of Industry Pursued in Scotland* (1790) and *Agriculture of Clydeside* (1813), is critical of *laissez-faire*, and makes strictures on the cotton manufacture as unhygienic and precarious. He is a strong supporter of the linen industry as essentially a native one.

Some at least of contemporary travellers had not so much a tourist interest as a deliberate intention of reporting on the economic situation. Most useful are the *Journey through the West of Scotland* (1793) of Robert Heron (1764–1807), a hack writer who was engaged in the editing of the Old Statistical Account and wrote one of the earliest lives of Burns ; and the *Beauties of Scotland* (5 volumes, 1805–8) by Robert Forsyth (1764–1845), a thrawn Edinburgh advocate and miscellaneous writer of humble origin, who passed from active sympathy with the French Revolution to high Toryism. His work comprises a " full account of agriculture commerce mines and manufactures, of population, of city towns and villages of each county ". Cockburn, with malicious exaggeration, declares that it was " produced sitting by his fireside, as the usual extent of his peregrinations was from his room to the Court ".

Before proceeding to the changes in industry, something may be said on the vexed topic of the Highland Clearances. Most that has been written on the subject has been polemical [1] : the attacks, e.g., by Donald Macleod (*Gloomy Memories*, 1857, revised 1892) and Alex. Mackenzie (*Highland Clearances*, revised edition, 1914) ; the defence by James Loch, the factor concerned, in his *Account of the Sutherland Improvements* (1820) and later by Harriet Beecher Stowe in her *Sunny Memories* of her patron the Duchess of Sutherland. A search study by Miss Margaret Adam was cut short by her premature death ; a

---

[1] I. Grimble, *The Trial of Patrick Sellar* (1962) reproduces the chief descriptions.

few articles by her appeared in the *Scottish Historical Review* (1921–2). An authoritative survey of the economic background has now been supplied by Malcolm Gray in his *Highland Economy 1750–1850* (1957). Some contemporary evidence can be extracted from such publications as Professor J. Anderson's *Hebrides and West Coast* (1786) and Professor J. Walker's *Economic History of the Hebrides and Highlands* (1808). Of the main problems involved, the legality of the action, the morality of the methods, and the economic causes and results, the third mainly concerns us.

Among the basic factors were the remoteness of much of the Highlands (despite Wade's roads and later transport by rail, sea and air, a difficulty today as then) and thus the slower adoption of the new methods. Little of the land was suited to arable, and the runrig system persisted. Such primitive implements as the cascrom (hand plough) remained in use, while rental was commonly paid in kind and casualties and services were exacted. Much of the controversy has turned on the alleged communal ownership of land by the clan, the chief being regarded as trustee. It seems clear that, whatever the primeval condition, feudalism had so far penetrated as to give virtual ownership to the chief. A threefold classification was common ; the " tacksman ", often a kinsman of the chief, served as middleman, or more euphemistically, as organiser, standing between the chief and the tenants or cottars, sometimes joint holders, who had at best leases secure for only a year.

The impact of the '45 is held responsible for an upheaval of the social system, partly due to the legislation which followed, penalising Highland customs and abolishing heritable jurisdictions. Considerable forfeiture of estates took place and involved absentee ownership ; many were sold, and the new landlords had little but a cash nexus with their tenants, while traditional relations became obsolete. Many were charged with rack-renting ; a tenfold increase is alleged in Wester Ross (1777–1815). The expansion of cattle rearing gave a temporary stimulus to prosperity, but declined early in the nineteenth century. The pressure of population on subsistence had long been considerable, and became acute as rapid growth was facilitated by the introduction of the potato, the diminution of disease and the stoppage of clan feuds ; that of the Hebrides doubled between 1750 and 1810. Attempts to introduce manufactures had little success, e.g. the efforts of the Board of Trustees to acclimatise the linen industry. One enterprise alone gave some prosperity for a period, and produced all the greater misery by its collapse. The collection of kelp (seaweed) was promoted by its industrial use as a source of potash for the nascent chemical industries. Mr. Malcolm Gray's studies indicate that the main benefit went to the landlords such as Lord Macdonald and Clanranald, who obtained middleman's profits as well as increased rents. Labour was paid by the piece. Collapse came in the 1820's through the competition of imported Spanish barilla, and prices fell from £20 to £2 a ton. This was responsible for further sales of estates.

The prime incentive to Clearance came however with the growth of sheep rearing. The suitability of Highland pastures for new breeds of sheep, especially Cheviots, came to be appreciated, and the demand for wool of the rapidly expanding Yorkshire industry made concentration on sheep farming profitable. As in sixteenth-century England, this meant a declining demand for labour and the chronic " concealed unemployment " became visible. Especially in Sutherland, an attempt was made to turn the crofter into at least a part-time fisherman, and this involved the more or less forcible removal of tenants from the interior to the coast ; this is vividly described in Neil Gunn's *Silver Darlings* (novel and film). Migration abroad, or to the industries of the south, was however the main outlet. Organised schemes had already been pioneered by tacksmen, e.g. in the North Carolina settlement of 1729 ; these were now taken up, notably by Lord Selkirk who founded colonies in Prince Edward Island and on the Red River (Kildonan) (1803–17).

There was much migration to the south, whence Greenock obtained its " Celtic " flavour. Employment was found in such rising industries as the textile works (e.g. New Lanark and Blantyre) and in " navvying " on the Forth and Clyde Canal. David Livingstone and Alexander Macdonald were among the descendants of such migrants.

Eviction was speeded up by enhanced war values ; the most notorious, those in Sutherland, took place mainly in the

decade 1811–20. The Marquis of Stafford who had inherited
the Bridgwater estates married in 1785 the Countess of Sutherland ; they sought as " improving " landlords to imitate
southern practice, e.g. in constructing roads and bridges. The
direct responsibility for clearance falls on the factors James
Loch and Patrick Sellar. These continued spasmodically
during the next half-century, e.g. at Breadalbane and in the
islands, where in the Uists and Barra an " absentee purchaser "
John Gordon of Braid (*d.* 1858), " the richest commoner in
Scotland ", was author of the deportation of 2,000 crofters to
Canada. The apathy and lack of resistance with which the
tenants submitted to expulsion has been variously attributed
to their disconcertment at the loss of the traditional leadership
of their chief, to the draining off already of the more virile
elements by emigration and military recruitment, and to the
attitude of the parochial clergy who were said to have preached
an identification of the will of the laird and that of the Lord.
The famine of 1846–7 and the contemporary introduction of
deer forests completed the process ; it was only by the legislation
of the 1880's that some belated attempt was made to reverse it.
Meantime the main economic effect was to stabilise the " crofter
system " with its prevalence of very small holdings, except on the
eastern arable strip of Ross-shire. The tacksmen were virtually
eliminated, runrig gave place to compact holdings, and
occasional experiments were made by improving landlords.

THE REVOLUTION IN MANUFACTURE

In its rapidity and completeness, the industrialisation of Scotland seems to approximate to that of Russia and Asiatic
countries in the present age rather than to that of contemporary England. The introduction of steam power and machinery
constitutes what has been termed the " palaeotechnic " phase.
The great inventions, save Watt's steam engine, were largely
of English origin.

TEXTILES

In the textile industries development was chiefly a matter
of applying these techniques. The linen industry, already

specialised, e.g. in the fine lawn and cambrics of the West and the canvas and sackcloth of Angus, suffered in the former case from the growing substitution of cheaper cotton wares for clothing and domestic use. Water power was applied to flax spinning in the Arbroath area in the 1790's ; here also, it is claimed, steam power was first introduced in the Brothock Mill in 1806. The use of steam advanced slowly until the 1820's, when in the Kirkcaldy area, at the instance of James Aytoun, considerable development took place ; Arbroath rapidly followed. There were about 170 spinning mills in the 'thirties. Some fine yarn continued to be handspun.

Here, as in the other textile industries, the use of steam power in weaving was later and slower. Hand-loom weavers continued active, notably in the smaller burghs of Fife and Angus, though pay slumped seriously in the 1820's ; in Angus the average fell from 21/6 to 6/- a week. Power-looms were first installed in Kircaldy in 1821, and by Maberley in his Aberdeen venture in 1824. The Jacquard loom was introduced to the Dunfermline damask industry about 1825.

About two million yards of linen were exported from the Clyde just before the American War ; the French wars obstructed the former export to the Low Countries, and the English market was opened up by James Fergus of Kirkcaldy. Regulations affecting the industry were abolished in 1823, and the payment of bounties and premiums ended nine years later.

The woollen industry, after unsuccessful efforts at promotion in the seventeenth century and a setback from English competition in the early eighteenth, now began to thrive, particularly in the Borders, where local supplies of wool and of water power gave it natural advantages. Galashiels developed the making of blankets and opened a Cloth Hall in 1791 ; its " shepherd checks " were given a vogue by Scott and Hogg, and the parish minister Dr. Douglas did much to foster the industry. Machinery was introduced from Yorkshire by George Mercer in the 1770's.

Knitting frames were also introduced from the Midlands to Hawick. In Melrose, Kelso, Peebles, Selkirk and Langholm the manufacture also grew. The Ochils were another centre ; John Christie of Tillicoultry about 1800 set up carding machinery, and the noted firm of Patons commenced as yarn spinners in Alloa in 1814. In Kilmarnock carpet manufacture was commenced by Maria Gardner about 1730, and expanded by the now paramount firm of Blackwood from about 1800. The short-lived British Wool Society (1791–4), one of Sir John Sinclair's numerous ventures, promoted sheep rearing for wool ; premiums were subsequently offered by the Highland Society. In the 1820's the Scottish woollen industry employed about 25,000 workers, with an annual output valued at almost half a million pounds.

In contrast to the two other textiles, cotton was a new and exotic industry ; its supplies were imported, the output of the American plantations being greatly increased about this date by the invention of Whitney's cotton gin. Almost from the outset its markets also were largely overseas, first on the Continent and, with the abolition of the East India Company's monopoly, in India. It is thus the chief example of the new type of factory industry. Its origins are obscure, but it appears that a mixture of cotton and other yarn was used in Paisley by about 1770, and muslins were manufactured by James Monteith at Anderston about 1780. The chief impetus seems to have been given by the American War, which encouraged a diversion of capital from the colonial trade to take advantage of the opportunities offered by the new machinery, such as the mule, just invented in England ; an example of what Professor W. R. Scott called " resiliency ". The utilisation of water power was responsible for an initial wide dispersion of spinning mills. Copartneries were formed, and the industry was encouraged on their own estates by landowners such as Sir William Douglas in Galloway, Claud Alexander in Ayrshire and George Dempster in Sutherland. The two former had made their wealth in America and India respectively.

Penicuik claims to be the site of the first mill (1778), closely followed by Rothesay and Neilston. The most famous, that at New Lanark, was established in 1785 on the estate of the notorious Lord Braxfield. The original partners were the English " inventor " (of contested authenticity) Sir Richard Arkwright and David Dale, who started as a dealer in linen yarn, and combined success as a company promoter with active participation in Glasgow public life and the pastorate of a small religious sect. They soon parted company, and New

4

Lanark was in 1799 acquired by a copartnery in which Robert Owen was the leading figure. Under his control, which lasted until 1824, it became famous as a model factory, the haunt of numerous visitors and under royal and aristocratic patronage.

Dale was an original partner also in the Blantyre mills (1787), later carried on for many years by the Monteiths ; in that at Catrine, with Claud Alexander, until its sale to Kirkman Finlay in 1801 ; and with Dempster in the unfortunate far-flung venture at Spinningdale (originally Spinziedale) near Dornoch. Most noted of other factories (like New Lanark, still in operation) was Deanston-on-Teith near Doune, also with a model village, soon acquired by Kirkman Finlay and still owned by the firm which bears his name. Other acquisitions by Finlay included Ballindalloch (Balfron) ; his commercial ventures and public activities will be described later.

Steam power was introduced by the end of the century. This promoted concentration in the Glasgow area, where 115 out of 134 mills were situated in 1833. Machinery was usually constructed by local woodworkers ; only gradually was specialisation in machine-making undertaken, notably by the Houldsworths. Weaving continued to be the sphere of the hand-loom ; the cotton weavers were the aristocracy of labour, though their position deteriorated in the 1820's. The occupation was widespread, though ownership and control generally centred in Glasgow. Frequent references in the Old Statistical Account often leave obscure which textile is involved, but it appears that the great majority of the 50,000 weavers in 1830 were engaged on cotton ; " every village in Renfrewshire and Ayrshire was employed in weaving cotton ", says Forsyth (1805), and he affirms that the " cotton manufacture has become the staple industry of the west of Scotland ", vying with Lancashire. Its output in 1814 was valued at £7 million, and it employed about 180,000 workers, according to a contemporary estimate.

Several subsidiaries of importance were attached to the cotton industry. Tambouring—the embroidering of cotton stuffs stretched over a frame or " tambour "—was a frequent domestic employment of women. The technique first applied to cambric by Flemish immigrants was applied to hand-woven muslini by Ruffini (1882) and was later undertaken in the West, flourishing till the mid-nineteenth century as " Ayrshire Needlework " on a " domestic " basis.[1] The supply of chemicals for bleaching was facilitated by the invention of bleaching powder by Charles Tennant, who took out a patent and founded the famous works at St. Rollox (Glasgow) in 1800. The dyeing of the fabric was pioneered by George Macintosh (1739–1807), partner in cotton enterprises, who established a cudbear works at Dunchattan (Glasgow) in the 1770's, and became associated with Jacques Papillon, a Frenchman from Rouen, who devised a Turkey red dye. Four firms were operating in the Vale of Leven by 1830. Calico printing was introduced at Pollokshaws about 1740, and the Vale of Leven soon became a centre for this also. Thornliebank and Campsie were the sites adopted by other noted firms. A cylinder printer was invented by Thomas Bell of Glasgow about 1780. Much of the printed cloth was exported to the colonies.

The gigantic cotton-thread industry, which has survived the other branches in Scotland, started in a small way in Paisley with several firms, including besides Coats and Clark, Carlisle & Co., whose head had the doubtful honour of being immortalised in *Das Kapital*, from his opposition to factory legislation, as one " in whose brain capitalist outlooks are engrained ".

Silk, introduced to Paisley by Humphrey Fulton about 1760, was closely allied, and continued frequently to be mixed with cotton threads in the weaving of shawls and other articles.

The cotton and associated industries were speculative, in the sense of producing for an uncertain market, largely overseas ; and were thus peculiarly liable to fluctuations of trade. Commercial houses and agencies were established to dispose of goods in London and abroad. The career of Kirkman Finlay, the leading figure in the second generation, original begetter of the far-flung " Finlay Group " of today, illustrates the lines of development. Born in 1773, son of a yarn merchant who commenced the export of cottons to the Continent, he not only acquired control of several factories and expanded the European trade, but earned repute as a blockade runner during the

[1] M. H. Swain, *The Flowerers* (1955)

Napoleonic " Berlin Decrees " and was later a chief agent in securing dissolution of the East India Company's monopoly of trade with India, thus extending export there. In a Home Office paper he is styled " an intelligent sensible man, who carries on trade to a very great extent, and has hitherto almost always got access with his commodities into the Continent ".

MINING AND METALLURGICAL INDUSTRY

Coal-mining. The mining of coal was still largely organised as incidental to estate management, as was also the case in e.g. Bohemia. Particularly in the Lothians and Fife, landowners such as the Dukes of Buccleuch were also coalmasters. Leases were increasingly given ; one of the most long enduring was that granted in 1815 by Lord Elgin to Spowart and Co. of the Elgin and Wellwood Collieries. Leases sometimes combined the agricultural use of the soil and the mineral exploitation of the subsoil, as in the famous cases of the Bairds and the Addies in Lanarkshire. Through leases, especially in the newer coal-fields of the west, mining came to be associated with tied houses and truck.

Industrial development as well as domestic requirements expanded demand, and a further impetus was given by the invention of the process for lighting by coal gas devised by William Murdoch (1754–1839), an Ayrshireman in the service of Boulton and Watt. Gaslight Companies were formed in Edinburgh (1817) and Glasgow (1818) ; the chairman of the former was Sir Walter Scott, who introduced the new illuminant at Abbotsford.

Transport of coal relied first on horse carriage or traction ; much was carried by sea, e.g. to London, Holland or Ireland. The development of canals interacted with that of the coal trade ; the Monkland pits and canal were interdependent ; the canal was designed primarily for the transport of coal to Glasgow.

Combination among employers goes back to the famous Fawside bond of 1620, and was revived by owners in the Glasgow area when a " participating cartel with a selling syndicate " was formed by William Dixon ; it was frustrated by the competition of the Monklands pits. An agreement to restrict output and maintain prices was again in force from 1813 to 1817.

Ironworks. The two charcoal-using works in the Highlands at Bunawe and Loch Fyne continued in operation ; but the use of coke on the Darby process challenged the advantage of the proximity of timber, and attracted the industry to the coal-fields. This consideration determined, after some hesitation, the eventual location of the first of the great modern works at Carron near Falkirk (1759).[1] The capital and expertise were at first mainly English. One of the original partners was John Roebuck (1718–94) of Sheffield, a medical graduate of Edinburgh, who first devoted himself to the rising chemical industry, and founded a sulphuric acid works at Prestonpans, and also leased coal and salt works at Bo'ness. A second was Samuel Garbett, a pioneer of Birmingham industry, already associated with Roebuck in his chemical works. The only Scot in the trio was William Cadell (1708–77) of the Cockenzie coal-owning family, who was also an importer of Swedish ore and timber. He became managing partner, and the company was reorganised when Roebuck became bankrupt in the early 'seventies. By this time capital had increased from £12,000 to £150,000. In addition to blast furnaces at Carron, a rolling mill was established at Cramond and a coal pit was acquired at Kilsyth. " Domestic " nail-making (important in the age of wood) [2] was organised at St. Ninians (Stirling). The Second Hundred Years' War with its demand for munitions proved a considerable stimulus to Carron and to the industry generally, which thus, as J. U. Nef suggested, came to be unduly dependent on an unstable and unhealthy war demand. The " carronade " utilised in the American War was a typical product ; the dubious honour of its invention is disputed between General Robert Melville (1723–1809) and Patrick Miller of Dalswinton (1713–1815), the landlord of Burns. About 5,000 cannon were turned out annually in Napoleonic times ; cannon balls and later shrapnel were also produced. The works were also more happily devoted to the arts of peace,

[1] R. H. Campbell's definitive history *Carron Company* (1961) appeared after this was drafted.
[2] cf. M. Flinn, *Men of Iron* (1962), p. 6

in the form of agricultural implements, household utensils and light castings such as the grates for fireplaces designed by the brothers Adam. A direct service of vessels to transport their wares to London was inaugurated after a few years, and the navigability of the Carron improved for the purpose.

A further impetus to the industry was given by Cort's " puddling " process, and about thirty furnaces were operating early in the nineteenth century. Of these the most noted were the Clyde Iron Works (1786) which produced bar and cast iron, and the Muirkirk Works (1787). The Scottish industry was for some time handicapped by the prevailing type of local coal which was less suited for coking and thus enhanced costs of production. Improvement came with the demonstration (1801) of the utility of the blackband ironstone of Lanarkshire, a rich ore containing a considerable proportion of coal and thus enabling the consumption of the latter to be diminished. This was due to David Mushet (1772–1847), originally of an iron foundry in Dalkeith and for a few years partner in the Calder Works. He made many other experiments, but his later activities were in England.

William Dixon (1753–1824), a native of Northumberland, previously associated with glass-making, was his partner in the Calder Works, and founded a famous dynasty of ironmasters. A " longterm stagnation " of the industry was terminated just at the end of this period thanks chiefly to the second of the peculiarly Scottish technical improvements, the invention of the hot-blast process (1828) by James Beaumont Neilson (1792–1865), the first manager of the Glasgow Gas Company. This " proved the salvation of the Scottish iron industry ".[1] His patent involved him in much litigation, especially with the Bairds, who opened their renowned Gartsherrie Works in 1828, and introduced the process as well as the use of the blackband. These were also adopted in the Shotts Ironworks, founded in 1801, and long managed by John Baird. The great expansion of the industry however falls within the early Victorian period, and is associated with the introduction of railways. One noteworthy feature is the prevalence of " interlocking directorates " in the conduct of the industry, effected through membership of temporary copartneries.

[1] H. Hamilton, *Industrial Revolution in Scotland*, p. 182

The Steam Engine. The earlier career of James Watt, and his epoch-making invention, belongs to Scottish economic history. Born in Greenock in 1736, he became a mathematical instrument maker, and eventually settled in Glasgow where, besides carrying on under the patronage of Professor John Anderson the experiments which culminated in his patent for the improved steam engine in 1769, he became a partner in Delftfield Pottery, and undertook tasks as a surveyor, making reports on the projected Forth and Clyde, Monkland and Caledonian Canals. The familiar story of the opposition of the Incorporation of Hammermen to his setting up shop in Glasgow seems unsubstantiated though not improbable. His main difficulty was rather the lack of engineering skill in constructing machinery, due largely to the lack of fine machine tools. After his removal to Birmingham, where he entered into partnership with Matthew Boulton of Soho Works to exploit his patent, he had little direct contact with Scotland. William Murdoch of coal-gas fame, and John Rennie the bridge-builder were among his Scots employees. His patent was at first operated by selling licences to erect engines ; of these 21 were set up in Scotland by 1800 and over 300 by 1825. This increase was facilitated by the improvements made in engineering tools and technique by inventors such as William Fairbairn.

Shipbuilding. The art of building wooden vessels had long been practised in Scotland, especially in east-coast ports. The *Great Michael* of James IV's reign remained a high achievement ; the great bulk of the output comprised small fishing and coastal boats. Encouragement to the industry in the West had been given by the colonial trade ; the pioneer firm of Scott of Greenock was founded in 1711, and yards were also established at Port-Glasgow and Dumbarton, but the majority of the vessels engaged on the Atlantic were built in America until the War of Independence necessitated reliance on home production.

A patent for a steam-driven vessel is said to have been taken out by David Ramseye in 1630, but no practical result followed. There were in the mid-eighteenth century experiments in steam navigation on the Avon and the Seine. On 14th October

1788, on Dalswinton Loch in Dumfriesshire, there was tried out a small steam-driven boat, designed by James Taylor (1753–1828), tutor in the house of the laird Patrick Miller, with an engine constructed at Carron Works on the patent taken out the previous year by William Symington (1763–1831), originally a millwright from Wanlockhead. Next year Symington put a boat on the Forth and Clyde Canal ; but it was only in 1802 that his paddle boat *Charlotte Dundas* demonstrated on the Canal the practicability of steam navigation. Like many other inventors Symington died poor and neglected ; and the new device was made a commercial success by Henry Bell (1767–1830), also a millwright, whose *Comet* in August 1812 made the voyage from Glasgow to Helensburgh. It was built by John Wood of Port-Glasgow, engined by John Robertson, with a boiler constructed by David Napier and a funnel by Pettigrew—all of Glasgow. Bell, who became a hotel and bath-house proprietor in the new residential resort of Helensburgh, ran this and other vessels on the Clyde and the Canal during the next few years. By 1818 eighteen steamboats were afloat, including the *Rob Roy*, built by Denny of Dumbarton and engined by David Napier, which voyaged to Belfast.

David Napier (1790–1869) became the real promoter of steam shipping, both as builder and shipper. He set up a yard at Lancefield in 1821, and established a regular service to Liverpool and Dublin, but shortly removed to London. The first iron vessel built in the Clyde area was the *Vulcan*, a barge launched by Thomas Wilson in 1819 on the Monkland Canal ; Napier followed with the *Cyclops* (1825) and the *Aglaia* (1827), both steam driven. His place was taken by his cousin Robert (1791–1876) who started as an engineer in 1815, and acquired the Lancefield yard in 1835. Other early shipbuilders included the Dennys at Dumbarton (1817) and the Stephens, who began at Burghead on the Moray Firth in 1750, and later founded yards in Aberdeen and Arbroath. So late as 1820, vessels built outwith Scotland constituted one-third of the tonnage engaged, and those built on the Forth were more numerous than those Clyde-built, though the latter comprised a large majority of the steamboats.

Shipping. There was considerable expansion of shipping at this period. A regular Irish mail service was established between Portpatrick and Donaghadee, which carried an average of 12,000 passengers and 20,000 livestock a year. The brothers Burns instituted in 1824 a service between Belfast and Glasgow —the germ of the famous Burns Line. The Aberdeen, Leith and Clyde Shipping Co. (*c.* 1790), the London and Edinburgh Shipping Company (1809), the Clyde Shipping Co. (1815) and Dundee, Perth and London Shipping Co. (1826), all contributed to the growth of coastal services. In 1818 Greenock led with nearly 350 vessels, of 46,000 tonnage. Its rapid expansion was due partly to privateering in the Napoleonic Wars, e.g. by Walter Ritchie and Sons, who also imported West Indian mahogany and Canadian timber. George Blake has celebrated the romance and prowess of the shipping of his native town in *Down to the Sea* and in his historical novels.

Chemicals. The great if inadequately realised importance of industrial chemistry has been indicated ; it primarily affected the bleaching and dyeing, glass and soap industries. " A galaxy of Scots gave a scientific direction to the Industrial Revolution, particularly to its non-mechanical aspects " (Clows), through the researches of the founders of the academic study of chemistry, William Cullen, Joseph Black and Francis Home, as well as of the brilliant amateur Archibald ninth Earl of Dundonald (1749–1831) who took out patents for chlorine, coal gas, etc., and established a tar works on his Culross estate (1782).

The sulphuric acid factory at Prestonpans (1749) has been mentioned ; it operated a lead chamber process invented by Roebuck, and exported vitriol. The permanent establishment of the chemical industry is mainly due to Charles Tennant (1768–1838), son of John Tennant of Glenconner (Ayrshire) farmer and friend of Burns ; he inherited capital from Governor Macrae. He obtained a patent for bleaching powder (1789), and set up a bleachworks at Darnley (Renfrewshire) ; he founded the St. Rollox Works in Glasgow in 1800 in partnership with Charles Macintosh who was also a partner in what became the Hurlet and Campsie Alum Co., which manufactured ammonia.

Meantime the old Scottish saltmaking industry dwindled almost to extinction, partly through increased heavy taxation but chiefly through effective competition from the growing imports from the Cheshire brine pits.

TRANSPORT

Transport, now recognised, through the emphasis given by Dr. Lilian Knowles, as essential to economic expansion, improved considerably.

Roads. The Scottish contribution to skilled road engineering is considerable. The respective claims of McAdam and Telford were disputed in their lifetime, and the dispute has been revived by their modern biographers. John Loudon McAdam (1756–1836), son of an impoverished Ayrshire laird, retrieved the family fortune by successful trade in New York. Returning to Britain after the War, he became a victualling agent to the Admiralty, and eventually a road surveyor in south-west England, where he developed the surfacing process which bears his name.

His rival Thomas Telford (1757–1834) [1] was of humble origin, son of a Dumfriesshire shepherd. Starting as a mason he gained the patronage of Sir William Pulteney, and became a surveyor and civil engineer, latterly in the service of the British Fisheries Society and Highland Roads and Bridges Commission. He is said to have constructed nearly 1,000 miles of roads and over 1,000 bridges. He was engineer for the Caledonian and other canals and consultant for the Göts Canal in Sweden. He constructed several east-coast harbours and the Dean Bridge in Edinburgh, advised regarding Edinburgh and Glasgow water supplies and surveyed an abortive railway from Glasgow to Berwick in 1810.

An Act of 1792 commuted statute labour for money payments ; outwith the Highlands, construction and maintenance continued to be mainly the work of Turnpike Trusts, for which General Acts were passed in 1823 and 1831. Mail-coach

[1] Full accounts of Telford have recently been given in L. T. C. Rolt's biography (1958) and A. R. B. Haldane's *New Ways through the Glens* (1962).

services were established between Glasgow and London in 1788 and Edinburgh and Aberdeen in 1798.

The most noted bridge-builder apart from Telford was John Rennie (1761–1821), whose bridge at Kelso has survived his more famous Waterloo Bridge on the Thames. He was of the noted East Lothian farming family ; his sons John and George also became distinguished as civil engineers.

Canals. This was, as in England, the heyday of canals. The Forth and Clyde, envisaged in the seventeenth century and later by Defoe, was the subject of several reports before its construction, roughly following the line of the Antonine Wall, was authorised by an Act of 1768, promoted by Sir Laurence Dundas, on whose estate was its eastern outlet. The engineer was John Smeaton (1724–92), a Yorkshireman of Scots descent. Operations were suspended for financial reasons between 1775 and 1784 ; it was completed in 1790 from Bowling on the Clyde to Grangemouth on the Forth, and was of commercial success and utility for half a century.

A direct link with Edinburgh was provided by the construction of the Union Canal (1817–22) which joined it at Falkirk and was much used for passengers and goods until superseded by the railway. The Monkland Canal, commenced in 1770 and completed in 1790, was, as already stated, of high importance in the expansion of the Lanarkshire coal and iron industries. Similar ventures were made on a small scale at Saltcoats, and more ambitiously but abortively between Glasgow and Ardrossan, to avoid the passage of the Clyde ; the incompleted channel was later partially diverted to railway uses. The Caledonian Canal (1803–22), proposed largely for strategic reasons, was never of economic importance, and the Crinan Canal (Kintyre) was a financial loss.

Railways. In the literal sense these began as " coal-pit accessories ", surface and underground ; " almost every railway in Scotland before 1820 was a colliery wagon road ".[1] The pioneer wooden railway, as already described, was laid by the York Building Company at Tranent in 1722 ; others followed, e.g. at Carron, Alloa and Fordell Collieries (Fife) ;

[1] cf. G. Dott, *Early Scottish Colliery Wagonways*

the last ran to the tiny export harbour of St. David's. Iron
rails were substituted early in the nineteenth century. These
lines " developed as a subordinate part of the canal system ".
The first " public " railways, still primarily for coal transport,
were those from Kilmarnock to Troon (1811) and the Monklands to Kirkintilloch (1826) ; these were horse drawn.
Charles Maclaren, first editor of *The Scotsman*, in several articles
in 1824 " forecast the value of railways " and made researches
in mechanics. The first locomotive in Scotland was introduced
in 1832.

Harbours. Glasgow set up a quay at the Broomielaw in 1688,
and established Port-Glasgow in 1662 as a landing-point for
vessels carrying on its trade. At length the city achieved the
long-projected expedient of making the Clyde navigable by
seagoing vessels by the deepening carried on under the
direction of John Golborne (1773–81). Regular steam dredg-
ing was later instituted, and the care of river navigation was
assigned to the Clyde Trust in 1809.

Landowners were prominent in building harbours largely
for the export of coal. That at Troon was developed about
1808 by the fourth Duke of Portland who had recently acquired
the estate of Fullarton in Ayrshire. The nearby port of
Ardrossan was the creation of the twelfth Earl of Eglinton, in
connexion with the frustrated canal project, about 1805 ; the
harbour works were completed by his grandson a generation
later. Grangemouth was developed from 1777 by Lord Dundas
of Kerse as a terminal for the Forth and Clyde Canal. Portpatrick Harbour was designed by Rennie in 1821 for the Irish
mail service, and Granton in 1835–7 by the Duke of Buccleuch
for his collieries.

In addition to Glasgow, other burghs such as Arbroath
undertook harbour improvements. The British Fisheries
Society established fishing harbours at Ullapool, Wick and
Tobermory, and the Highland Roads and Bridges Commission
those at Dundee and Peterhead. John Gibb (1776–1850) was
engineer for Leith Docks and Aberdeen harbour.

Lighthouses. The ruin on the slopes of Arthur's Seat, known as
St. Anthony's Chapel, is said to have served as a primitive

lighthouse for the Forth. The first modern building was erected on the Little Cumbrae in 1756. The Commissioners for Northern Lighthouses were established in 1786 by an Act promoted by George Dempster ; the members included the Sheriffs, hence the famous visit of Scott to the Orkneys on a tour of inspection in 1814, which bore fruit in *The Pirate*. Another literary association was afforded through the appointment as engineer of Robert Stevenson, whose son and successor Thomas was father of " R.L.S.". The chief achievements of the Commission included the erection of lighthouses at Kinnaird Head in 1787 and on the romantic Bell Rock in 1811, described in one of Stevenson's essays.

BANKING AND FINANCE

During the later eighteenth century there was some development of branch banking by the Chartered Banks, but local facilities were much more provided by a considerable increase in private banks both in the capital and in the rising industrial towns ; foundations took place between 1760 and 1790 in Dundee, Perth, Aberdeen, Stirling, Greenock, Falkirk and Paisley. Some of these were precariously based and failures were not infrequent, due either to undue speculation or to a crisis such as was occasioned by the outbreak of the American and French Wars ; the latter brought down the Arms Bank in 1793. In 1797 the example of the Bank of England in suspending cash payments was followed by the Scottish banks, chartered and private ; this policy, agreed on by their representatives, though without legal sanction, was pursued until the termination of inconvertible currency in 1821. Owing to scarcity of small change, the issue of notes of 5/- value was temporarily authorised. In 1810 the Bank of Scotland initiated the system of deposit receipts.

In the late eighteenth century " the expansion of private banking began again on rather sounder lines ", and partners in the private banks often sat on the Boards of the Chartered Banks ; Ramsay Bonar & Co. were thus associated with the Royal Bank and Mansfield & Co. with the Bank of Scotland. This popularity was however short-lived ; in the early nineteenth century " public opinion hardened against the private bankers ", on the grounds that they were unstable and speculative, added to costs as mere intermediaries and abused their position on the boards.[1] A rival type of banking successfully emerged ; the joint-stock banks, with their large capital and unlimited partnership, " sounded the death knell of the private banks " with their small partnerships and resources. The first of these was the Commercial Banking Co. (1810) with £3 million capital and over 500 partners, which was independent of the private banks, and instead set up its own branches, soon about 30, and made advances to industry and commerce. It was followed by the National (1825), with over 1,200 shareholders. Their success in Scotland encouraged the establishment of the joint-stock system in England, to which it was particularly commended by Thomas Joplin in his *Principles and Practice of Banking* (1822). There were however in the postwar boom several new local banks, of which the most notorious was that formed in 1818 in Aberdeen by John Maberley, an English speculator who also engaged in textile manufacture there ; he went bankrupt in 1832.

Scottish banks suffered less than English in the crisis of 1825, when only three failed. One result, the proposed abolition of the One Pound Note, evoked much opposition in Scotland, on nationalistic rather than economic grounds, since the note had become a symbol of Scottish independence ; this was voiced in petitions from County meetings, and in Scott's famous " Letters of Malachi Malagrowther " in the *Edinburgh Weekly Journal* (1826). A Parliamentary Committee reported against the proposal, but an Act of 1828 prohibited the circulation in England of Scottish notes under £5. At this date there were 32 recognised banks in Scotland, with about £20 million deposits. Perhaps the leading figure in Scottish banking during this period was Patrick Miller (1731–1815), an Edinburgh merchant who became laird of Dalswinton, and was thus, as we have seen, associated with the beginnings of steam navigation and also with the Carron Company. He became a Director of the Bank of Scotland in 1767, and served as Deputy Governor from 1785 till his death.

The source of capital for commercial and industrial

---

[1] *Three Banks Review*, Sept. 1951, pp. 28–34

expansion remains obscure ; much, it seems, must have come from the " thrift and abstinence " of those engaged in private and family concerns and the " ploughing in " of profits. Some importance is traditionally attached to the " cash credit " system in enabling individuals without personal capital to obtain advances from the banks ; this is said particularly to have aided farmers in making improvements, and also applied to the cattle trade and fisheries. The profits of the colonial trade, the estates of richer craftsmen and agricultural rents have been suggested as other contributory factors.

Most of the earlier enterprises were one-man businesses or small copartneries. Joint-stock companies existed from the seventeenth century, and were readily recognised by Scots law, for which " every company was a distinct persona " (Rankine). These early companies, of which Professor W. R. Scott made a meticulous study, were based on the unlimited liability of their partners. Company form was usually limited to banks, insurance, gas and canal companies, but was adopted by the Carron and Shotts Iron Companies.

The first great speculative mania affected Scotland as well as England in 1824, and was particularly stimulated by the opening of the South American market after the Spanish colonies attained independence. Over £20 million is said to have been invested in companies ranging from brewing to whaling. The collapse of 1825 " brought a period of magnificent expansion to a dead stop ".[1]

The " Tontine " system of annuities, commonly used for government loans in the eighteenth century, was used in Scotland for *inter alia* the establishment of hotels, e.g. at Greenock and Peebles.

The profession of accountancy developed during this period in municipal service, banking, etc. A notable pioneer was George Watson, who became accountant to the Bank of Scotland on its foundation and endowed a well-known Edinburgh school.

Examples of speculative enterprise, chiefly in the form of public contracts, are found in such careers as those of Sir William Forbes, Sir Lawrence Dundas and Sir William Fettes. Forbes (1743–1815), son of an Aberdeen merchant of landed

[1] L. J. Saunders, *Scottish Democracy*, p. 88

family, became a tinsmith in London and acquired a large fortune through naval and military contracts, and was thus enabled to purchase the forfeited Callendar estates (Falkirk) in 1783. Dundas (*d.* 1781), also of a landed family, was an Edinburgh merchant who also attained wealth as Commissar General to the army in the mid-century wars ; he became M.P. for Edinburgh and a Baronet, was Governor of the Royal Bank, 1764–77, bought the superiority of the Orkneys and Shetlands from the Earl of Morton for 60,000 guineas, and the estate of Kerse in Stirlingshire, where he promoted the foundation of the Forth and Clyde Canal and of the port of Grangemouth. Fettes, an Edinburgh wine and tea merchant (1750–1836), also flourished on army contracts, became Lord Provost and a Director of the British Linen Bank, feued the Comely Bank estate and left his fortune to found what has become one of the few Scottish " public schools ".

COMMERCE

Customs records indicate a fourfold expansion in the value of Scottish overseas trade in the 'seventies and 'eighties despite war restrictions. Coal and wheat were among the main exports to England. One item of particular concern to the Scottish traders was the monopoly of the East India Company ; thanks partly to the agitation headed by Kirkman Finlay and the Greenock merchants, India was opened to all British trade in 1813.

The history of retail trade is almost virgin soil. There are indications that in the eighteenth century reliance on markets and fairs diminished, and there was a growth in Edinburgh and the larger towns of shops, dealing in food, clothing and domestic goods, apart from the booths attached to craftsmen's workshops. It is noted that it was not uncommon " for men of good family to have a retail shop "—e.g. Dundas of Fingask in the Luckenbooths, the Earl of Hopetoun in the Lawnmarket. At the end of the century Robert Heron gives a glowing account of the wealth and variety of Edinburgh shops, " which it possesses as the seat of fashion and the commercial centre of intercourse for Scotland ". He notes the extent of the area from which the commodities are drawn, foodstuffs from " the circumjacent country ", manufactured wares from England, linen from Ireland, a variety of imports from France, Russia, the Mediterranean and the West Indies.[1]

SOCIAL CONSEQUENCES

The social consequences of industrialism, as was largely the case elsewhere, may be summed up as the dislocation of a " custom society ", the disruption of communal life, the intensification of distinctions of classes and the loss of their direct intercourse, the growth of individualism and materialism, and the separation of work and home, of labour and leisure.

The population aspect has been particularly studied by Professor D. F. Macdonald. The lack of definite statistics prior to 1801 handicaps comparison between the eighteenth and nineteenth centuries. Church registrations provide uncertain evidence, but Dr. Alexander Webster's survey for the Society for Propagating Christian Knowledge (1743–55), published only recently, seems reliable ; his estimated total was about 1¼ million, which tallies adequately with that presented by the Old Statistical Account (1790–8) of about 1½ million ; the first census (1801) revealed a population of 1,600,000, which by that of 1831 had grown to 2⅓ million. The birth-rate appears to have increased, and this is attributed to improvements in agriculture and food supply. The death-rate declined, perhaps largely due to better medical care, by which ague and smallpox were much diminished. Epidemics however continued, and with the growth of urban congestion the Glasgow death-rate increased in the early nineteenth century.

The Midland Belt, comprising one-seventh of the area, contained about 1,750 over one-third of the population ; half a century later, nearly two-thirds. The average density of population increased about two-thirds.

Irish immigration became an important factor ; it has been fully investigated by Dr. Handley in his *Irish in Scotland*. At first it was mainly seasonal, for harvest work, and later was

[1] R. Heron, *Journey through Western Counties* (1793), vol. ii, pp. 488–9

facilitated by the cheap passages offered by the early steamboats in the 1820's. Occupation was now readily found in navvying, textiles and mining. The 1841 census showed about 125,000 of Irish origin, 5 per cent of the whole. There was some contemporary emigration, notably to Canada where Galt the novelist was a promoter.

Increased urbanisation is indicated by the fact that a town dwelling population of a quarter (1800) had become a third by 1850. Glasgow, with a population of 28,000 in 1765 had tripled it by 1801, and by 1831 it rose to over 200,000. Edinburgh, with 100,000 in 1800 by 1825 increased this by 50 per cent.

One obvious result was the increase in ground values. The landowners were estimated at about 8,000, half of whom held entailed estates. Feuing was prevalent ; long leases were infrequent. The " Feuar " " acquired the use of land within the conditions of the deed, under secure perpetual tenure ". This perhaps encouraged speculative building, especially in the traditional " intensive " tenement style. A notorious example is the Blythswood estate, originally part of Common Lands of Glasgow, but acquired by the Campbell family. Much of it was developed for building in the early nineteenth century by William Harley, the pioneer of water supply, and James Cleland, the burgh official and statistician, and became the business quarter of Glasgow. Land bringing a rental of £220 in 1800 produced £25,000 about 1870. An Edinburgh example is afforded by the Broughton estate, in which the Heriot Trust made a very far-seeing and prosperous investment in 1636, when they acquired the superiority from the Crown in lieu of debts ; its value rose rapidly with the extension of the New Town. The Earl of Moray's estate in Edinburgh and the Powis estate in Aberdeen show similar features.

There was much expansion of building, industrial and domestic, but it remained a small-scale craft, of almost unchanged technique ; Hugh Miller's early experiences as a stonemason illustrate its characteristics. Much new building was paternalist, promoted by the industrial entrepreneur to house his workers, as at New Lanark and Deanston. Some was speculative, as in the well-known case of James Brown, who built George Square and other southern suburbs of

Edinburgh ; and in Glasgow, the Glasgow Building Company (1787) who feued in the George Square locality, and Thomas Binnie who commenced building on the south side of the Clyde.[1]

The traditional " Scots baronial " architecture was at the time giving way before the Classical Revival, of which the brothers Adam were the principal figures ; though much of their important work was in England, they were responsible for the Register House, the first South Bridge, Charlotte Square and the original plans for the University of Edinburgh, completed by Playfair.

The latter eighteenth century was also an era of planning, an idea familiar to the Classical world and to some extent practised in the medieval burgh. The New Town of Edinburgh is the best-known example, at first laid out on James Craig's plan (1767), but the capital had been anticipated by Greenock under Lord Cathcart (c. 1750), and was imitated in the layout of the newer part of Alloa by Erskine of Mar, of Stonehaven by Barclay of Ury and of Langholm by the Duke of Buccleuch, the pupil of Adam Smith. Helensburgh was planned virtually *ab initio* by Sir Ian Colquhoun, as a watering-place and residential centre. Many villages were laid out on their own estates by lairds ; the first probably at Ormiston by the Cockburns (c. 1726), Charlestown (1761) by the fifth Earl of Elgin, New Pitsligo by Sir William Forbes the banker (1787), Letham by George Dempster (c. 1790) are familiar examples. The idea was unfortunately ignored in the subsequent rapid industrialisation. Regulation of individual buildings remained a duty of the Dean of Guild in royal burghs.

Housing. Scottish housing standards, always low, were worsened in the industrial towns by the sub-division of already crowded tenements, now deserted by the better-off classes, and by the building up of " backlands " (open spaces) thus leaving inadequate air space and sunlight. Congestion reached its peak in the old central area of Glasgow, with 5,000 per acre (1821). Sharing of dwellings was frequent, so that the average

[1] J. R. Kellett's article in *Sc. Journal of Political Economy*, Oct. 1961, pp. 211–32, discusses " Property Speculators and the Building of Glasgow, 1780—1830 ".

there was 1·3 family per house while the average size of family was 6·1. Jerry-building was common, e.g. in the " miners' rows ", and was encouraged by the shortness of leases ; professedly " temporary " dwellings became semi-permanent. Probably a growing proportion of agricultural workers were housed in the " bothies " of mid- and northern Scotland, where unmarried men " fended " for themselves in barrack-like huts, and received allowances in kind.

The insanitary conditions have been demonstrated by contemporary reports, especially that of 1842, on " the Sanitary Conditions of the Labouring Population " and analysed by modern authorities such as Ferguson and Brotherston. Workplaces—e.g. textile mills, collieries—were unhygienic and also polluted air and water by their effluvia. The lack of drainage and sewerage, proverbially illustrated in the Edinburgh cry of " Gardyloo ", continued, despite sporadic efforts of civic authorities ; open sewers, sometimes used to irrigate and fertilise meadows, existed ; pigs and other stock roamed the streets ; the shambles and fish markets deteriorated the amenity of the neighbourhood. Water supply was derived mainly from public wells, at which daily queues formed. William Harley, the Glasgow builder, instituted a supply by carts as well as public baths (1804).

Endemic diseases included rheumatism and consumption. Epidemics of smallpox and typhus occurred in the 1810's, and a visitation of cholera vied in public interest with the Reform agitation in 1831–2. The widely circulated *Domestic Medicine* of Dr. William Buchan, which passed through about twenty editions, was " a principal means whereby medical thought influenced health ".

Food. Food supply was also inadequate ; such " deficiency diseases " as rickets were prevalent. Truck was often responsible for worse and dearer food. Intemperance was a prime social evil, encouraged by the cheapness and accessibility of potent liquors, whose sale was first regulated by the Home Drummond Act of 1828, which gave licensing powers to magistrates.

Such lawlessness as the activities of the " resurrectionists ", culminating in the notorious Burke and Hare episode of 1828, immortalised in Bridie's macabre play, display the seamier side of social life. The lack of open spaces and entertainment for the town dweller, transferred from his rural habitat with its customary amenities, have been graphically described by the Hammonds ; in the " Bleak Age " the " pub " was almost his only resort for leisure. Such Fairs as survived tended to become places and times of amusement. The Presbyterian discipline with its observation of the Sabbath and " Fast Days " was ignored or despised by many. Against much clerical resistance theatres were opened in several towns.

Conditions of Labour are indicated by the Factory Reports ; as those in Scotland differed little from English, little consideration is necessary. A main reason for the unsuitability of factories in respect of light, heating, ventilation, etc. was that many were adaptations of buildings designed for other purposes ; perhaps, as in more recent wars, as has been suggested, war conditions enhanced costs and limited supplies for new building. The introduction of coal-gas lighting enabled working hours to be lengthened.

Woman and child labour, certainly no novelty, was common, often a matter of sub-contracting by adult male workers, virtually employers, especially in the mines. Long-term contracts, such as the miners' " Yearly bond ", continued. Payment in cash was often made at long intervals, advances in kind being made meanwhile ; hence a chronic liability to debt, and consequent " arrestment of wages " by the creditor. Fines for lateness and damaged goods, " offtakes " for tools, medical care, etc., diminished real wages. The operation of the trade cycle made employment insecure, as in the 1790's and 1825.

There was a lack of public control ; the trend was towards desuetude of public regulation ; fixation of wages was abolished in 1813. The preoccupations of war and fear of Jacobinism militated against reform.

LOCAL GOVERNMENT

The varied composition, generally unrepresentative character and limited activities of burgh corporations have already been indicated. Burghs of Barony continued to be created, and occasionally some degree of self-government was conferred by the superior for specific purposes—e.g. Greenock, Falkirk, Kinross, Stornoway. Rates were originally levied for national purposes, as the contributions for which royal burghs were responsible ; they were allocated by the Convention of Burghs, and the varying proportions exacted in individual cases are a measure of their prosperity. There was no definite statutory basis for rating for local purposes, though the power might be inferred from the Acts of 1592 and subsequently, and was confirmed by judicial decisions. Levies for special purposes were specifically authorised on occasion—e.g. that for the stipends of the burgh clergy in Edinburgh (1633), the origin of the controversial " Annuity Tax ". " Stent masters " were commonly appointed, and these sometimes became an administrative body. Loans were latterly raised for public enterprises —e.g. harbours ; and inadequate security brought even Aberdeen (1817) and Edinburgh (1832) to admit insolvency.

Economic and political grievances in the late eighteenth century stimulated a demand for burgh reform, both for its own sake and because Parliamentary representation was based on the unrepresentative Councils. A convention was held in Edinburgh in 1784, and Archibald Fletcher, an advocate, became the protagonist. Draft Bills were drawn up, and a petition submitted to Parliament, but the French Revolution postponed action. The campaign was revived after the War by Lord Archibald Hamilton, M.P., and received a fillip from the Montrose case (1817), where elections were voided because of unconstitutional procedure, and a new charter gave an extended franchise.

Meantime the inertia and vested interests of the Burgh Corporations were in many cases circumvented by the establishment through Private Acts of elective bodies with rating powers and limited functions, usually relating to street cleansing, lighting, watching, etc., what Adam Smith called

" the regulation of inferior parts of government ". Bo'ness (1744) and Dalkeith (1759) appear to be early examples. A similar " Police Commission " (police in the Scottish sense, as in Smith's lectures on " Police Justice and Arms " ; i.e. administration, not constabulary) was set up for the new town and suburbs of Edinburgh in 1771 and extended in 1805. Aberdeen and Glasgow and several other burghs followed ; in the Glasgow area the device was adopted of giving burgh status to some of the suburbs, e.g. Anderston, Calton.

Local Improvement Acts were also passed at the instance of burgh councils, notably those inspired by Lord Provost George Drummond of Edinburgh (1687–1766), by which Commissioners were appointed (1752 et seq.) ; thus were effected the planning and building of the " New Town ", the erection of the North, South and George IV Bridges, the draining of the " Nor' Loch ", etc.

In the " landward " parishes there was no secular authority ; such administration as there was remained mainly in the hands of the Church, through the minister and kirk session, little subject to control save in the form of Court of Session decisions on disputed points. Their activities concerned mainly education and poor relief. Knox's *Book of Discipline*, which outlined a national system of education, remained inoperative, but an Act of 1696 eventually secured a minimum provision by enacting the establishment of a school in every parish. In the burghs there was usually more civic control ; High or Grammar Schools, sometimes of medieval origin, gave something of a secondary education. The parochial system, rather idealised by tradition and Ian Maclaren, was inadequate, both in quantity and quality, as modern research has demonstrated ; in 1815 the 942 parish schools had 54,000 scholars ; about two-thirds were being educated otherwise in over 2,000 schools. These included the 130 to 140 established in the Highlands by the Society for Propagating Christian Knowledge ; over 100 " Sessional " Schools, set up by the Church to supplement the parish schools ; denominational schools, resulting from the schisms in the Church (Secession and Relief), over 300 ; and about 30 each under the aegis of the Roman Catholic and Episcopalian Churches. Besides the endowed " Hospitals " or boarding schools such as Heriot's there was a wide variety of

" adventure " or private enterprise schools, ranging from the
" Academies ", opened in several burghs in the eighteenth
century to provide a modern commercial education, in contrast
with the classical and professional bias of the Grammar Schools,
to the " hedge schools " kept by discharged soldiers or decrepit
dames.   Despite all these, considerable illiteracy persisted,
estimated about 1820 as amounting in some Highland parishes
to from 30 to 70 per cent of the population.

Poor Relief, like education, has been well and fully
described by several authorities. It had " assumed the nature
of an ecclesiastical institution " in contrast with its " civil
character " in England.   Legislation can be traced to the Act
of 1424, instituting " licensed begging ", which inaugurated
the principle preserved until the twentieth century, that right
to relief was confined to the " impotent poor ". For the able-
bodied, penal discipline and compulsory labour were the
prescription asserted by post-Reformation enactments (1579 et
seq.).   The Act of 1597 came to be accepted in practice as
committing the responsibility for relief to kirk sessions in rural
areas ; functions were in the burghs shared with the Councils.
While rating powers were granted in 1579, reliance till the
eighteenth century was usually had to " voluntary " church
collections and other ecclesiastical revenues.   When with the
growth and shifts of population these methods became unsatisfactory, pooling of parochial resources was tried in larger
towns, e.g. Aberdeen, Glasgow ; and by 1800 nearly 100
parishes had resorted to assessment, mainly in the industrial
areas.   Chalmers's experiment in St. John's Parish, Glasgow
(1819–32), was a belated attempt to reverse the trend away
from the voluntary system and Church control. Liability for
its own destitute lay wholly on the parish ; the ambiguity of
the Law of Settlement occasioned much litigation, and even
physical strife.

Relief was mainly " outdoor " ; in the larger towns
" workhouses " were sometimes founded, usually by a combination of voluntary and municipal effort. That in Edinburgh
(1749) sought to distinguish classes of destitute, and to provide
separate and appropriate treatment for aged, children, " sturdy
vagabonds " and lunatics. There was " an entire absence of
any central government control ".

The County remained essentially a judicial and military unit. A county rate, " rogue money ", was introduced in 1724 and county magistrates were made responsible for prisons. They also acted frequently in the eighteenth century to enforce the maintenance and improvement of roads.

SOCIAL MOVEMENTS

Contemporary movements for political reform were explored in the pioneer research work of Dr. H. W. Meikle. Their leaders appealed to the " rebel tradition " of the Reformers and Covenanters. The demand for franchise reform, at first favoured by Pitt, was thwarted by the anti-Jacobin frenzy evoked by the French Revolution ; repression and persecution of any advocacy followed, culminating in the trials and transportation of Thomas Muir and the other " Political Martyrs ".

The post-war revival of agitation had a more economic and working-class tinge, especially in the general strike and " Radical Rising " (alleged to be instigated by *agents provocateurs*) of 1820. The succeeding decade witnessed the conversion of the Whigs, stimulated by the intellectuals of the *Edinburgh Review*, to the need of constitutional reform, and the accomplishment of economic reforms by the Canning and Huskisson Tories.

More immediately practical efforts to reform social conditions were made by the philanthropic movements which emerged in the later eighteenth century. In Scotland the influence of the Church was paramount. The medieval Catholic doctrines of the duty of charity and the deprecation of wealth-seeking had given place to the Calvinistic insistence on the vocation of labour, with property as its due reward ; but the social discipline exercised by the Church survived the Reformation and reached its apex in Geneva and New England. Calvinism was now modified by the rise of Evangelicalism, with its individualistic bias, its teaching as to the trusteeship of wealth and depreciation of the social causes and consequences of behaviour. Evangelicals were thus able to unite with secular reformers like the Utilitarians in practical schemes for penal reform, abolition of slavery, child welfare, etc. All these had their adherents in Scotland, but here peculiar importance attaches to the " voluntary hospital " movement, by which infirmaries, dispensaries and asylums were set up in the principal towns. The encouragement of thrift by the institution of savings banks is particularly associated with Rev. Henry Duncan of Ruthwell, afterwards a leader of the Disruption.

This period also witnessed the beginnings of mutual aid organisation among those who themselves suffered from social evils. The decline of the gild system was accelerated by industrial change, and among the journeymen of skilled trades whose opportunities of becoming masters were disappearing, notably the tailors, efforts at independent action were made. Strikes led to prosecutions for violation of the law (1617) which assigned the fixation of wages to the justices. This law was however sometimes invoked with success by the employees against their masters, as in the case of the Edinburgh printers (1805), but the last attempt, made on a nation-wide scale by the hand-loom weavers in 1812, though their case was upheld by the Court of Session, was frustrated by the recalcitrance of the employers, and resulted only in a disastrous strike, the imprisonment of its leaders and the repeal next year of legal fixation of wages.

Meantime unions were also appearing sporadically in the newer non-craft industries such as cotton-spinning and coal-mining. The application of the Combination Laws of 1799–1800 to Scotland has been disputed ; it appears that combination was sometimes regarded as an offence under Common Law.[1] Unions however survived clandestinely or in the guise of Friendly Societies. The Glasgow Cotton Spinners Union was credited with great power in the 1820's and was associated with the national organisation of the period. The best-organised workers were those of the printing trades with their " Chapels ". Miners were organised ephemerally in local unions, and there are traces of unionism in the building trades, reflected in Hugh Miller's early experiences as a stonemason. Owenite influence at the end of our period is evidenced in the attempt to set up a national general union, with sections for each trade.

[1] cf. J. L. Gray in *Economica*, Dec. 1928

Friendly Societies developed, somewhat on the model of the Incorporations as regards procedure and benefits. Some were virtually trade unions. Some were designedly temporary, many collapsed from lack of actuarial soundness. They attracted some public attention, and as an outcome of investigation by a House of Commons Committee an Act was passed in 1829 to regulate their position and protect their funds. They were in general approved by the authorities.

Examples of small-scale retail co-operation are found in the later eighteenth century, when local groups—e.g. Fenwick Weavers (1769), Govan Victualling Society (1777 ; it survived till 1909)—were formed to buy staple provisions wholesale and distribute them to members, thus eliminating middlemen's profits, and offering some assurance of quality of goods. Owen, at first a successful self-made industrialist who made New Lanark a model factory and village, the cynosure of aristocratic and even royal patrons, developed his co-operative doctrines first as a palliative for unemployment in the post-war depression, rather on the model of Bellers's projected Colleges of Industry a century earlier. After his breach with the governing classes and virtual relinquishment of New Lanark, he devoted himself to preaching the panacea of producers' co-operation.

The one full-fledged scheme in Scotland was the Orbiston Community [1] in Lanarkshire of 1826–8, directed chiefly by Abram Combe (brother of the phrenologist) ; among the active participants was Alexander Campbell (1796–1870) who here initiated his lifelong career as the most fervent and consistent exponent of Owenism. He later professed to have devised at this time the expedient of " dividend on purchase " later made the basis of their success by the Rochdale Pioneers. Labour Exchanges and bazaars and co-operative stores had a brief vogue, chiefly in the Glasgow area.

The movement for Adult Education was also pioneered at this time by John Anderson (1726–96), Professor of Natural Philosophy in Glasgow, patron of James Watt and sympathiser with the French Revolution. He conducted a special class for artisans, and bequeathed his estate to found a college for the

[1] cf. Cullen, *Adventures in Socialism* (1910), ch. xix–xxxii, for full account.

popular teaching of science. Anderson's College was accordingly formed, and its teachers included such well-known personalities as Andrew Ure, the apologist of the factory system, and George Birkbeck, commemorated in the college in London. An offshoot was one of the first Mechanics' Institutes (1823). Two years earlier Leonard Horner, brother of the Edinburgh Reviewer, had founded the Edinburgh School of Arts on similar lines ; and several such institutes were started within the decade.

Subscription libraries were also coming into fashion ; those at Leadhills and Dumfries are early examples. Samuel Brown of Haddington established about forty " itinerating " libraries in East Lothian. Popular " tracts " of an edifying character were published to vie with the earlier " chapbooks ". The periodical press became firmly established in town and country, despite the artificial raising of costs by the " taxes on knowledge "—e.g. the *Glasgow Advertiser* (later *Herald*, 1783), *The Scotsman* (1817), the *Dumfries and Galloway Courier* (1809) ; while the *Edinburgh Review* (1802) and *Blackwood's* (1817) expressed and moulded opinion on public issues ; the influential character of the former's articles on economics as well as its literary criticism has been noted by recent students.

The Universities, though their academic standards were low and their curriculum limited, offered a more " democratic " opportunity for education than most other countries did, and their repute in the natural sciences, in medicine and philosophy grew, and attracted students from south of the Border, including those excluded by their nonconformity from Oxford and Cambridge, but also men of such social standing as Henry Brougham and Lord John Russell. A Royal Commission of 1826–30 proposed drastic reforms, which were effected a generation later.

3

The Victorian Age

(c. 1830-1900)

MAIN CHARACTERISTICS

THE period of about seventy years which can conveniently if inaccurately be entitled " the Victorian Age " constitutes a stage in economic development marked by well-defined characteristics. These may be summarised as : the primacy of heavy industry, the growth of large-scale combination, the trend to the absorption of the Scottish economy within that of Great Britain, and the growing subordination of both to world economy.

The heavy industries—coal, iron and steel, shipbuilding and engineering, mineral oil—attain a growing ascendancy and increase the concentration of Scottish industrial strength in the Clyde area. " Consumptional " industries, with the partial exception of cotton, continue to flourish, and agriculture also retains its prosperity until the 'eighties.

The growth of large-scale organisation is stimulated by technical advance, involving higher capitalisation, and by the increased vogue of the limited liability company (finally legalised in 1862), both in the floating of new enterprises and in the reconstruction of old. The banks and the railways are particular examples, followed by the dyeing, distilling, tobacco and thread industries, and by the establishment of multiple and department stores.

The trend to absorption in British economy is one outcome of this concentration, and is also facilitated by financial developments and such legislation as the Bank Act of 1845, and by collectivist enactments, all-British in scope, e.g. the Factory Acts.

Subordination to world economy gave a rather precarious

basis to Scottish stability, in virtue of dependence on foreign markets for disposal of its leading products—coal, ships, machinery, textiles, etc.—and on overseas supplies of basic foodstuffs, especially grain, and increasingly of raw materials, such as iron, wool and flax, as home production became inadequate. Scotland was thus particularly liable to the " trade cycles " of boom and slump, which became almost regularly recurrent in decennial periods. There was also much Scottish enterprise and investment, especially in Asia and North America ; while there are a few notable instances of foreign initiative in Scotland—rubber, sewing machines, tramways and explosives.

While the period has these common features, various phases may be distinguished within it. There is an initial period of dislocation and unrest, to which the familiar phrase " the Hungry 'Forties " may be applied. There follows the period of rapidly expanding industry and rising standards of living, when Britain is most nearly " the workshop of the world ", the mid-century Years of Plenty (c. 1850–75). Then comes a time of retardation of growth if not of setback, of falling prices and wages, of foreign competition through the rapid industrialisation of Germany and U.S.A. ; this seems to have been particularly acute in the west of Scotland. The shock to the apparently assured progress of the economic system promoted the revival of Protectionism and Socialism. In the late 'eighties and 'nineties there is a slow recovery, and the rise of prices becomes evident by the end of the century.

LAND AND AGRICULTURE

One outstanding fact is the declining proportion engaged in agriculture, from nearly a half in 1831 to about one-quarter of the population in 1891. By the end of the century the total had fallen to little over 200,000. Rural depopulation, a kindred but not identical phenomenon, proceeded apace ; between 1851 and 1891 the proportion of country dwellers fell from about two-thirds to one-third. The Highland counties contained about one-third of the population in 1801 ; a century later about one-fifteenth.

According to Dr. D. F. Macdonald, much of the migration was short-distance. Early industries were often semi-rural, and rural employment includes much not directly dependent on agriculture. Industrial concentration gave the Clyde " conurbation " about one-sixth of the population by 1891.

Of landownership we have a unique statistical account in the official " Return of Owners of Lands and Heritages " (1874). This together with other evidence brings out the concentration of economic power and social prestige in some 8,000 proprietors, among whom the Duke of Buccleuch with two-thirds of Selkirkshire, as well as much in Dumfriesshire, and the Duke of Sutherland, with four-fifths of that county, are outstanding. About 400 had rent rolls of at least £2,500 per annum. These aggregations were fostered by the growth of entail early in the century ; by 1825 about half the acreage was thus bound, though later the Rutherford Act of 1848 and the Dunlop Act of 1860 facilitated disentail. Criticism of land monopoly recurred in the propaganda of the Anti-Corn Law League— e.g. by the East Lothian tenant farmer George Hope of Fentonbarns ; and the land-tax agitation of Patrick Dove and later Henry George and the Land League.

Rentals were increased by agricultural improvement up to the 'eighties, when bad harvests and foreign imports provoked decline. For those with estates in the developing areas the rise in site values for industrial and residential use brought profit. The Warrender and Pilrig estates in Edinburgh, Cranstonhill and Dennistoun in Glasgow, illustrate the effects of urban expansion. Much land was feued, or long leases given, and speculative building grew.

The original attitude of landlords to railways varied, some resenting intrusion, but most reaped gain from the compensation paid for land acquired, and it became realised that improved transport might enhance land values. Mineral royalties and wayleaves were another prolific source of " unearned increment " to those fortunate in their subsoil. The Royal Commission of 1888–94 demonstrated that iron-stone paid 6d. to 2/6 per ton, coal 4d. to 1/3, shale 4d. to 10d. in royalties ; wayleaves varied from 1d. to 3d. a ton. Leases for exploiting minerals were commonly for twenty to thirty years, and no compensation was due on the expiry of the lease for buildings or other improvements. Litigation sometimes occurred as to responsibility for damage to buildings by subsidence due to underground workings, and as to terms of royalties, as in the famous case of the original working of " torbanite " shale, in which the amateur theologian W. H. Gillespie was involved as the local laird.

Shooting rights were now protected by the Game Laws, supplemented by Poaching (1828) and Trespass Acts (1832), ultimately limited by the Ground Game Act of 1880 for protection of crops. Thus from the 1830's it became advantageous to establish deer forests ; by the end of the century some $2\frac{1}{2}$ million acres were thus demarcated, the largest being that of Mar in Aberdeenshire (c. 80,000 acres). A rental of nearly £200,000 per annum was estimated to accrue from the summer let of shooting rights.

It may be noted that there was no distinct cleavage between the landed and industrial interests. As earlier, landlords, notably the Duke of Portland, the Earls of Eglinton and Zetland, fostered and participated in industrial development, while the recurrent process of the *nouveaux riches* of industry and commerce laying out their wealth in acquiring land is illustrated by the Finlays, Bairds, Houldsworths and Mathesons. Some, perhaps of Scots descent, made their money in England or overseas, like John Ferguson (1787–1856) " the heaviest American fundholder in Great Britain " and James Morrison (1790–1857) the leading dry-goods merchant in London. Towards the end of the century the American magnate appears in the person of Louis Winans whose attempts at rigid enforcement of trespass on his Kintail estate afforded a *cause célèbre* of the 'eighties.

Several enactments modified conditions of land tenure. The Agricultural Holdings Act of 1883 gave compensation for improvements, and limited the right of Hypothec (eviction for arrears of rent). More conspicuous was that of 1886, the result of agitation in the Highlands, especially Lewis and Skye, against belated Clearances, and the subsequent Crofters' Commission of 1883, presided over by Lord Napier. The Crofters' Holdings Act gave a legal definition of crofters and cottars, numbering about 40,000, with rentals under £30, and occupying holdings in the seven " Crofting Counties ", which comprised nearly half the area but only 6 per cent of the population. Like contemporary Irish legislation, this provided for security of tenure, fixed " fair " rents with compensation for improvements. To implement these provisions a permanent Crofters' Commission was established of three members, as an executive and judicial body, which during its quarter of a century's existence dealt with about 22,000 applications.

These measures were supplemented by the Common Grazings Regulation Act (1891), designed to prevent over-stocking of pastures ; it proved ineffective. A Royal Commission on Deer Forests (1892) scheduled as available for new holdings over 300,000 acres, fully 10 per cent of the total " forested " area. Two later Acts of little effect were the Small Holdings and Allotments Act (1892) which empowered the new County Councils to acquire land for sale or lease ; and the Congested Districts Board Act of 1897 setting up an executive authority for similar aims.

Turning to agricultural development, of which a full and authoritative account has been given by J. A. Symon, we note progressive improvement, due partly to the stimulus of the Napoleonic wars and to better transport. Professor Saunders sees in the earlier part of the century the creation of a new rural society. By " conjunction of tradition and experiment . . . agriculture was become a business and a scientific art as well as an occupation. . . . Landholding became more than ever a multiple business, and estate management a very varied art ".[1] The latter function was performed increasingly on the larger estate by the " factor ".

" High farming ", arable and mixed, became more common ; longer leases were granted, often with " good Husbandry " clauses. The acreage under arable and pasture increased from $3\frac{1}{2}$ million acres in 1857 to $4\frac{2}{3}$ million in 1877. 1872 was the peak year for tillage ; wheat output declined thereafter. Land drainage was promoted by the Scottish Drainage and Improvement Co., and government loans were given for the purpose. James Smith, manager of Deanston cotton mills, was a pioneer in this field ; tile draining was practised on the Duke of Portland's estates by 1830.

Further improvements were made in technique. Smith

[1] L. J. Saunders, *Scottish Democracy*, 8, 17

was responsible also for an improved reaping machine. That which proved most satisfactory is attributed to Rev. Patrick Bell of Carnoustie (1828). He took out no patent, and manufacture was largely monopolised by Cyrus McCormick, founder of the International Harvesting Co. in Chicago. A notable Scots producer was the firm of Alex. Jack and Sons, Maybole (1852). A threshing machine devised by George McCartney early in the century was produced at the rate of about 100 a year at his works in Cumnock. A rotary churn for milking was introduced from France about 1850 and manufactured at Kilmarnock. Premiums for a steam plough were awarded by the Highland Society. Among successful inventors was James Usher of the Edinburgh brewing firm, at the Exhibition of 1851.

An important development was the growing use of artificial fertilisers, chiefly derived from South American guano. The firm of Alex. Cross and Sons, Glasgow, founded in 1830, became the leading supplier.

Experiments in plant breedings were carried out, e.g. by Patrick Shireff of Mungoswells, East Lothian, especially the " Hopetoun oats ". Improved strains of potato, securing immunity from virus, were obtained by William Paterson of Dundee (the " Victoria ", c. 1850) and Nicol of Arbroath (" the Champion ", c. 1870).

A regional variety, resulting from geographical factors, is manifest.

(i) The Lothians. This comprised much of the most fertile soil, and supplied the demand of the local city and of wider markets, especially London, for potatoes. The average farm was of 200 to 500 acres. Landlords usually were responsible for farm buildings and cottages. A free hand as regards crops and marketing was frequently given to the tenant. A common rotation, according to Professor Saunders, was an " alternate succession of grain and greens, which produced a marketable commodity, fattened stock and kept up the fertility level ".[1]

The labour force was supplied by the " hind " usually hired for six or twelve months at the " feeing market " held in such centres as Dalkeith and Haddington. This in practice meant considerable turnover, especially among the younger

[1] Saunders, op. cit. p. 37

men. They were paid both in money and kind, including perquisites such as milk and potatoes. There was a nucleus of skilled artisans for ditching, hedging and smithing, a " local reserve of semi-skilled labour ", supplemented by " unskilled seasonal harvest labour ", chiefly migrant Highlanders and Irish. A graphic account of the life of the agricultural worker is given in Alex. Sommerville's *Autobiography of a Working Man.* Blackfaced sheep were bred on the Moorfoots. Firms of nurserymen and seed merchants grew up in Edinburgh.

(ii) In the South-west meat and dairy produce were the staples. " Medium " family farms of 50 to 150 acres predominated. There were many small occupying owners, such as the Prydes of Lochwinnoch, whose papers have been published. Among the notable types of stock were the Clydesdale horses, apparently of Flemish origin ; shorthorn cattle in Dumfriesshire ; and blackfaced sheep, indigenous to Ayrshire. Cheese-making, especially of the " Dunlop " type, had flourished in Ayrshire since about 1700 ; a Dairy Association was formed about 1880 to improve processes and an " Ayrshire Cheddar " was produced.

There was a considerable development of orchards on the Upper Clyde in the latter part of the century—gooseberries, apples and pears, commonly sold by auction to town dealers. Strawberry cultivation on a large scale was introduced about 1870 and a boom followed. William Scott of Carluke became a leading producer and established a jelly factory in 1878. Glasshouse rearing of tomatoes was introduced at Braidwood about 1880. Vines and orchids were grown at Clovenfords from about 1870 by William Thomson, previously gardener at Dalkeith Palace.

(iii) In Aberdeenshire cattle rearing predominated, and has been described fully in the work of Miss I. M. Bruce. Shorthorns, introduced about 1780, displaced the native black cattle. Fame as a breeder was achieved by Amos Cruickshank (1808–95), a leader in the local Quaker community, who kept a pedigree herd at his farm of Sittyton. The " Aberdeen-Angus " hornless cattle were bred by William McCombie of Tillyfour (1802–80) from about 1830.

(iv) In central Scotland there were many large farms, where the bothy system was introduced from England about the

1830's. Despite relatively high wages and allowances in kind living conditions were bad, and the system was much assailed by social reformers such as Dr. James Begg.

Generally speaking, the trend was to stock rearing at the expense of arable as imports of grain increased. Market gardening, fruit farming (in Perthshire as well as Lanarkshire) and horticulture flourished.

Scientific study continued to be fostered by the Highland Society with its publications and annual shows. An Edinburgh Professorship of Agriculture had existed since 1790 ; a lectureship in forestry was added in 1889. The " Dick " Veterinary College was founded privately in 1823 and received recognised status in 1839. The Edinburgh College of Agriculture was founded at the end of the period (1901), and was preceded by the Glasgow and West of Scotland (1889).

The fisheries at the outset of this period lost their long-standing government supervision and support ; bounties were abolished in 1830. A public Fishery Board was established in 1882. Attempts were made to control the chronic competition with foreign vessels, formerly Dutch, now mainly Norwegian, by agreements, culminating in the North Sea Convention of 1882, which sought to preserve coastal rights but did not eliminate litigation.

Herring fishing was carried on from such ports as Fraserburgh, Peterhead, Wick and Stornoway. Drift nets were used and most of the fishers owned their boats. Curing was helped by the repeal of the salt duty in 1817. The chief export markets were the West Indies and latterly Germany and Russia. Of the white fishery (cod, haddock, etc.) Aberdeen was the chief centre. In the mid-century 4,000 to 5,000 boats and 20,000 to 30,000 men were engaged. The fresh-fish trade grew in the latter decades, with quicker transport and better preservatives. A net loom was invented by James Paterson about 1812 and a factory set up later in Musselburgh ; thus home production was superseded.

The fishing communities were usually isolated and largely self-contained. Fishing was much of a hereditary craft. Women had their essential part, in (at first) weaving nets, preparing bait and selling the catch. The Newhaven fishwives were long familiar, and their life in the early Victorian period was described by Charles Reade in his *Christie Johnstone*. The Moray Firth fisherfolk are vividly portrayed by a later novelist Neil Paterson in *Behold Thy Daughter* ; and have found an artist as well as a historian in Peter F. Anson.

By the end of the century a seasonal migration of female labour developed for the gutting, salting and packing of herring—Wick and Fraserburgh in the summer, Yarmouth and Lowestoft in autumn. Anson describes and illustrates varied local types of boat ; the *Zulu* constructed at Lossie-mouth about 1880 was the finest design. Steam trawling was introduced about this date, and began a tendency to company ownership—e.g. Richard Irvin & Sons, Aberdeen—because of higher costs. The catch was auctioned in harbour—in the open, as at Eyemouth, or in the large market-hall built in Aberdeen in 1889.

Salmon, plentiful in the eighteenth century, declined in numbers owing to river pollution. Despite protective measures poaching was rampant on the Tweed. Lobster and crab fishing was practised in the northern and western isles. The whale " fishery " was pursued, chiefly from Peterhead and Dundee, but declined after the mid-century, owing to the competition with whale oil of gas and mineral oil ; whalebone and ambergris remained in demand. Expeditions to the Antarctic were sponsored in the 'nineties by Chr. Salvesen & Co. of Leith and the Tay Whale Fishing Co. of Dundee.

INDUSTRIAL DEVELOPMENT

HEAVY INDUSTRIES

Considerable information about coal-mining is obtainable from the Reports of the Commissions on Coal of 1871 and that on Mining Royalties of 1888–91 ; and from the annual reports on mines, notably those of the distinguished public servant Hugh S. Tremenheere (1804–93), who was " Commissioner for Mining Districts " from 1843 to 1858. There are also accounts of particular areas by A. S. Cunningham, and more recently of companies by J. L. Carvel and others.

" Paternalist " organisation continued during the earlier Victorian period in the older areas of Fife and the Lothians.

An example is the Earl of Buckinghamshire's pits at Fordell (Fife), including the famous " William " pit, opened in 1843 and operated for over a century. A private rail conveyed trucks to the tiny port of St. Davids, crossing the main northern line between Inverkeithing and Aberdour. There was a rapid development in the West, thanks to the great industrial demand, and by the mid-'seventies some 70 per cent of output came from the Lanarkshire and Ayrshire fields. Total output rose from 7½ million tons in the 'fifties to nearly 33 million in 1900 ; and exports from 1½ million to nearly 17 million, largely from the ports of Granton and Burntisland. Some export was undertaken direct by the coalowners, but firms of exporters such as D. M. Stevenson of Glasgow grew up. Large contracts were made, e.g. with Italian State Railways.

With the legalisation of Limited Liability the joint-stock company developed as in other industries from the 'seventies. Outstanding was the Fife Coal Co., founded in 1872, which rapidly acquired other pits throughout the county ; its expansion was largely due to Charles Carlow (1849–1923), manager from 1873. The Arniston (1874), the Lothian (1890) and the Wemyss (1894) illustrate old family concerns which took joint-stock form. The Niddrie and Benhar Co. (1882) had varied enterprises and chequered progress. James Nimmo & Co. (1897) and Gavin Paul & Sons (1898) are examples of the newer entrepreneurs. Mining " dynasties " include, besides the Carlows and the Nimmos, the Hoods and the Moores in the Lothians.

Vertical combines became frequent, bringing coal-mines under the control of iron and steel magnates like the Bairds, Addies and Dixons, and the Coltness and Shotts Companies. Coalmasters' Associations were formed in the main coalfields, largely to deal with the rising trade unions.

Improvements in technique were made, as regards ventilation, drainage, transport, etc. ; coal-cutting machinery was introduced by the Fife Co. in the 'eighties. Deeper strata were tapped ; the chief methods of working were the " stoop " or pillar, and the " long wall " (continuous face). Scotland is credited with a lower accident rate than England, owing to freedom from " fire damp ". A common type of coal was the " cannel " or " parrot " which yielded gas and oil ; anthracite was mined in Stirlingshire. Attention was called to the problem of subsidence by damage sustained on the Duke of Hamilton's estate at Motherwell in 1888 ; an abortive measure to ensure compensation was introduced into Parliament.

Employment almost doubled, rising from about 40,000 to nearly 75,000. The underground labour of women and children was prohibited by an Act of 1842. Regular inspection commenced in 1850, and by the " Miners' Charter " of 1872 improved working conditions were given legal protection.

Iron-mining was stimulated by the discovery of the black-band ironstone and the hot-blast process, but output declined as the better ores were exhausted ; local supplies fell by nearly one-half in the last decade and employment was reduced to about 3,000. Raw material was obtained from Cumberland, and from abroad, especially from Spain, where the Coltness and other companies acquired control of mines.

Shale-mining had a period of expansion and prosperity. Mineral oils had been known in the Middle Ages, and used chiefly for medicinal purposes. The experiments of the ninth Earl of Dundonald in the late eighteenth century led to some industrial utilisation. The development on a large scale of the mineral-oil industry must be attributed to James Young (1811–83), a Glasgow man who carried on experiments and production in Derbyshire before utilising the " torbanite " discovered on the estate of W. H. Gillespie, with the resultant litigation already mentioned. Young's patents also involved him in several lawsuits to maintain his rights. The bituminous shale of the Lothians proved a satisfactory source and much activity ensued in the Bathgate area in the 'fifties, occasioning a threefold increase of population in a few years. Here and at Addiewell extraction of shale was combined with distillation of oil and manufacture of naphtha candles and other by-products. Technical improvements were made by Young and others ; the Beilby retort was introduced about 1880. Some 5,000 were employed by 1900.

Young's success attracted competitors and the " Scottish Oil Fever " set in in the 'sixties. About fifty companies were started, of which only seven survived by 1900. Young converted his own business into a large joint-stock company in which he retained a large interest. The leading figure in the second generation was Robert Bell who founded the Broxburn Co. in 1877 ; the Pumpherston Co., started by Archibald and William Fraser in 1883, became the nucleus of the present Scottish Oils combine. In the later decades the brief prosperity of the new industry was challenged by the competition of the natural oilfields of U.S.A., and later of Asia. The price of oil dropped from 3/6 a gallon in the 'sixties to 6d. in 1887. A Scottish Mineral Oil Association was formed in 1887 to regulate output and prices ; it came to an agreement with the Standard Oil Co. next year, but this was terminated in 1892 and the Association collapsed.

Some unsuccessful ventures in mining copper were made, e.g. by the Marquis of Breadalbane in Perthshire (*c.* 1840–60). The mining of lead was continued intermittently with varying fortune in the Leadhills, latterly by the Silver Lead Mining and Smelting Co. (1876). Alum was worked at Hurlet till supplies were exhausted about 1880.

Granite quarrying was carried on in Aberdeen. Previously small-scale, it expanded early in the century to provide paving and monumental stones. Material was supplied, e.g. for Waterloo Bridge and the Bell Rock Lighthouse. Export reached 50,000 tons in the 'sixties, and saved Aberdeen from depression in the 'eighties. Galloway was another centre, and thence came the stone for the Thames Embankment. Edinburgh sandstone found chiefly local use. Easdale and Ballachulish were noted for their slates. Large firms of quarry masters, operating throughout the country, were founded.

METALLURGICAL INDUSTRIES

A common feature is the liability to be affected by the trade cycle, owing to elasticity of demand. Hence selling prices fluctuated frequently and considerably. The iron trades expanded rapidly after the general introduction of the hot-blast process, in which improvements were made by John Condie of Blair Ironworks. The rapid growth of railways enhanced demand, e.g. for rails. Output increased sevenfold between 1835 and 1845, and by 1848 a fourth of British production was in Scotland. Over-investment probably occurred. The competition of South Wales and later of the Cleveland area was felt later in the century.

The iron industry developed mainly in Lanarkshire [1] and Ayrshire, where blast furnaces abounded. Several large-scale enterprises soon operated. The brothers Baird commenced the famous works at Gartsherrie (Coatbridge) in 1828, and within the next thirty years acquired Eglinton, Muirkirk and other works in Ayrshire. The outstanding figure was James (1802–76), a strong Tory and Churchman, a doughty foe of trade unionism, a " rough diamond " of whom many anecdotes are preserved. Active control passed to their nephews Alex. Whitelaw (1823–79) and William Weir (1834–1913), and subsequently to Sir William Laird (1830–1901) and Andrew K. McCosh (*d.* 1916) ; the firm became a private company in 1894 with a capital of £800,000.

James Merry (1805–77), lessee of Carnbroe Collieries from 1833, joined with Alex. Cunninghame, twelfth laird of Craigends, to establish ironworks at Glengarnock, Ayrshire, in 1843, to which furnaces at Ardeer and Stevenston were soon added. Merry became a chief rival of the Bairds in politics as well as industry, and was a noted sportsman. After Cunninghame's death a limited company was formed in 1872 with £1 million capital. The directorate comprised several landowners and industrialists ; John Cunninghame, nephew of the co-founder, was managing director. The company was reconstituted in 1891 when Beardmore of Parkhead joined the board. John C. Cunninghame (1857–1917), son of Alexander, became chairman.

Henry Houldsworth (1770–1853), who had come from Lancashire to Glasgow to engage in the cotton manufacture, established the Anderston Foundry and Machine Works to make textile machinery, and eventually abandoned the cotton industry. In 1836 his brother Thomas bought Coltness estate from the Stuart Denhams, the family of the economist, and established his nephew John (1807–59) in an ironworks there. Another works was founded at Dalmellington in 1846, and collieries and ironstone-mines acquired, latterly in Spain. In the Coltness and associated Dalmellington Companies Houldsworths predominated for several generations.

Another notable family was that of the Dixons, whose

---

[1] *The Monkland Tradition* by T. R. Miller (1958), a veteran industrialist, gives a rather rambling history of the iron industry of Lanarkshire.

" Blazes " at Govanhill were long a familiar landmark in south Glasgow. Other firms in various branches of the iron industry were the Glasgow Iron Co., whose manager Thomas Morton took out patents for refining and puddling ; the Blochairn Iron Co., Glasgow, which had much ill-success until acquired by the Steel Co. ; and Smith and McLean, Mossend and Gartcosh, who specialised in galvanised iron and sheets.

The pioneer Carron Co. retained its position as a manufacturer of light castings and other ironware, though suffering from litigation, occasioned by the alleged over-predominance and nepotism of successive managers of the same family. The Shotts Iron Co., managed for many years by John Ormiston, remained one of the leading producers. It became closely associated with the Fife Coal Co. ; at one of its pits occurred the great Mauricewood disaster (1889).

The Falkirk Iron Co., an offshoot of the Carron (1819), came into the hands of the Kennard family in 1848, and manufactured munitions and a variety of goods from bridges to pots and pans. Several other companies were founded in the later decades, and the Falkirk district became the centre of the light-castings industry.

A special type of product was the stove, on the American model, introduced by James Smith and Stephen Wellstood, whose works were transferred to Bonnybridge in 1871. Wellstood was an Edinburgh Radical politician, associated with the Society of Friends. The manufacture of sanitary appliances was undertaken by James Shanks (d. 1895) at the Tubal Works, Barrhead.

The manufacture of iron tubes was commenced in Glasgow in the 'thirties, stimulated by the demand for pipes to convey coal gas on Murdoch's patent. The most notable firms were the Clyde Tube Works of A. & J. Stewart (1860) who soon absorbed other works and ultimately shared in the great combine of Stewarts & Lloyds, and the North British Tube Works, founded in 1868 by Sir David Richmond, afterwards Lord Provost of Glasgow.

Wire manufacture, long a handicraft, was mechanised ; the firm of Brunton at Musselburgh (1876) took a leading place.

Towards the end of the century the use of steel partially

superseded that of iron, especially in shipbuilding. About 1 million tons were being produced annually by 1900, giving employment to about 6,000. This was largely due to the Siemens process, introduced by the Steel Co. of Scotland, founded in 1871 by the chemical magnate Sir Charles Tennant, with works in the Glasgow area. With it was closely associated the Tharsis Co. (1863) which owned and worked copper mines in Spain and factories in Glasgow, South Wales and on the Tyne. Another notable firm was that of Colvilles, whose works at Dalziel (Motherwell) dated from 1871 ; they began steel-making in 1880. Stewart and Menzies, Clydesdale Works (1890) were founded by Andrew Stewart of the Tube Works, with which they soon amalgamated. The Parkhead Forge, established by Robert Napier in 1842, was developed for steelplate for armoury by the Beardmores, associated with it since the 'sixties. Merry & Cuninghame introduced the Bessemer process at their Glengarnock Works in 1884.

Engineering. The amorphous and relatively unexplored engineering industry can hardly be distinguished sharply from the iron and steel industry. It includes complex and varied forms of enterprise. The early engineers, such as Watt, Telford and Rennie, were essentially versatile in their scope. The origin of the engineer may be found in the crafts of the millwright and the smith, and also in the military expert in fortifications such as Vauban. There have been gradually differentiated such branches as the civil, mechanical, electrical and marine engineer.

The mechanical engineer was most conspicuous at this period through the growth of " machinofacture ". The millwright who had constructed windmills, water wheels, flour mills, etc. extended his range to steam engines, pumps, tools and machinery. His was still a handicraft, relying on manual dexterity. His material was chiefly wood ; little iron was used ; the commoner metals for fittings were brass and copper. The early machines were usually set up in the works where they were to be used, by local labour, on specifications supplied under patent—e.g. Watt's steam engine.

The first real steps in advance came with the growing use of iron ; " almost all the great engineers—e.g. Henry Maudsley

(1771–1831)—started in an iron foundry " ; and with the transformation of tools and introduction of precision instruments such as the lathe and plane (c. 1800–40), thus removing the previous handicap of inaccuracy which had hampered Watt. The principal Scottish contributions were those of Sir William Fairbairn (1789–1874), the steam-riveting machine (c. 1838), and James Nasmyth (1808–90), the steam hammer (1839) ; both inventors settled in Manchester. There followed the establishment of machine-making factories—in Gordon Bottomley's phrase, " machines for making more machines ".

Within this came fuller specialisation—e.g. sugar machinery, chiefly for the West Indies, pioneered by James Cook of College Works, Glasgow, a business later acquired by McOnie, Harvey & Co. ; associated with the latter was the Mirrlees Watson Co., which after 1885 entered other branches of engineering also. Textile machinery was made, as already noted, by the Houldsworths of Anderston, chiefly for cotton factories : the needs of linen were supplied by Carmichaels of Dundee, of woollens by Melroses of Hawick. Locomotive engineering was undertaken by the Neilsons at Hyde Park Works, Glasgow, while the larger railway companies produced their own rolling stock. Babcock and Wilcox, of American origin (1867), became the leading producers of boilers and heaters ; the business became a limited company in 1891, dominated by Stewarts and Arrols. It operated thirty two British patents, and had an agreement with a sister firm in New York. George & James Weir at the Holm Foundry, Cathcart, made improvements in boiler construction.

Sir William Arrol, who set up works at Dalmarnock in 1868, attained world repute as a bridge-builder ; the Tay and the Forth Bridges were among his achievements. Alex. Findlay of Parkneuk (Motherwell) and P. & W. Maclellan of Clutha Works, Glasgow, also attained success in this field.

Smaller local firms, such as Jack of Maybole and Shanks of Arbroath (inventor of the lawn mower), devoted themselves to agricultural machinery.

A great variety of specialised types grew up, among whom may be noted the machine-tool works of Shanks at Johnstone (c. 1820) and the Rivet, Bolt and Nut Co. of Glasgow, a combine of several firms (1900) : Glenfield and Kennedy, Kilmarnock, hydraulic appliances (of which firm Dr. Robert Munro the archaeologist became head) ; Barr and Stroud, scientific instrument-makers, Glasgow ; Bertrams of Edinburgh, paper-making machinery ; Henry Balfour of Leven (Fife), rice machinery ; and Bruce Peebles of Edinburgh (1866), electrical machinery.

The sewing-machine was another invention of American origin. That patented by Elias Howe (1846) was manufactured in Glasgow between 1873 and 1897. His more successful rival, Isaac Singer (1851) formed a company, associated with Babcock and Wilcox, which came under the direction of the Scots immigrant George Mackenzie. Under his auspices retail shops were established in Glasgow, pioneering the hire-purchase system, and a factory set up at Bridgeton, and soon transferred to Kilbowie (1882) where along with Thomsons' shipyard it was responsible for the emergence of the new industrial town of Clydebank.

Two noted Glasgow firms, Kelvin and White, of which Lord Kelvin the eminent physicist was a partner, and Mavor and Coulson, pioneered electrical engineering. Members of the Mavor family became famous also in economics and drama.

Marine engineering arose from " a fusion of interest between the iron industry and shipbuilding with the development of the marine engine ". Robert Napier (1791–1876) had commenced marine engineering in 1823, and set up works subsequently at Lancefield and Parkhead ; he was associated with the Burns Line and Cunard Co., and held Admiralty contracts. Parkhead passed to the Beardmores in the 'sixties, but was reunited with the marine engineering works in 1900. The original firm passed from the Napiers to a partnership in which the leading role was that of Dr. Alex. Carnegie Kirk, an able inventor. John Elder (1824–69), a brilliant experimenter, became partner in an engineering firm at Tradeston in 1852, and set up a shipyard at Fairfield (Govan) in 1864 ; after his premature death the Fairfield Company was formed, headed by Sir William Pearce. Dennys of Dumbarton also combined engineering and shipbuilding in two closely associated family firms. William Denny (1847–87) contributed much both to technical advance and to better labour relations, in which he was matched by Robert Duncan (1850–1924) an avowed Carlylean who introduced profit-sharing in his Govan works ; as a politician he was a Chamberlain imperialist.

Shipbuilding.[1]   Marine engineering, as already indicated, is closely linked with shipbuilding, even when the firms concerned remain separate.   There was a great expansion from the middle 'forties, when " the use of the marine steam engine began to give the Clyde its great predominance " (I. F. Grant).   This was displayed in successful competition with the Thames ; a final triumph was achieved in the transfer of Yarrows in 1906. In the 'eighties two-thirds of British tonnage was being built on the Clyde.   There was some building in east-coast ports but on a smaller scale, and the leading-east coast firm, Stephens, transferred their activities to the West about 1850.   Much of the output, reaching half a million tons by 1900, was built to foreign orders, especially German.   The prosperity of the industry was however variable, owing to its special liability as a constructional industry to the trade cycle.

Two chief features of the period were the substitution of iron and steel for wood as material, and of steam for wind as motive power.   (i) The former, depicted in drama by Bennett and Ervine, was heralded by David Napier's *Aglaia* (1827) and Neilson's *Fairy Queen* (1832).   Iron building was developed mainly by smaller employers, and more slowly than on the Thames.   Progress was retarded by the opposition of timber merchants, the imperfections of technique and the distrust shown by underwriters.   Tod and McGregor, founded in 1834, were the firm who first specialised successfully in iron vessels, launching the first iron ocean liner, *The City of Glasgow*, in 1851. The introduction of the propeller, the local accessibility of iron, and the training of skilled metal workers ultimately assured the victory of iron.   In the 1850's, of about 100 vessels launched only six were of timber.   Steel was first used in shipbuilding on the Clyde at Fairfield in 1877 ; by 1890 steel-ship output had risen to 97 per cent.   (ii) Overseas steam shipping expanded in the 1840's, after the first Atlantic crossing

---

[1] J. Shields, *Clydebuilt* (1949), gives a detailed factual account ; G. Blake, *Down to the Sea* (1937), a popular impressionistic one of Clyde shipbuilding.

by the *Sirius* (1838). It was employed by the P. & O., Canadian lines, etc. The sailing ship however held its own : in 1850 there were still 3,500 afloat, against 170 steamers ; in times of depression there was a tendency to revert to sail. The famous " Clippers ", of which Alex. Hall and Duthies of Aberdeen were the chief builders, had their brief ascendancy in the 'sixties and 'seventies ; they were particularly used in the China tea and Australian wool trades, where speed of voyage was not essential. Names of vessels such as the *Thermopylae* and the still-preserved *Cutty Sark* became household words, and their races a theme of popular interest. The opening of the Suez Canal (1869) was the main cause of their supersession ; improved methods of using fuel made steam more economical, steam construction trebled in the 'sixties and constituted 95 per cent of output in the 'nineties.

Output embraced all classes of vessels—passenger and cargo boats, " tramps ", dredgers (in which Simons of Renfrew specialised) and yachts (especially for the annual Clyde Regatta ; George L. Watson (1851–1904) was a noted designer) and war vessels. Napier secured the first Admiralty contract in 1838 and supplied floating batteries and ironclads for the Crimea. The Fairfield and other south-bank yards obtained the bulk of naval work and produced many vessels for foreign powers, including Russia and Japan. Blockade runners were fitted out during the American Civil War, occasioning friction with the United States government. In 1900 naval output constituted two-fifths of the total.

In that year about 25,000 men were employed in the shipyards. Among the chief shipbuilding firms were that founded by Robert Napier : the Fairfield Company, Govan, and J. & G. Thomson, who began shipbuilding in 1851 and transferred their yards to Clydebank in the early 'seventies ; they were bought up in 1899 by John Brown of Sheffield. They built for the Cunard, P. & O. and Union Lines. Tod and McGregor, the pioneers of iron-shipbuilding, were acquired (1872) by D. and W. Henderson, who had close family con-nexions with the Anchor Line. Barclay Curle and Co., engineers, Stobcross, were developed as shipbuilders by James Gilchrist, principal partner from 1880. The Stephens, moving from the east coast in 1851, were a family firm for many generations ; the tale of the Glasgow builders is completed by A. and J. Inglis of Pointhouse (1846).

At Greenock and Port-Glasgow were two long-lived family firms, the Cairds and the Scotts ; the yard of John Wood, builder of the *Comet*, was acquired by Robert Duncan & Co. Russell and Co., commencing in the yard of an earlier firm at Cartsdyke in 1874, became within a decade the largest builders on the Clyde ; control soon passed to William T. Lithgow (1854–1908). Dennys of Dumbarton and Lobnitz of Renfrew were the other major firms on the Clyde. There were several small firms at ports such as Troon and Campbelltown on the west coast, Alloa and Leith on the east. Hall, Russell and Co. maintained the industry in Aberdeen and W. B. Thompson and Co. that of Dundee.

Timber was the basic material for many products used in house and ship building, in mining as pit props and later for paper-making. Estate owners planted trees for the market as well as for amenity. Local supplies came especially from the valleys of the Spey and the Findhorn, " one of the chief centres of Scottish lumbering," [2] where it was usually floated downstream by lumberers,[1] and were supplemented by import, notably through the " St. Lawrence trade " with Canada, in which Pollok Gilmour & Co. of Glasgow and Liverpool were leading importers. Colonial products enjoyed a " preference " until 1860 ; thereafter the Baltic and Swedish trade expanded and Grangemouth became the chief port. Large sawmills grew up, e.g. in Falkirk, Glasgow and Grangemouth, where Brownlie & Co. introduced the circular saw. The making of wooden boxes and barrels—originally for fish—was developed by Wm. Fiddes & Son, Aberdeen, from about 1870.

Chemicals. Various branches of chemical industry developed in this period. The pioneer firm of Tennants of St. Rollox, producing bleaching powder, sulphuric acid, soda, etc., expanded under the long leadership of Sir Charles Tennant (1823–1906), grandson of the founder, who became one of the leading industrialists of Victorian Scotland, as well as a Liberal

[1] T. Henderson, *The Findhorn* (1932), p. 79
[2] *The Scotsman* 9.4.1960, " Logs on the River Spey "

politician, father of a Secretary for Scotland and of a woman Life Peer, and father-in-law of a Premier (Asquith). Tennants became associated with the Tharsis Co., owning copper-mines in Spain, and the Steel Co. of Scotland. In 1890 the firm was absorbed in the United Alkali Co., a union of forty-five firms, headed by Muspratts of St. Helens, which utilised the Leblanc process and had protracted rivalry with Brunner Monds combine, utilising the alternative Solvey process, until they finally united in I.C.I. (1926). The Hurlet and Campsie Co., now controlled by the family of King, continued to manufacture alum, ammonia, cyanide, etc.

Alfred Nobel, the Swedish inventor who bequeathed the famous " prizes ", in 1871 formed " the British Dynamite Co. ", which acquired the British rights in his dynamite patents, and established a factory at Ardeer ; Nobel retained half the capital, the rest being taken up by Glasgow capitalists, of whom Charles Randolph of Fairfield became chairman. In 1877 this was transformed into Nobel's Explosives Co., with a much larger capital, particularly to develop a new process for gelatine blasting, on which Nobel was to receive 5 per cent royalty ; this acquired other companies in Britain and overseas. In 1886 two trust companies were formed, of which the Nobel Dynamite Trust Co. with £2 million capital acquired the shares of Nobel Explosives and some associated foreign companies. On its reorganisation in 1900 Sir Charles Tennant became chairman.[1]

Artificial fertilisers were developed by Alex. Cross & Sons, Glasgow, originally seedsmen and manure merchants, who imported American phosphates, notably Peruvian guano. J. & J. White, Rutherglen, manufacturers of soap and soda, came to specialise in chrome for leather working. Lord Overtoun (1843–1908), long head of the firm, was prominent in the Free Church and other religious activities, and acquired less desirable fame through the exposure by Keir Hardie of oppressive and insanitary conditions in his works (1899).[2] Other varieties of the chemical industry included the Cassel Gold Extracting Co. (1884), holding patents which superseded

[1] I.C.I. published *A History of Nobel's* (1938)
[2] A satirical sketch of Overtoun is included in D. Carswell's *Brother Scots* (1927).

that of the original American inventor ; the Scottish Cyanide Co. (1894), utilising the patents of James Readman ; and T. & H. Smith, Edinburgh, founded by two doctor brothers in 1827, who produced pharmaceutical goods such as chloroform.

The British Oil and Cake Mills Co. combined in 1899 twenty-eight mills and twelve oil refineries, some in Scotland. Leading Scottish makers of paints and oils were Craig and Rose, Edinburgh (1820), and Alexander, Fergusson & Co., Glasgow (1854).

TRANSPORT

Shipping. The close connexion with shipbuilding is obvious, and has already been exemplified. There may be further noted the share of the Stephens in the Dundee Whale Fishing Co., and that of William Pearce of Fairfield in the New Zealand and Pacific Steamship Co.

The outstanding Scottish shipmasters were G. and J. Burns, who established services from the Clyde to Ireland and Liverpool in the 1820's, and in 1831 formed the City of Glasgow Steam Packet Co. in partnership with David McIver of Liverpool and David Napier the marine engineer, who built for them till the 'sixties, when their patronage was transferred to J. & G. Thomson. Along with Napier and the Canadian Samuel Cunard they were founders of the Cunard Co. in 1840, and members of the family continued to hold a leading role up to the present. There were several short-lived Glasgow firms in the mid-century. Those of longer life included the City Line, founded by George Smith, and largely engaged in the India sea trade, and latterly associated with the Ellerman Line ; the Donaldson Line (1854), chiefly in the American trade ; the Clan Line (1854), also connected with America, afterwards with New Zealand (developing the meat trade) and Africa, and passing under the control of the Cayzers of London and Liverpool ; and the Allan Line, founded by a Canadian in 1820, specialising for some time in the emigrant traffic. Long a family concern, it absorbed the Shire Line in 1891. The Anchor Line, founded as Handyside & Henderson in 1852, was acquired in 1875 by two brothers of D. & W. Henderson the shipbuilders and combined Atlantic and Indian trade.

Other shipping centres were Aberdeen (Geo. Thompson & Co., whose clippers were for a while famous), Dundee and Leith. Here the doyen was Geo. Gibson & Co. (1797), originally in the West Indian trade, later sailing to North Sea ports. The Leith and Hamburg Steam Packet Co. passed under the control of the Currie family, of whom Sir Donald, founder of the Union Castle Line, was the most eminent, and became the Currie Line. Salvesen & Co., of Scandinavian origin, concerned with the North Sea trade, were also prominent.

Local and coastal services included the London and Edinburgh Shipping Co. (1809), and the Orkney & Shetland & North of Scotland Co. (whose origins went back to 1790), both centring in Leith ; and a complex variety of shippers plying to the Western Isles, ultimately absorbed by the MacBrayne Line, formed in 1851 and dominated from 1879 to 1902 by David MacBrayne (1814–1907), who obtained mail contracts in the 'fifties, and a government subsidy, ultimately of £10,000 per annum. The three chief railway companies running to the Clyde established their own steamers, especially for holiday traffic " down the water " ; among these was great rivalry. On the Clyde, Tay and Forth were ferry services, in the latter two cases much reduced by the building of the railway bridges in the 'nineties, when in particular the Granton to Burntisland train ferry was superseded.

Railways. There was a rapid expansion of railways, especially during the " mania " of the mid-'forties when Britain was " an island of lunatics, all railway mad " (Cockburn). In 1846 fifty-eight Scottish railway Bills were promoted. About 1,200 miles were laid down at this period. These were mostly small local schemes promoted by the magnates of the district, sometimes with the support of neighbouring landowners ; industrial and commercial leaders frequently sat on the boards. The costs of Private Acts, surveys and compensation were high and loaded most companies with debt. There was much speculative investment, facilitated by the " Exchange Banks ". Stock Exchanges were established in Edinburgh and Glasgow, primarily to deal in railway stocks ; and the device of the joint-stock company was popularised.

Longer-distance projects emerged, especially to link London with Scotland. This was achieved piecemeal ; rivalry developed between the chief lines, e.g. the " Aberdeen Race " of the late 'eighties. The building of the Tay and Forth Bridges permitted direct communication between north and south. Despite popular criticism and legal obstacles, much amalgamation had been achieved by 1870, when railways in the Lowlands had largely assumed their present form and most services were in the hands of the Caledonian, North British, Great North of Scotland, Glasgow and South Western, and Highland Companies. The growth of residential suburbs encouraged, and was perhaps facilitated by, the opening of the Glasgow City and District (1886) and the Edinburgh Suburban Lines (1885). The mileage in 1900 was well over 3,000 and about 90 million passengers per annum were carried. The railways incurred charges of vandalism, e.g. in the demolition of Berwick Castle and Trinity College Church, Edinburgh.

Among contractors for the building of railways John Waddell (1828–88) was the best known ; " navvying " was largely done by immigrant and peripatetic Irish. Railway construction enhanced the demand for steel, bricks, etc. Originally both passengers and goods were transported mainly under contract, made with the railway's " agents " ; this system survived for the carriage of coal in colliery trucks. A recurrent dispute in the mid-century was over the running of Sunday services ; the collapse of the first Tay Bridge (1879) during the passage of a Sunday train was regarded by some Sabbatarians as an act of divine vengeance. Sir Andrew Agnew, a Free Churchman, was the protagonist of prohibition, both as an M.P. and a railway shareholder.

Canals tended to be superseded, especially when they came under the control of railways. The Union Canal was acquired by the Glasgow and Edinburgh Railway Co. in 1849 ; the Forth & Clyde, together with the Monkland which it had bought in 1846, and with Grangemouth Docks, by the Caledonian in 1867. A Mid-Scotland Ship Canal was proposed by Charles Wilson, a Hawick industrialist, and a National Ship Canal Co. formed in 1889 to promote the scheme, without avail.

Harbours were regulated by the Burgh Harbour (Scotland) Act of 1853. Those at Granton, Burntisland and Methil were constructed chiefly for the coal trade ; those at Grangemouth, Greenock and Ardrossan were extended. Much expansion took place in the docks on the Clyde, at Leith and at Dundee.

Roads. On the roads turnpikes were largely superseded through the Roads and Bridges Act of 1878, which re-established public responsibility and set up Road Trustees, whose powers were transferred to the new County Councils in 1889. In the towns experiments were made in Edinburgh and Glasgow with horse-omnibus services and rival enterprises arose ; most of those in Glasgow were combined by Andrew Menzies (1822–73).

The establishment of tramways was authorised by an Act of 1870. Municipalities adopting the Act usually leased the operation to private companies. An American, George F. Train (1829–1904) had a large part in promoting such companies, though perhaps exaggerated in his own egotistical accounts. In Glasgow a company in which Menzies had a prominent part leased the main system until its municipalisation in 1894. Horse traction was used until electrification in 1898. The company continued a light omnibus service to the suburbs, trams outwith the city bounds, cab hiring and undertaking. The Edinburgh transport service embarked on its career of chronic controversy and inefficiency in 1871. The central services were acquired by the Corporation in 1893, the outer services leased until 1919. The Corporation also bought in 1897 another cable service for the northern areas established in 1884. The Vale of Clyde Transport Company established services in the Glasgow " conurbation " ; these were bought by the Corporation in 1896. The Glasgow Subway Railway Company, a circular underground route linking the north and south of the Clyde, was founded in 1896.

Occasional attempts to establish " steam car " services were unsuccessfully made, e.g. at Paisley in the 'thirties, by J. S. Russell, afterwards eminent as a shipbuilder.

The cycle was first made in Scotland about 1840 by Kirkpatrick Macmillan of Dalswinton ; the first factory however was opened at Coventry in 1868. A rubber tyre was invented about 1845 by Robert W. Thomson of Stonehaven, but was almost ignored for a generation. The " safety cycle " came into use about 1885 and popularised cycling as a recreation ; a Scottish Cyclists' Union was formed. John Boyd Dunlop (1840–1921), a native of Ayrshire, then practising as a veteri-nary surgeon in Belfast, patented a pneumatic rubber tyre in 1887. There was much rivalry and litigation between the company formed to utilise his patent, ultimately known as the Dunlop Rubber Co., at one time manipulated by the notorious speculator E. T. Hooley but developed successfully by the Du Cros family ; and those who promoted and improved the earlier device of Thomson, which was eventually utilised by the Dunlop Co. after Dunlop's own patent expired and he severed his connexion with it.

The first motor cars, driven by the internal combustion engine, were produced in France about 1890 ; use was encouraged by the growing availability of petrol. Progress in this country was retarded by an Act of 1865 limiting speed to four miles per hour, until its repeal in 1896. The first Scottish motor vehicle was invented by William Peck, afterwards astronomer at Edinburgh Observatory. A manufactory was founded at Granton, later taken over by John Stirling. The Rossleigh Cycle Co., Edinburgh, formed in 1889, fostered cycle and motor transport ; the first annual exhibition was held in Edinburgh in 1898.

Local transport of goods was largely conducted by carriers, whose " quarters " were established in the centres of the main towns. Large-scale carriers included Cowans and the Globe. Cabs and coaches for private hire were supplied, e.g. by Croall of Edinburgh, dating from the 'twenties. They had mail contracts, and were also coachbuilders and undertakers.

THE CONSUMPTIONAL INDUSTRIES

Textiles, with the exception of cotton, continued to expand, though losing in relative importance. About 100,000, of whom two-thirds were women, were employed towards the end of the century.

Cotton became concentrated in the Glasgow area by the 'thirties : of 192 spinning mills, 175 were in Lanarkshire and Renfrewshire by the end of that decade. *St. Mungo's City* by " Sarah Tytler " gives a graphic picture of the industry in mid-century Glasgow.

Hand-loom weaving underwent a disastrous decline ; Parliamentary inquiries were promoted by the weavers' champions, the Maxwells of Pollok, but without avail. There were still some 10,000 in the 'seventies, mainly in a parlous condition, but few survived the century. Wholesale dealers such as D. & J. Macdonald of Glasgow organised production by some 30,000 in the west of Scotland and the north of Ireland until their collapse in the late 'fifties. The last employer in the trade is said to have been James Calder of Kirkintilloch (1834–1912) whose employees diminished from 160 to 20.

Factory production was carried on in Glasgow, e.g. at the Adelphi Works and the Broomward Works, Bridgeton. The most important branch was the " fancy goods "—muslins, gauzes, etc. " Tambouring " by home workers continued for decades. Decline was attributed chiefly to the competition of both Lancashire and foreign (especially Swiss) goods, and to relatively backward technique. The financial crisis of 1857, when the Macdonalds went bankrupt, was a severe blow, and the " cotton famine " occasioned by the American Civil War completed the disaster. There was however some recovery, and firms such as the Glasgow Cotton Spinning Co. (1883), headed by Thomas Reid, a shrewd entrepreneur, and D. & J. Anderson introduced modern spinning machinery and successfully maintained output of the finer qualities, such as zephyrs and shirtings. The notable factory at Blantyre, latterly controlled by the Hannans, closed in 1888 and much of it was demolished ; the surviving fragment is now incorporated in the Memorial established to David Livingstone, its most famous employee. New Lanark Mills continued under the family of Walker, one of Owen's later partners, and later of the Birkmyres, eventually becoming a subsidiary of the Greenock Ropery ; the great Finlay combine still owned the works at Catrine and Deanston. The total employment remained fairly steadily from the 'sixties at 30,000 to 35,000.

Among subsidiaries the Paisley shawl manufacture, introduced about 1800 and developed in the 'twenties, flourished in the earlier half of the century. Improvements in technique were made by John Roxburgh, who introduced the " lashing frame " ; and in 1835 the value of the output was estimated at about £1 million. Its collapse in the 'seventies was attributed mainly to a change of fashion in women's wear.

Its place was taken by the cotton-thread manufacture which had started on a small scale at the end of the past century and was encouraged by the growing use of the sewing-machine. A number of small firms were competed out of existence or absorbed by those of Coats and Clark, both prolific families, who came to a selling agreement in 1889 and amalgamated in 1896. Clarks established a factory in New Jersey in the 'forties. The other main survivor was R. and J. Alexander of Neilston, eventually a component of the English Sewing Cotton Co.

Calico printing was carried on mainly by three large firms, Crum of Thornliebank, Stirling of Renton and Dalglish Falconer of Campsie, all of whom were absorbed in the Calico Printers Association of 1899, a combine with £6 million capital, including fourteen Scottish firms. About 8,000 adults and 7,000 children were employed in the 'forties. The chief market was at first in the West Indies ; this declined after Negro emancipation.

The making of lace curtains by steam-power machinery was introduced into the Irvine Valley about 1870 by Alexander Morton (1844–1928), originally a handloom weaver. He later established carpet factories at Darvel (Ayrshire) and in Carlisle and Northern Ireland, and engaged in fruit growing and horse breeding. A Weaving College was founded in Glasgow in 1877 to give technical training.

Linen. With the abolition of bounties in 1832 the industry became dependent on its own efforts. Machine spinning by Kay's process developed in the Dundee area. Manufacture was increasingly concentrated on the east coast. Hand-loom weaving declined, owing, it is said, rather to excessive supply of labour than to power-loom competition. The latter was introduced by Baxters of Dundee in 1836, but its use did not become general until the 'sixties, when numbers of looms were more than doubled in five years. The industry, after a period of depression, was then revived by the demands of the American

Civil War, during which export expanded enormously. A mechanical " heckler " was introduced by John Sharp, according to legend to eliminate the factious operatives who have left the name of their craft to ardent politicians like themselves.

Angus continued to be the centre of the coarser branches —canvas, sailcloth, etc. Two leading firms were Baxter (1822) and Cox. Sir David Baxter (1793–1872) was the chief agent in promoting the former. William E. Baxter (1825–90), son of the founder, held office under Gladstone, and Dundee University College was endowed by members of the family (1883). Cox of Lochee originated in 1741 as merchants and bleachers, and was developed by the grandson of the founder. Steam weaving was introduced in their Camperdown works in the 'forties.

In Arbroath the Websters (1793) were the doyens ; two firms founded by the Corsar family were prominent, and Andrew Lowson, founded in 1836, became the largest. Brechin, Montrose and Forfar were other centres. In Aberdeen the Broadford Works, conducted for some time by the versatile but unsuccessful John Maberley, passed into the hands of the Richards who about 1860 employed some 2,000 flax spinners.

The Glasgow industry was revived by limited companies later in the century. The production of table linen was fostered by the introduction about 1830 of the Jacquard loom, invented in France thirty years before. Beveridge of St. Leonards (Dunfermline) introduced the power-loom about 1850. There were 130 to 140 linen works at the end of the century, with about 45,000 employees, two-thirds women. This was a considerable fall since the 'sixties, attributed to partial displacement by jute and linoleum, and later foreign competition. Rather unsuccessful attempts were still sporadically made to stimulate home growing of flax, e.g. in Caithness about 1850. Most supplies were imported from Russia.

Jute. Small imports of jute began about 1800 at the instance of the East India Company, and experiments in its use were made in Dundee in the 'twenties. During a failure of the Russian flax crop jute was mixed with flax ; the same technique was found applicable. Pure jute fabrics were first woven by James Aytoun about 1845.   Manufacture advanced considerably in the 'fifties and 'sixties owing to the Crimean and American wars' demands for sackcloth and bags ; " during the siege of Sebastopol all belligerents were using Dundee sackcloth " (Compton Mackenzie).   Import of material grew from 9,000 tons in 1848 to 60,000 by 1868 and 170,000 in 1900. The Coxes of Camperdown Works went over largely to jute. The number of factories tripled between 1862 and 1875, and employment rose to a peak of 40,000 (three-fourths women) in the 'eighties.   Hence the Dundee sobriquet of Juteopolis and the building from the 'sixties of the " jute palaces " of Broughty Ferry.

Dundee however raised up a competitor by fostering Indian manufacture with its own capital and skill.   The first jute spinning factory was established at Serampore in 1855, on " the site of Warren Hastings' country residence ".   In 1859 the power-loom was introduced by Thomas Duff.   £1¾ million was invested in three companies.   Output became competitive with Dundee in the 'nineties and surpassed it early in the twentieth century.

Linoleum.   The linoleum industry was pioneered by Michael Nairn of Kirkcaldy (1804–58) who commenced making canvas in 1828, and in 1847 designed a floorcloth of flax yarn, handpainted ;   a few years later block-printing processes were adopted.   A patent for linoleum had been taken out by Walton of Staines in 1862, and on its expiry in 1877 Nairns adopted the process, and successive generations expanded the firm. Other firms which gave Kirkcaldy its virtual monopoly and characteristic odour included Shepherd and Beveridge (1862) and Barry and Ostlere (1882), which amalgamated in 1899. The leading figure was John Barry (1845–1921), of Irish birth, in youth a Fenian, who sat for Wexford as a Nationalist and was a devout Catholic and leading opponent of Parnell after his divorce case.   Three to four thousand were employed at the close of the century.

Woollens.   There was an increase in import of wool, especially from Australia where sheep ranching was introduced by a Scots immigrant John Macarthur.

The tweed section of manufacture flourished ; according to tradition, partly because of the appeal of the name, originally " Tweel ", said to have been altered thanks to the " inspired error " of a clerk of Messrs. Watson of Hawick. Output doubled in about fifteen years ; in 1865 there were 85 firms, with nearly 14,000 employees, and an output valued at £2 million. There was a setback towards the end of the century, owing to the competition of factory ready-made clothing, utilising cheaper materials, and to American and other tariffs. About half the output was exported, partly through London agents.

New factories were built, and improved machinery diminished the demand for juvenile labour. Galashiels remained the centre ; other factories were almost confined to the Border burghs, but a notable exception was Kynochs of Keith who entered this branch in 1860.

The hosiery branch of the industry was developed by several Hawick firms, particularly offshoots of Wilson and Watson. Walter Wilson (1796–1890) was also prominent in burgh life as a political reformer and railway promoter. Others included Robert Pringle and Sons, Innes Henderson & Co., makers of " Braemar " underwear, and Peter Scott & Co., makers of " Pesco ". In Edinburgh, Munro & Co. founded their well-known factory at Restalrig in 1899. In Greenock, Fleming Reid & Co., originally spinners of worsted yarns, founded in 1833 the Scottish Wool & Hosiery Co. to retail their products through chain stores, of which about 120 had been opened by the end of the century. John Paton & Sons of Alloa expanded considerably as yarn spinners.

Hand-loom weaving retained a precarious life, particularly in the making of tweeds in Harris and of jerseys in Shetland.

In the woollen industry there were in 1900 about 30,000 employees, of whom men predominated in the skilled crafts associated with spinning, and women in the weaving factories. A Scottish Woollen Textile School was established in Galashiels in 1883.

Carpets. In the carpet branch of the industry there were three Scottish inventions. The " three-ply carpet " invented by Thomas Morton of Kilmarnock was manufactured by his firm.

The " patent tapestry carpet " was the device of Richard Whytock of Lasswade (1834) ; his factories there and at Roslin were later carried on as Widnell & Stewart. The " patent Axminster " was devised by James Templeton, a former shawl manufacturer in Paisley, who set up a carpet works in Glasgow in 1839.

Dyeing was still extensively carried on in the Vale of Leven, where the three chief firms, the Stirlings, dating from the late eighteenth century, and two firms of Orr-Ewing, who commenced in early Victorian decades, amalgamated in 1898 as the United Turkey Red Co. In April 1900 was formed the British Cotton and Wool Dyers Association, a fusion of about forty firms, including thirteen Scottish from the Borders, Dunfermline and the Glasgow area. Pullars of Perth were a noted family firm, long headed by Sir Robert Pullar (1828–1912). A. & J. Macnab of Slateford, founded in 1773, in 1849 acquired a bleachfield ; their dyeworks came under the control of Alex. Stevenson, an Edinburgh draper, and at the end of the century was reorganised as a limited company, in the hands of his family.

Tailoring and Clothing was long carried on mainly under the " domestic " or home-working system, liable to " sweating " against which recurrent agitation arose, as in the 'eighties by the Tailors' Trade Union. The higher class output was generally " bespoke ", made to individual order, but with the improvement of machines for cutting and sewing, and rising working-class standards, " ready-mades " came into vogue in the latter half of the century. The pioneers were Leeds firms, sometimes Jewish, still relying partly on home workers ; but the chief advance was due to John Barran, who obtained materials from Border manufacturers. Mass-produced clothing retailed through multiple stores was pioneered in Edinburgh by M. A. Levy, who set up his " Cosmocapaleion " in Edinburgh about 1850. He was followed a decade later by Hyams. Native firms included Mann Byars and R. W. Forsyth, both of Glasgow. The ready-made " unique " shirt was popularised by James Webster of Glasgow about 1850.

Footwear. The making of footwear was an old handicraft practised by the Cordiners, whose Edinburgh Incorporation dated from 1450 ; they were in close relationship with the Skinners, who tanned the leather. Forrest Alexander, a founder of the Commercial Bank, was the pioneer of large-scale production in Edinburgh (1783) ; his firm subsequently became James Allan and Sons. Thomas Duncan, also of Edinburgh (1797), remained a high-class producer of bespoke goods. In the later nineteenth century factory mass production by machinery developed, as in clothing, to meet a new working-class demand, and was associated with multiple retail stores. Machines were at first leased from the American Shoe Machinery Co. Glasgow and Kilmarnock were the main centres. R. and J. Dick, pioneers of rubber soles, much of whose resources were derived from successful speculation in Australian mining, established a factory in Glasgow in the 'forties, and ultimately owned about seventy retail shops ; later they undertook the manufacture of " Balata " rubber belting, on a patent of Robert Dick, and finally discontinued shoe manufacture and retail. Bayne & Duckett, Greenlees and Sons and A. & W. Paterson of Glasgow, and the Saxone Co. of Kilmarnock, were other leading producers.

Leather. The leather industry has been described as " one of the forgotten occupations ",[1] probably more important than metals till the eighteenth century. The " heavier " types were carried on by the currier and tanners ; the lighter by the skinners. They prepared the material for such products as footwear, saddles, belts and gloves. Large-scale tanneries grew up in this period, chiefly in Edinburgh and Glasgow ; in 1871 there were about 120, employing about 2,700.

Rubber. The Scottish rubber industry is largely due to American enterprise. Charles Goodyear (1800–64) of Philadelphia took out patents for a vulcanising process, which were acquired by a company which decided to undertake manufacture in Scotland, where the similar patent of Thomas Hancock (1786–1865), who manufactured waterproof goods in Manchester in

[1] L. A. Clarkson in *Econ. Hist. Review* Dec. 1960, p. 245 ; cf. *Glasgow Chamber of Commerce Journal*, Dec. 1954 for Scottish details.

partnership with Charles Macintosh, was not valid. The Castle Mills in Edinburgh were bought in 1856, and the style of the North British Rubber Co. adopted, under the direction of Henry L. Norris (1813–81). Shoes, belting, hot-water bottles, etc. were manufactured, under the management of William E. Bartlett, who devised various improvements. The works became mainly British owned in a few years. Several other works, notably the Victoria Rubber Co., Leith, were established in the next few decades. The history of the rubber-tyre branch of the industry has already been described in connexion with the cycle. The Dunlop Co. eventually acquired Bartlett's patents and absorbed the Macintosh concern.

Rubber supplies were at first obtained from natural growth, chiefly on the Amazon and Congo. Experiments in artificial cultivation were made in Ceylon and the Malay peninsula in the 'nineties.

Food-processing Industries. The growth of large-scale factory production of food is even more characteristic of the period than is that of dress. Flour milling had of course for centuries been a specialised craft, and the miller a prominent and usually unpopular figure in rural economy. The Water of Leith, with seventy in all, especially at Bonnington, and the Kelvin had mills of long standing. Large concerns were developed in Glasgow by the Whites and Ures ; and the Scottish Co-operative Wholesale Society acquired the Chancelot Mills in Edinburgh in 1894.

The baking of bread, regulated by an Act of 1836, was in the main carried on in small units. Complaints of the insani-tary conditions of frequently underground working led to the passing of the Bakehouses Act of 1863, which also prohibited night employment of juveniles ; agitation for its extension to adults was unsuccessfully pursued. Large enterprises were established in Glasgow by Neale Thomson at Crossmyloof in the 'fifties, and by Bilsland Bros. in the 'seventies. J. W. Mackie (noted for " shortbread ") commenced in Edinburgh in 1832. The United Co-operative Baking Society was a federation of retail societies which produced bread and other cereal products for its members (1868). The manufacture of biscuits was encouraged by the growing supply of imported grain.

Gray Dunn, one of whose founders, William Gray (1812–80), was a pillar of Scottish Quakerism, began in 1853, and in the ' nineties became associated with Bilslands. Wylie Barr & Ross soon followed, and were joined by Macfarlane Lang thirty years later. Lindsay & Low, Dundee (1872), R. Middlemass & Son, Edinburgh (c. 1860), William Crawford, Edinburgh (1852), and McVitie & Price, Edinburgh (1888), combined bread and biscuit baking. Charles Price, a partner in the latter, was an active Liberal politician and latterly M.P.

The making of cornflour was initiated by Brown & Polson of Paisley, a combination of J. & W. Polson, muslin manufacturers, and Wm. Brown & Son, bleachers, who joined to make sago and starch in 1842. John Polson (1825–1900) took out patents for starch and cornflour. Semolina, another popular dish with Victorian mothers, was produced by Marshall of Glasgow in 1885 ; and porage oats by A. & R. Scott, Colinton, 1891.

The preserving of meat in tins was rendered practicable by the device of Michael Appert (1757–1811), a Frenchman, and was undertaken by John Moir & Son, Aberdeen, from 1822 ; the firm obtained government contracts. Much however was imported, particularly from Chicago.

The preservation of fruit and making of " preserves " was carried on so successfully by Keillers of Dundee as to enable one partner to leave £2 million (1899). They commenced the making of marmalade from Spanish oranges in 1797. James Robertson, a Paisley grocer, successfully experimented in the " Golden Shred " variety (1866). Fruit jellies were factory made in the fruit-growing centres of Carluke and Crieff.

The consumption of sugar increased with the prevalence of tea drinking and jam making, and the abolition of protective duties in 1846. West Indian output declined after Negro emancipation. Refining on the Clyde expanded for a time, thanks partly to improvements in machinery due chiefly to James Duncan of Greenock ; output rose from 50,000 tons in 1854 to a quarter million in the early 'eighties, but thereafter declined. Some leading firms, including Fairries and Macfies, transferred their headquarters to Liverpool or London. Abram Lyle (1820–91), originally a maker of barrels for the

West India trade, became a shipowner as well as a sugar dealer and refiner ; in 1881 he established works in East London ; his firm was the nucleus of the modern combine of Tate & Lyle, constituted by a merger with the Liverpool firm associated with the founder of the Tate Gallery. Late in the century came the import of foreign refined sugar, and eventually only three refineries survived in Greenock. The extraction of sugar from beet was first achieved in Silesia in 1801 and was fostered by Napoleon's Continental System. Imports to Britain began in the 'fifties, and competition, stimulated by bounties from the German government, became acute in the 'eighties. After long negotiations an International Convention for the elimination of bounties was signed in 1902.

" An enormous recent increase in the consumption of confectionery " was noted by Bremner in the 'sixties ; one factor was the reduced price of sugar. David Ridpath of Edinburgh was already noted about 1820 for his peppermints, and Keillers of Dundee somewhat later for " lozenges, comfits, candies and gum goods ". Alex. Ferguson of Edinburgh Rock fame started business about 1820. The leading Glasgow manufacturer was John Buchanan & Sons of Phoenix Works (1857).

Dairy products improved in hygiene and purity with the establishment of some large-scale multiple concerns, notably United Creameries of Wigtonshire (1892) ; four dairies amalgamated in 1900 to form the Glasgow Dairy Co. The making of margarine commenced on the Continent before 1870 and was stimulated by the Franco-Prussian War. The Netherlands became the chief centre, where the two large firms of Jurgens and Van den Bergh developed rivalry. The basic material was animal fat, until with the opening up of West Africa towards the end of the century coconut and palm-kernel oil were utilised. Local manufacture was pioneered by the Craigmillar Creamery Co. in 1884. Import of Danish butter was inaugurated by Beveridge of Leith in 1862.

The popularity of tea drinking was encouraged by the abolition of the East India Company's monopoly in 1833, and consequent cheapening. China tea was directly imported thereafter by Andrew Melrose of Edinburgh and others. India tea was introduced about the same time, and its import increased fourfold in the last two decades, constituting five-sixths of the total import as against one-tenth in 1870. Tea plantations in India were acquired by the " Finlay Group " and by Liptons.

The vogue of coffee declined somewhat until recently, in contrast with its popularity on the Continent and in U.S.A. Wm. Law of Edinburgh was the chief firm ; its head, who became Lord Provost, improved grinding machinery. The bottling of coffee essence was begun by Thos. Symington & Co., Edinburgh, about 1880 ; Robert Paterson of Glasgow introduced " Camp Coffee " in 1897.

Brewing employed about 3,000 at the end of the century ; its labour costs were exceptionally low, being estimated at 16 per cent. There were about 200 licensed brewers in the 'sixties ; there was some concentration in Edinburgh, attributed partially to the suitability of its water. Wm. Younger & Co., Holyrood, became the outstanding firm, producing about 200 million barrels per annum, of which 7 per cent was exported ; trade with the colonies and U.S.A. developed from the 'forties. Brewing also expanded in the Duddingston area towards the end of the century. The Edinburgh United Breweries combined four firms in 1889. John Jeffrey & Co., who migrated to Murrayfield in 1862 ; Thos. Usher & Son, St. Leonards, and Wm. McEwan, Liberal M.P. and founder of the McEwan Hall, were other leading Edinburgh firms. Archibald Campbell & Co., Argyle Brewery (1770), amalgamated with Hope & King of Glasgow ; their works absorbed the old Tailors Hall in Cowgate. Alloa remained another centre, with the veteran firms of George Younger (1760) and Andrew Roy (c. 1740) which expanded under the name of Arch. Arrol & Son (1870), also operating in Glasgow, where Tennents of Wellpark (c. 1750) survived as doyen. Technical improvements encouraged large-scale production, and the growth of the industry was affected by excise duties and licensing laws.

In the Distilling [1] industry two main types of whisky are distinguished. " Malt " whisky was probably of Irish origin and was produced from home-grown barley and burn water,

---

[1] The history of distilling is described in R. B. Lockhart's *Scotch* (1951) and R. Wilson's *Scotch Made Easy* (1959).

flavoured by peat. Distillation and consumption was almost confined to the Highlands in the eighteenth century. Much was illicit, and there was great opposition to excise until the Act of 1823 improved administration. Thereafter large distilleries grew up, notably the Glenlivet (Banffshire) founded in 1820 by George Smith, an architect and cattle breeder ; the " Glenlivet case " of 1880 gave modified sanction to a monopoly of the name.

The distilling of " grain " whisky was introduced by the Steins of Kilbagie (Kincardine-on-Forth) in the 1820's. Their " invention of the patent still led to the conquest of the English-speaking world ". An overseas trade developed in the late nineteenth century and Japan became a leading market. Six Lowland firms formed in 1851 a trade agreement, which evolved into Distillers Company Ltd. in 1871, including Haigs & McNabs. The manufacture of yeast was undertaken in the 'nineties, and later that of industrial alcohol. A protracted lawsuit (the " What is Whisky ? " case) of 1905 was followed by a Royal Commission, whose report was a triumph for the grain distillers.

Several firms undertook the blending of whisky, including Andrew Usher & Co., Edinburgh (c. 1825), one of whose partners endowed the Usher Hall ; thus Edinburgh's two chief halls were floated on alcoholic liquor. Other noted firms were J. & T. Dewar of Perth (1846), who introduced bottled whisky and acquired distilleries ; Alex. Walker of Kilmarnock, founded by a licensed grocer about 1820, and known by their " Johnnie Walker " brand, and James Buchanan of " Black and White " fame. There were about 160 distilleries in 1900, also employing a relatively small labour force.

The manufacture of Mineral Waters was begun by James Dunbar, Edinburgh, in 1868 ; A. G. Barr & Co., Glasgow, produced " Iron Brew ".

Tobacco is usually associated for statistical purposes with " Food and Drink ". A number of small firms, chiefly in Edinburgh and Glasgow, prepared the finished article and produced various brands of cigarettes as these came into vogue. Much juvenile labour was employed. John Cotton of Edinburgh, founded about 1770, combined manufacture and retail.

Stephen Mitchell & Son migrated from Linlithgow to Glasgow in 1825 ; Stephen Mitchell the third (1790–1874) is commemorated by the library for which he left a bequest. The Imperial Tobacco Company founded in 1901 included among its thirteen components three Glasgow firms, Mitchells, D. & J. Macdonald (1839) and F. & J. Smith (1858). The chief Scottish firms who retained their independence were Geo. Dobie & Sons, Paisley (1809), noted for " Four Square " products, and Fairweather & Son, Dundee (1835). The manufacture of snuff boxes was common in Ayrshire in early decades, and the making of pipes was undertaken in Glasgow.

Building. Turning from food and clothing to the other primary necessity of dwelling, we note the growth of the speculative builder, encouraged by the feuing of estates, as already illustrated. The most detailed account so far published appears to be the booklet on *Architecture in Dundee* of the Abertay Society (1955), where in particular the layout of Broughty Ferry in the 'sixties and the building of mansions for the " Merchant Princes " of the jute industry is described.

While building remained largely a small-scale handicraft industry, with an average employment of ten workers per firm (1891), some large firms of general contractors grew up, like Thomas Cubitt in London. In Glasgow, John Carswell (1767–1856), pioneer of internal water supply, and Thomas Binnie (1792–1867) built many large blocks of residences. Sir James Steel (1830–1904), Lord Provost of Edinburgh, was responsible for much of the industrial quarter of Dalry and of the new West End mansions and flats. James Young & Sons, Edinburgh (1846), and Sir Robert McAlpine & Sons, originating in Motherwell in 1868, were among those who undertook contracts for factories, railways, drainage, etc.

Speculative building was carried on mainly on borrowed capital ; dwelling houses constituted about one-half of normal building. The industry as a " constructional " one was particularly liable to boom and slump ; it was much affected by variations in the rate of interest and responded rapidly to fluctuations of trade. Cairncross, discussing its course in Glasgow, remarks that " launchings and lettings went together ". The collapse of the late 'seventies followed on over-expansion.

The idea of town planning was virtually ignored ; in rapid urban growth buildings were erected haphazard.

Much building was still in stone ; the Aberdeen granite industry flourished accordingly. In the " *age of grey ashlar* " (J. M. Reid) the growth of Glasgow was largely in sandstones. Brick was increasingly used, and considerable manufacture developed e.g. at Garnkirk and Bonnybridge.

Some erection of dwellings continued on " paternalist " lines, especially in the coalfields and the newer shale-oil industry. Experiments in co-operative building were made in several towns, notably by the Edinburgh Co-operative Building Co. which in the 'sixties erected several rows of two-storey working-class dwellings, e.g. at Abbeyhill and Haymarket.

Painting and decorating remained mainly the sphere of the small tradesman, but George Dobie of Edinburgh (1824–98), the subject of a brochure by W. M. Parker, developed a large business in paper hangings and undertook large contracts, e.g. for the Caxton and Liverpool Harmonic Halls.

Household goods were usually produced and retailed by the same firms. Among large-scale establishments were those of Wylie & Lochhead, Glasgow (1828), who combined cabinet-making with carriage-hiring and undertaking ; and A. H. McIntosh & Co., Kirkcaldy (1827), upholsterers and cabinet-makers, who had a wholesale establishment in London and also made equipment for ships.

The old craft of clock-making was pursued by such firms as Ritchies and Brysons of Edinburgh. The former, founded in 1807, were responsible for the " time ball " on Calton Hill (1852) and the one o'clock gun on the Castle (1861) and for the clocks of the University and the city churches.

Glass-making and pottery were kindred trades, to which J. Arnold Fleming has devoted much research. The former was carried on mainly in Edinburgh and Glasgow. The Holyrood Works, started by John Ford in 1825, were carried on by successive owners ; bottles were made at Baileyfield (Portobello.) The industry in Glasgow suffered a severe setback in the depression of the 'seventies. There pottery had a chequered career ; the Britannia Works, St. Rollox, appear to have been the most successful. In the 'fifties it was rather optimistically affirmed that " Glasgow rivals Staffordshire in the last twenty years ". In 1868 fourteen firms are recorded, employing about 5,000. The raw material was brought from England ; export was mainly to the colonies and U.S.A., where it was dislocated by the Civil War.

The old industry of soap-making as a domestic necessity may conveniently be referred to here. The most noted firm was Alex. Ogston & Sons, Aberdeen, which combined in 1898 with the soap-making section of Tennants, when the latter's works at St. Rollox were burnt down ; a new joint factory was built at Renfrew. Isdale & McCallum of Paisley (c. 1870) was another leading maker ; the S.C.W.S. started manufacture at Grangemouth in 1898. As E. S. Turner's lively work has demonstrated, the soap industry was a pioneer in modern advertising methods, thanks largely to the ingenuity of Thos. J. Barratt of Pears.

Laundering, dependent on soap, was introduced about 1880 ; William Paul, an Aberdeen advocate, was a chief promoter and pleaded the interests of public health.

The manufacture and sale of drugs was regulated by the Pharmacy Acts of 1852 and 1868 ; professional qualifications for dispensing were required. J. F. Macfarlane & Co. (1780) produced surgical dressings and morphine. Duncan, Flockhart & Co., Edinburgh (1828), catered for the Edinburgh Medical School. T. & H. Smith, Edinburgh (1827), founded by brother surgeons, were the first makers of chloroform. Production and retail were usually associated, but production of " proprietary " goods came to be done on a large scale by manufacturers such as Allen & Hanbury of London and Beechams of St. Helens. Towards the end of the century Boots of Nottingham combined multiple retail with manufacture.

Paper-making, Printing and Publishing may be regarded as ministering rather to the mental than the physical needs of the community. The expansion of paper-making is directly linked with the growth of literacy and was encouraged by the abolition of the excise duty (1860). With the growing insufficiency of the principal raw material, linen rags, much experiment was made to find a substitute. Esparto grass, chiefly from North Africa, was utilised by Routledge of Oxford whose patent occasioned lawsuits. It was adopted in Scotland at Kinleith Mill, Currie. Wood-pulp, chiefly from Sweden, came into use in the 'seventies, with the machinery devised by Bertrams of Edinburgh (1862). Another problem was the pollution of rivers, caused by effluvia from the works, which sometimes was met by an interdict from local landowners and produced rather unsatisfactory legislation.

A main centre of the industry was Midlothian, with twenty-two out of a total of fifty-seven mills. Outstanding was that of Cowans at Valleyfield (Penicuik), prospering under the control of a distinguished Edinburgh family. The Annandale Mills, Polton, passed through several hands, and mills at Lasswade and Polton came into the possession of members of the Tod family. The other chief localities were Aberdeenshire, where Pirie & Sons and the Culter Mills both originated in the eighteenth century, and Fife. Tullis of Markinch and the Guardbridge Co. in Fife, and Trotter of Chirnside and Duncan of Denny were notable firms.

Macniven & Cameron commenced as stationers in Edinburgh about 1780, and undertook the making of steel pens (the once-famed " Pickwick, Owl & Waverley ") in the mid-century. Geo. Waterston & Sons, dating from the mid-eighteenth century, combined the manufacture of stationery with bookbinding, engraving, etc. A. B. Fleming & Co. set up an ink factory in Leith in 1852, and transferred it to the historic mansion of Caroline Park, Granton.

Edinburgh remained the principal home of Scottish printing. Bell & Bradfute (1734) were the oldest firm and specialised in law publishing. Most leading firms of publishers printed their own books. Another veteran was Neill & Co. (1749) whose history has been related by Moray McLaren ; they introduced steam presses in the 'forties and linotypes in the 'nineties. The employment of women caused much friction in the last decade. A. & C. Black (1806), long headed by Adam Black, Lord Provost and M.P., acquired the copyrights of the *Encyclopaedia Britannica* and of Scott's works ; they transferred their headquarters to London in 1891 ; much of their printing was done by R. & R. Clark. Oliver and Boyd, also headed by a Lord Provost, were noted for their Almanac. Blackwood's continued their well-known magazine, and issued the *New*

Statistical Account; they remained a family firm. T. & T. Clark specialised in theological works, again under the direction of a Lord Provost. The brothers William and Robert Chambers, the former active in municipal life, the latter as a historical writer, published a journal and an encyclopaedia, and pioneered cheap popular editions. Thos. Nelson & Sons, latterly of St. Leonards, achieved many improvements in technique.

Glasgow publishers also attained civic dignities. John Blackie in addition to managing the firm of his name was a housing reformer. William Collins the second was associated with the Temperance cause ; the firm (depicted in a volume by David Keir) pursued the policy of cheap editions, and undertook also the manufacture of stationery. Robert Maclehose & Co. were booksellers before becoming also printers and publishers to the University.

Another specialty of Edinburgh became the publication of maps and other geographical material. W. & A. K. Johnston and Bartholomews (associated with Nelsons) attained world repute. John Valentine of Dundee was a pioneer of the pictorial postcard and Charles Drummond of Leith of the Christmas card, both in the 'forties.

The increase of leisure and its separation from labour stimulated and facilitated the vogue of regular holidays, particularly for the dominant industrial and professional middle class, but also on a smaller scale for the proletariat at the annual " Fair " ; the " week-end habit " also grew. Thus the provision for holiday-makers by hotels and restaurants, and the organisation of sport and entertainments, etc., becomes a matter of economic importance, involving considerable capital, labour and expenditure.

Holiday resorts were developed, notably on the Clyde, e.g. by David Napier at Kilmun and by James Craig at Dunoon, and on the east coast, e.g. at Carnoustie and Dunbar. Organised excursions were pioneered by Thomas Cook and became a regular feature in some industrial works. Day cruises were arranged on the Clyde and the Forth, especially in the summer. Shooting holidays in the Highlands were fashionable with the upper classes, following the royal example at Balmoral. Hotels of a luxury type were established, e.g. by Peter Chalmers, a retired army officer, at Callander, St. Andrews and elsewhere. The North of Scotland Railway opened a hotel at Cruden Bay in 1899 in connexion with a golf course.

More modest were the " Commercial " hotels, catering primarily for the " traveller " who became a familiar figure with the expansion of wholesale trade. Notable is the growth of the " Temperance " (non-licensed) hotel, chiefly an outcome of the Total Abstinence movement of the 'forties. More than one was the result of Chartist devotion to this cause, most notably those founded in Edinburgh and later in London by Robert Cranston.

A peculiarly Victorian institution was the Hydropathic, originally designed for treatment in accordance with the " water cure " by internal and external application, propagated by the German Priessnitz and adopted in Scotland by medical men such as Dr. Wm. Paterson and Dr. John Balbirnie, as well as by clergy like Rev. John Kirk of Brighton St. Chapel, Edinburgh. One of the most famous was that founded by Paterson at Glenburn, Rothesay (1843). There was considerable flotation of companies in the 'sixties and 'seventies when the imposing buildings at Dunblane, Peebles and elsewhere were erected. These retained religious and temperance associations ; a facetious account of the mode of life is given by J. J. Bell in his *I Remember*, while a critic deprecated the advisability of " porridge and prayers " as a " motto for a hostelry ".

The Temperance movement also produced a temporary vogue for coffee houses, frequently utilised as meeting-places by trade unionists and Radical politicians ; they sometimes provided a reading-room equipped with periodicals. Lang of Glasgow experimented with a " self-service " restaurant in the 'eighties. The modern type of lunch and tearoom was originated there by Stuart Cranston and his sister Kate, whose premises were adorned with decorations by the architect Charles Rennie Mackintosh.

As sport, especially " Soccer " football, became commercialised and professionalised after the manner of the later Olympic Games in Greece, gate money, players' fees and the acquisition and upkeep of grounds and implements assumed economic importance. The Scottish Football Association was formed in 1873, and such well-known teams as Heart of Midlothian and Hibernians came into being.

The traditional Highland Games were reorganised, especially on Deeside, as an entertainment for spectators and a source of revenue for promoters and athletes.

Higher ranges of culture were catered for by music sellers and promoters of concerts, including the three well-known Edinburgh firms of R. & W. Paterson, R. W. Pentland and Methven Simpson. Theatres in Edinburgh and Glasgow were founded and carried on with growing support ; the partnership of Howard and Wyndham became leading proprietors.

TRADE AND COMMERCE

The development of an exchange economy is the obverse of industrialisation. It involves the increase of " tertiary " employment, e.g. in transport and distribution, as is borne out by census returns ; and the growth of middlemanship, whereby the cost of selling a commodity may bear an increased ratio to that of producing it.

Trade may be divided into Home (Retail and Wholesale) and Foreign.

I *Home*

(a) *Retail trade* has been rather neglected by economic historians, though some attention has been given recently to an economic analysis of distribution, e.g. by Finer, Braithwaite and Jeffreys. The latter's broad survey of modern developments may be taken as a basis, and illustrated from a few local descriptive accounts and from the contemporary press.[1]

The modern shop, as distinct from the craftsman's booth, came into being in the seventeenth century, especially in London, and is in evidence in eighteenth-century Edinburgh, e.g. in the Luckenbooths. In the early nineteenth century there are differentiated pure retailers such as drapers and grocers, producer-retailers such as shoemakers and tailors, stallholders at markets and fairs, itinerant pedlars, chapmen, etc.

Pure retailers were in a sense craftsmen, self-employed and

---

[1] These are elaborated in my article on " Shops in Edinburgh " in *The Book of the Old Edinburgh Club*, v. xxx (1959).

" processing " their wares, e.g. blending tea, cutting sugar. They were linked with the wholesale producers by the commercial traveller.

For the best part of the century " effective market demand was limited ", says Jeffreys, by the low standards of the masses. Purchases of non-perishable goods, even of some foodstuffs, were often made in large quantities at infrequent intervals. The ancient practice of " higgling " over prices survived ; liability to adulteration and light weight was a frequent complaint.

During the last quarter of the century there was considerable transformation. New types of goods, factory-made or imported, came on sale. " Marked " or " branded " proprietary goods became common, and these were increasingly packaged in quantities ready for sale. Advertisement and display flourished ; fixed prices became usual. With rising standards of life there was an expansion especially of working-class demand. Hence there was an increase in the total of both general stores and specialised shops, a decline of the independent produce-retailer, a separation between the shop and the dwelling. A stress on salesmanship rather than the technical knowledge of goods, growing dependence on the wholesaler, and growth of the large-scale producer-retailer and of the multiple shop and department store as well as of the retail Co-operative, are other characteristics.

These trends may be illustrated by Scottish references. In addition to the old-established goldsmiths, jewellers and watchmakers there grew up retailers of cheaper articles, sometimes branches of producers such as H. Samuel.

Oil dealers were prominent in earlier days of its use as an illuminant, e.g. Smith and Co., Blair St., Edinburgh, who held a contract for street lighting. Thos. Smith the founder undertook lighthouse contracts, and was succeeded by his son-in-law Thomas Stevenson, the first of the eminent lighthouse engineering family.

Pharmacists sometimes concocted their own drugs. Frazer and Green were the leading Glasgow firm, of which Sir James Frazer the anthropologist was a scion.

There were various grades of grocers, utilising such designations as cheesemongers, provision dealers and Italian warehousemen. Sir William Fettes was the first notable figure ; R. & T. Gibson of Princes St. was one of the well-known family firms.

With the growth of public meat markets and abattoirs, butchers became primarily retailers, though sometimes also interested in wholesale trade, e.g. Brechins, associated with Swans the stock auctioneers ; imported meat, though known by the mid-century, did not become common till the twentieth.

Seed merchants, nurserymen and florists included two Edinburgh Lord Provosts Henderson and Lawson, and one of the oldest surviving Glasgow firms, Austin and McAuslan.

Booksellers were naturally numerous in Edinburgh. Blackwoods had a selling department which served as a literary centre in the days of Scott. Robert Grant's dates from the beginning of the century, absorbed other firms and engaged in publishing and the making of stationery. Douglas & Foulis and Macniven and Wallace were later comers to the New Town ; while Thins (1848), Baxendines, Bryce, John Grant and W. F. Henderson were associated with the University quarter and acquired repute with book collectors as second-hand dealers. The wholesale trade was also undertaken by John Menzies & Co., originally agents for Chapman & Hall, who established railway bookstalls in the 'fifties ; and by Love of Glasgow. William Love (1810–65), originally a newsagent, was active among Radicals who made his shop a " howff " ; after his death his younger brothers developed the wholesale trade.

The drapers, mercers and hosiers were among the most numerous and flourishing retailers. Among the earliest was Alex. Cruickshanks, an Aberdeenshire Quaker, established in the New Town by 1800 ; the firm continued in his family in George St. until the 1930's. To him, as to other Quakers, is attributed the rejection of the practice of " prigging " or haggling about prices. This reform is also mentioned as characterising the early career of Duncan McLaren, who set up in the High St. in 1828 and was afterwards noted as Lord Provost and M.P. " for Scotland ". His son and namesake became a partner in Rentons in Princes St., founded by Wm. Renton, Sen. (c. 1815) ; the business was eventually transferred to the latter premises to make way for the extension of the Municipal Buildings in High St. in the 'nineties. This firm had a rather involved connexion with that of Alex. Clapperton, cloth merchant, High St. (*c.* 1800), through John Oliver, son-in-law and partner of McLaren, who also became a partner in Debenhams, London. Another old and long-continued firm was founded by James Spittal, the first Lord Provost after municipal reform (1833) ; after various changes it passed with other firms into the hands of J. & R. Allan, South Bridge (1883). Three noted firms of later origin were Kennington & Jenner (1838), subsequently carried on in the name of the latter by the Kennedy family ; Cranston & Elliot (1865), of which the prominent Volunteer and Lord Provost Sir Robert Cranston (1843–1923) was head ; and Robert Maule, transferred from Kincardine-on-Forth in 1872.

In Glasgow, Arthur and Fraser (1849) separated, the former becoming wholesalers, the latter the nucleus of the huge retail combine of today. Catering for a popular trade were such firms as Daly's Tron House (1846) and Bow's Emporium (1873). Copland & Lye (1873) and Pettigrew & Stephens (1888) established themselves in the more " fashionable " Sauchie-hall St. In Dundee, D. M. Brown was outstanding.

The department store seems to have originated in France during the Second Empire (as depicted in Zola's *Au Bonheur des Dames*) ; the example was followed in London by such establishments as Gamages, Harrods and Whiteleys. A claim to have anticipated these may be made for John Anderson who established his " Polytechnic " in Glasgow in 1837, and instituted regular " bargain sales " of most varied goods. He was emulated by Walter Wilson (1849–1917), originally a hatter, who founded the Colosseum in 1873 and the Tréron in 1896 ; he arranged " Christmas Fairs ", introduced tearooms and sold cheap reprints of books. He had towards the end of the century less successful branches in Edinburgh and elsewhere.

Two early examples of the multiple shop originated in Glasgow. Cooper & Co., grocers, was founded by Thomas G. Bishop (1871) and went in for direct buying from producers, afterwards supplemented from its own factories ; the firm pioneered the use of electricity for advertising signs. Sir Thomas Lipton, an Ulsterman by birth, started his first shop in Glasgow in 1871, and within ten years had twenty. He later acquired tea plantations in India, established a limited company in 1898, in which he retained half the capital, and became an intimate of Edward VII ; in his later years he sought new fame as a yachtsman. Of more local scope was the chain of groceries founded in the West by Wm. Galbraith of Paisley in the 'nineties. With the increased import and consumption of fruit, Malcolm Campbell of Glasgow developed a large-scale retail trade.

Manufacture and retail were, as already mentioned, combined by clothing, hosiery and footwear firms. The Co-operative movement proper was partially imitated by such enterprises as " Dick's Co-operative Institution " of Dunfermline, which shared profits with customers.

(b) *Wholesale Trade*. The decline of the Fair as a commercial medium was accelerated by the growth of railway transport. Glasgow Fair, e.g., degenerated into a periodic entertainment, and the name survived as that of the annual " trades holiday ".

Live-stock auction marts continued, e.g. at St. Boswells, and large wholesalers such as Oliver & Son of Edinburgh and John Swan & Sons (1856) acquired much of the business ; the latter was associated with American ranching. Special produce markets for grain, fruit and vegetables, meat and fish, grew up in the main centres, under the provisions of Burgh Charters, supplemented by later Acts. The other chief example of a commodity market in Scotland was the Glasgow Iron Exchange, dating from the 'forties ; " warrants " were issued for material in store, and these gave rise to considerable speculation and some " cornering ". Some well-known firms were associated, including a branch of Connals, previously in the West India trade, Jas. Watson & Co. (linked with heavy industry companies) and Wm. Jacks & Co., a partner in which was A. Bonar Law, the " unknown " Tory premier of a recent biography.

Coal, formerly often retailed direct or through an agent by the colliery owner, became a sphere of middlemanship. In the textile trades, particularly linen, there were noted wholesalers such as Armitages of Dundee, whose founder was an intimate of Gladstone and was raised to the peerage ; and the

Linen Thread Co. of Glasgow and Belfast. Warehousemen of
" soft goods " included J. & W. Campbell, of which family
Sir Henry Campbell-Bannerman, the Liberal Premier, was a
scion ; Stewart & McDonald and Arthur & Co., all of
Glasgow.

In the auctioneering of miscellaneous and other household
goods, Dowells of Edinburgh became prominent. Its founder
was a cabinet-maker who set up as an auctioneer and
" appraiser " about 1830.

(II)   *Overseas Trade : Import and Export.*   As we have seen,
several Scottish firms, such as Coats, Cowans and Nairns, had
their subsidiary factories as well as trading agencies overseas.
In addition there were large-scale trading concerns engaged
in import and export, who may conveniently be treated with
reference to their particular spheres of operation.

Eastern.   Here the great firm of Finlays were pioneers.
Kirkman Finlay, as already described, was a leader in the
opposition to the East India Co.'s monopoly, and on its with-
drawal engaged in export of cotton and other goods to India.
This was developed by his successors such as James Clark.
Subsidiary or related firms undertook varied enterprises in
India, including cotton and jute factories and later tea
plantations.   The latter were consolidated as the " Finlay
Group ".[1]

Wm. Graham & Co. of Glasgow and associated firms
engaged in similar activities and also in the Portuguese wine
trade.   The Scottish Assam Tea Co. (1865) also developed tea
plantations in that area.   The Irrawaddy Flotilla Co., and its
associates, closely identified with Dennys the shipbuilders,
opened up trade with Burma, where Steel Brothers promoted
rice and timber plantations.

Sir William Mackinnon and Lord Inchcape (a native of
Arbroath) were successive heads of an enterprise engaged in
shipping and banking in Calcutta, Burma and Zanzibar.   The
banking activities were transferred (1897) to the Chartered
Bank of India, Australia and China, founded in the 'fifties by
James Wilson (of the Hawick family and of the *Economist*)

---

[1] A bi-centenary account of *Jas. Finlay & Co* was issued by the firm in
1951.

with several Scottish directors ; its centenary history has been written by Compton Mackenzie.[1]

The other notable firm in Oriental trade was Jardine Matheson & Co., of which a full account based on their papers has recently been given by Greenberg.[2] Dr. Wm. Jardine and James Matheson, both scions of Scottish landed families and in the East India Co.'s service, after the freeing of the China trade established their own business in 1824 at Canton, and soon extended it to Hong Kong, Shanghai, etc. They engaged in the import of opium and textiles, and export of silk, tea, etc. Subsequently they established cotton mills, railways and warehouses, undertook banking and insurance and made loans to the Chinese government. They held about one-tenth of British investment in China.

The subsequently famous Burmah Oil Co. was formed in 1886 by David S. Cargill, a Glasgow merchant engaged in the East India Trade.

The eighteenth-century connexion with America and the West Indies continued, though the decline of the sugar plantations affected the fortunes of such old-standing firms as Wm. Connal & Co., who branched into the India tea and local iron trades, and James Ewing & Co. Other firms were interested in the cotton trade, which also declined after the mid-century ; J. A. Dennistoun & Co. after over a century's existence was a victim of the 1857 crisis. Scottish links with Canada were strong, through settlement especially in Nova Scotia, Prince Edward Island and Manitoba. Besides the connexions established by the shipping firms of Cunard and Allan, there may be noted the activities of Pollok Gilmour & Co. as shipowners and timber merchants ; their headquarters later passed to Liverpool under the Rankin family, one of whom wrote *A History of Our Firm.*

They also participated in the still older Scottish trade with the Baltic, the import of tar, hemp and flax. Other firms engaged in this field were chiefly located in Leith, e.g. James Miller & Sons. In this and other ports, such as Bo'ness and Grangemouth, export of coal and import of timber expanded.

Scottish explorers from Bruce and Mungo Park to Livingstone

[1] C. Mackenzie, *Realms of Silver* (1954)
[2] M. Greenberg, *British Trade and the Opening of China* (1951)

and Kirk did much for the " Opening Up of the Dark Continent ". In the footsteps of Livingstone came the African Lakes Corporation, founded in 1878 by Glasgow commercial magnates such as James Stevenson, James Young of oil fame and the Whites of Overtoun, most of whom were also prominent members of the Free Church, which set up a " Livingstonia Committee " of similar personnel. They took as their motto " to advance the kingdom of God by honest trade ". Some of their agents, like the brothers Moir, were also lay missionaries ; clergymen such as Drs. Laws and Hetherington undertook the civil government of the area ; roads were constructed, a steamship service instituted on Lake Nyasa, coffee and tobacco plantations established, the Arab slave raiders suppressed. A community inspired by the ideals of Calvin's Geneva and reminiscent of the Jesuits in Paraguay persisted until the British Protectorate of Nyasaland was formed in 1891 ; two years later the company became a subsidiary of the British South Africa Company of Cecil Rhodes.

Contacts with the east coast were developed by Sir William Mackinnon through the British and East India Steam Navigation Co. (1856) and later by Sir John Kirk, the associate of Livingstone. The British East Africa Co. (1888), the result of their efforts, was financially unsuccessful and gave place to the British colony of Kenya. Association with what is now the Union of South Africa was rather religious and educational, e.g. Lovedale Institute, through missionaries like John Philip, Robert Moffat and John Mackenzie, who exerted an active influence especially on the abolition of slavery and protection of native rights.

In West Africa climatic conditions were unfavourable for white settlement and land remained in native ownership ; thus the economic situation differed basically from that in the East and South. Early British contacts were mainly associated with the slave trade. After its abolition trade developed especially in the export of vegetable oils, used for lubricants and illuminants and latterly in margarine production. The trade was usually on a small scale ; Glasgow and Liverpool firms were involved. Abuses arising from the sale of liquor and firearms, and disputes with native chiefs, evoked protests from missionaries, chiefly engaged at the United Presbyterian stations in Calabar (S. Nigeria), among whom Mary Slessor, a native of Dundee, became famous. The Royal Niger Company was formed in 1886 and British protection was followed by annexation in 1900.

Meantime an " economic revolution " began, fully described by Dr. Allan McPhee.[1] Native cultivation was increasingly devoted to production of cash crops instead of to subsistence economy, e.g. palm-kernel oil, cocoa ; consequently an expanding market for European manufactures—e.g. cycles— was provided, at the risk in some areas of monoculture, of a buyers' monopoly and of excessive dependence on fluctuating price levels, for which a dubious remedy was ultimately found in the establishment of semi-governmental marketing boards. Meantime the chief trading firms were merged in the United Africa Co., which became a subsidiary of Unilever.

Scottish participation in Australasian trade is chiefly associated with the export of wool and frozen meat, and was most conspicuous in the days of the " clippers ".

Scots played a prominent part in the colonisation and settlement of the Dominions, especially Canada and New Zealand. From the days of Lord Selkirk and the Red River settlement, and the rather ill-fated schemes of John Galt, Scottish immigrants, such as Lord Strathcona (Hudson Bay Co.) and Lord Mount Stephen (Canadian Pacific Railway), were prominent in the economic expansion of the former.

FINANCE AND INVESTMENT

The device of the joint-stock company was popularised by its utilisation in the " railway mania ", in connexion with which " Exchange Companies " had a brief vogue ; these made advances on the security of stock. They were introduced by George Kinnear of Glasgow, who founded the " Commercial Exchange Co." in 1845 with £1 million capital, and wrote in their defence. Another in Edinburgh was promoted by Duncan McLaren. They fell out of favour with the end of the boom and most soon closed.

Stock Exchanges were opened in Edinburgh (1844) and Glasgow (1845). With the legalisation of limited liability (1862) there was a rapid growth of companies ; many existing

[1] A. McPhee, *The Economic Revolution in British West Africa* (1926)

partnerships adopted this form, which became general in the major industries towards the end of the century.[1]

Much Scottish capital was invested overseas,[2] particularly in U.S.A. where a " ranching mania " developed in the 'seventies and 'eighties. Rufus Hatch of Wall St. was a chief promoter. " Scotland revels in foreign investment," said *Blackwood's Magazine* (Oct. 1884) ; " three fourths of foreign and colonial investment companies are of Scottish origin." Several of these " land and cattle companies " were registered in Scotland. The best known were the Swan, organised by a Scottish immigrant of that name in Wyoming (1883), the Prairie (Kansas) and the Matador (Texas) whose office was in Dundee. Other enterprises were concerned with mines or railways, e.g. Arizona Copper Co. (1882), Oregon Railway Co. (1880). Many were highly speculative and had chequered careers, partly due to the vagaries of American State laws, but largely to their financial methods, especially excessive reliance on debentures for raising capital. These evoked the strong censure of W. R. Lawson, editor of the *Edinburgh Courant* (1884).[3]

There was also considerable investment in Australian estates ; the depression of the early 'nineties there had reper-cussions on the Scottish economy. Prominent as directors of such enterprises were Sir George Warrender who had profitably developed his own Bruntsfield (Edinburgh) estates, and Colin Mackenzie of Portmore, son of the legislator of " Sunday Closing ".

The Investment Trust, as an expedient for the spreading of risks, was apparently devised in Belgium early in the century, but was given a vogue in Scotland largely in relation to this export of capital. The two chief promoters were Robert Fleming of Dundee (1845–1933) and Wm. J. Menzies, an Edinburgh W.S., who in the same year 1873 launched the Scottish American Trust Co. and the Scottish American Investment Co. respectively.[4] About fifteen Trusts were

---

[1] This is elaborated in my article in *Economic History*, Feb. 1937
[2] cf. my article in *Scottish Bankers' Magazine*, July 1935 for details
[3] W. R. Lawson, *The Scottish Investors Manual* (1884)—articles reprinted from the *Courant*
[4] G. Glasgow, *Scottish Investment Trust Companies* (1932) ; J. C. Gilbert, *Investment Trusts in Dundee* (1939).

formed by the end of the century, mainly holding shares in overseas investment concerns ; several operated from Dundee.

Another type of investment which expanded in the latter part of the century, and had a boom in the 'seventies, was the Property Investment Society. Its popular name, the Building Society, was more appropriate to its early form, that of a small local group who pooled their resources to obtain the means of building houses for themselves in turn. When this object was accomplished the society usually dissolved. Illustrations are found among Lanarkshire miners and weavers ; they were sometimes associated with schemes of co-operative building, and were encouraged by housing reformers such as Dr. Begg.

Some of the larger of these " mutual " societies were converted into " proprietary " form after the mid-century ; i.e. they allotted shares to the general public, and lent to prospective houseowners, increasingly for purchase rather than for building. A report of 1892, the year in which the leading society, the Scottish Amicable, was constituted, shows a total of 68 Scottish societies with 13,000 members and about £1 million capital.

Insurance Societies increased and expanded, mainly also on a proprietary basis, e.g. Scottish Widows' Fund (1815), Standard Life Assurance (1832). In 1872 there were 16 Scottish companies, estimated to hold three-tenths of British policies and a quarter of the funds. A late-comer was the General Accident Fire and Life Assurance Corporation, which started as a small local concern in Perth but, under the direction of Francis Norie-Miller (1859–1947) who became manager in 1887, it built up a world-wide business. Increasingly as they accumulated funds in premiums, the Insurance Companies became important media of investment.

Banking. The history of banking in early nineteenth-century Scotland is largely that of the decline of the private banks which closed down or amalgamated, and of the rise of the joint-stock banks which competed with and superseded them. Following on the establishment of the Commercial Bank in 1810 and the National in 1825, both in Edinburgh, several were founded, mainly in the West, including the Union (1830), the Western (1832), the Clydesdale (1838) and the City of

Glasgow (1839). Two of these ultimately failed. The Western, which had set up many branches and encouraged small depositors by paying a high rate of interest, succumbed to the crisis of 1857, having made excessive loans and maintained inadequate reserves ; it was in some degree a victim of the hostility which it had inspired in the more orthodox banks.

The City of Glasgow pursued a similar course, which involved its temporary suspension in the same year ; its resounding crash in 1878, which has left a singular impact on the Scottish mind and on Scottish fiction, was hastened by the Great Depression, but was probably unavoidable, in view of its excessive grant of loans on inadequate security. Inquiry demonstrated that these were largely given to directors of the bank, several of whom, with the manager, were prosecuted and sentenced for fraud. It had about £8 million in deposits, made at over 130 branches, chiefly in small sums. The deficit of £5 million, in view of their unlimited liability, involved a ruinous call of over 2,000 per cent on the 1,200 shareholders, of whom Robert Craig, paper manufacturer, Caldercruix, was the largest. A relief fund raised £400,000, and an " Assets Company " was formed to take over the tangible properties of the bank, which included Glasgow houses and Australian land ; by careful development of these resources some recompense was ultimately made available.

Amalgamation advanced considerably, and by the end of the century the twenty-four banks of 1837 had been reduced to ten ; several of the older and better known such as the Thistle, the Ship and Wm. Forbes & Co. were absorbed by the Union Bank. " Peel's Bank Act " of 1844 stipulated that no new bank of issue should be established in Great Britain ; a special Act the next year, the Bank Notes (Scotland) Act, preserved the right of note issue to the existing Scottish banks or those with whom they might amalgamate, but denied Scots notes legal validity in England. A maximum fiduciary issue of about £3 million was enacted. This provision evoked the same criticism as was made in England by the " banking school " ; e.g. from Sir Archibald Alison, Hugh Miller, in virtue of his early experience as a bank agent, and Robert Somers a Glasgow journalist, who were insistent in their prophecies of deflationist disaster.

The Bank of England increased its influence on the Scottish banking system, symbolised by the agreement of the Scottish banks to accept " bank rate " as a guide to their own rates (1863). In the same decade most of them opened offices in London, and the " English raid ", despite the abortive opposition of English banks, extended to Cumberland, where the Clydesdale Bank, at the instance of its manager, George Readman, set up three branches, chiefly in view of the close relation between the Scots and local iron trade. The City of Glasgow disaster induced the banks finally to accept complete limitation of liability in terms of a special Act of 1882 ; and they agreed on the definitive adoption in 1892 of the distinction between current accounts, bearing no interest but to be drawn on by cheque; and deposit accounts, receiving interest but not thus to be drawn upon.

An attempt was made in 1849 by several Scots, headed by John Macgregor, M.P., to establish a bank in London on the " Scottish system ", e.g. advancing cash credits. After about seven years this " Royal British Bank " failed, largely through excessive lending, and the Directors were prosecuted and sentenced. They included Henry D. Macleod, afterwards well known as a financial writer, and candidate for the Edinburgh Chair of Political Economy on its foundation.

An " Investment Bank " was formed in 1875 in Hawick by Provost Ewen, with a view to diverting the deposits of savings banks from government securities to local industry ; it was later taken over by the Standard Investment Trust. The People's Bank was founded in Edinburgh in 1888 under Co-operative auspices. It acted as banker to working-class organisations, and made advances for house purchase.

Unorthodox financial theorists were active in Victorian Scotland. Sheriff Sir Archibald Alison in *England in 1815 and 1845* condemned " Peel's Bank Act " for its deflationary tendencies. John Crawford, a Paisley solicitor, interested in emigration schemes, in his *Philosophy of Wealth* (1837) attacked the " Dutch system " and " money power ". John Gray of the *North British Advertiser* in *Lectures on Money* (1848) advocated nationalisation of banking and a paper currency. Robert Somers, a Glasgow journalist, in his *Scottish Banks* (1873) commended unrestricted issue of notes.

In concluding this section, by way of summing up main features of economic development, stress may be laid on the recurrence of the trade cycle and the trend to combination. Periods of depression affected Scotland at almost regular decennial intervals, notably those of 1847, with its influence on the following " Year of Revolution " ; 1857, when dislocation arising mainly in U.S.A. brought down several Scottish firms ; the prolonged slump of the late 'seventies, apparently more severe in Scotland than in England ; and that of the early 'nineties due partly to Australian influences.

The Great Depression is particularly noteworthy for its political repercussions, in that it stimulated distrust of the existing economic system. The challenge of foreign competition revived Protectionist agitation, as in the British and Irish Fair Trade Society formed in Glasgow in 1887 ; to this movement some leading industrialists, especially in the threatened industries, gave support. A more far-reaching criticism of private enterprise was made by the nascent Socialist societies of the 'eighties.

Facilitated by the spread of the joint-stock company, industrial combination took place on both vertical and horizontal lines ; the former notably in the heavy industries, the latter most completely in such varied spheres as distilling, thread, dyeing and calico-printing, and tobacco. The growth of the professional entrepreneur, or managerial class, sometimes an accountant or lawyer rather than business man, is a concomitant ; interlocking directorates became frequent. Where independent identity was preserved, a price agreement might be in force, as on occasion in the iron and shale-oil industries. Joint action, especially in dealing with organised labour, became common among employers in mining and the metallurgical industries. More general associations such as Chambers of Commerce and Trade Protection Societies sought to act as legislative " pressure groups ". The role of government in economic life was enhanced.

SOCIAL CONDITIONS, PROBLEMS AND MOVEMENTS

The population of Scotland increased from about $2\frac{1}{3}$ million in 1831 to over 4 million in 1901. The birth-rate reached its maximum (35) in 1876, and has since declined.

(Social factors contributing to this decline in Britain are discussed in J. A. Banks's *Prosperity and Parenthood*.) The death-rate has also fallen since 1864, when it attained its peak for the period at 23·5. In 1861, 25 per cent were under ten years of age, 9 per cent over sixty. There was much internal migration ; less than 50 per cent of the urban population were natives of their burgh. The population of the Highlands was at its height in 1841, with nearly 400,000 (over 15 per cent of the total) ; by 1901 it had fallen to about 350,000 (less than 8 per cent). This is partially attributable to the famine of 1846.

Immigrants came chiefly from Ireland, and became a " flood " after the Famine when about 50,000 per annum came to Scotland ; the fare is said to have fallen as low as fourpence. Some Lithuanians were brought over in the 'eighties, primarily, it is said, as strike-breakers ; by 1891 they numbered about 500, mainly in Lanarkshire.

There was much emigration, especially to U.S.A., in which about half a million Scots settled between 1861 and 1901. This was sometimes organised and assisted, especially in the Highlands after the famine. Scottish colonisation schemes, with which were associated Patrick Matthew, the Chartist and pre-Darwinian exponent of Natural Selection, and John Crawford, solicitor and economic theorist, were particularly concerned with New Zealand. The most famous and successful was that in the South Island district of Otago, promoted by George Rennie, a Radical M.P. of the East Lothian family, and headed by Rev. Thomas Burns, nephew of the poet ; its Scots origin is commemorated in the name of Dunedin (1848).

The trade unions, particularly in times of depression, encouraged emigration to relieve the labour market ; Alexander Campbell the Owenite was for a time organiser of a New Brunswick emigration agency.

Conditions of employment were by and large those common to periods of industrialisation, when stress is laid rather on accumulation of capital than on consumption. A few Scottish features may be illustrated.

Craft gild privileges, long obsolescent, were abolished by the Burgh Trading Act of 1846. The older " craft " trade unions sought to maintain such rules as those regulating apprenticeship.   Particularly in the mines, features of " paternalism " survived for some time.

The chief feature was the growth of the factory, which increasingly involved an urban environment, the divorce of labour and leisure, of work and home.   " Domestic " work, notably that of the hand-loom weavers, declined ; the making of food and clothing tended to leave the home for the factory. Purely industrial towns such as Coatbridge, Addiewell and Clydebank grew up rapidly.   Buildings, originally used for other purposes, were frequently adapted for factories ; hence some of the deficiencies in lighting, heating and ventilation. There were some 600 underground workshops in Glasgow in 1901.   New buildings designed for the purpose were erected by progressive industrialists like those at Deanston ;   the Border textile industry followed, and the jute mills of Dundee are credited with inspiring a " school of mill design ", whose work " remained the standard form of construction till the end of the century ".[1]

The labour of women and children was investigated by Commissions of 1842 and 1862 ;   the latter showed that 77,000 under 15 were at work.   The limitations imposed by the series of Factory Acts and the Mines Act of 1842 were common to Great Britain.   Considerable juvenile employment survived in industries not covered by these Acts, e.g. bleaching, tobacco. Some restriction was put on child labour by the Education Act of 1872, which made schooling compulsory to the age of 13 (raised to 14 in 1883) ;   exemptions from attendance were however freely given in some rural areas, and sometimes for part-time factory work.

About one-fourth of the women employed in Dundee mills were married ;   to this was attributed the peculiarly high infantile-mortality rate.   Some protection for women was secured by the efforts of the Scottish Council for Women's Trade founded in 1895 under the Chairmanship of Rev. (afterwards Principal) Geo. Adam Smith ;   Miss Margaret Irwin was secretary throughout its existence.

The duration of the working day was probably no longer than had been common in " domestic " work, but the intensity

[1] D. M. Walker, *Architects and Architecture in Dundee*—one of a useful series of booklets published by the local Abertay Society.

of labour and discipline were undoubtedly more severe. The average working week was about 70 hours in the 'forties ; it was reduced to 55–60 by the 'nineties. The Saturday half-day became more common in the later decades ; Thomas Wingate of the Adelphi Factory, Glasgow, was a pioneer (c. 1850). A Shorter Hours movement was effectively promoted by unions in the building and heavy industries in the 'seventies. There was recurrent agitation for earlier closing of shops, especially drapers, in the 1890's, when shopkeepers and employees collaborated ; a Bill was unsuccessfully introduced by A. D. Provand, a Glasgow M.P. (1892).

Some industries—e.g. mining, textiles, chemicals—were peculiarly liable to accident and industrial disease ; a Departmental Committee investigated the matter in 1893.

Wage rates varied considerably as between skilled and unskilled workers, and were liable to fluctuation with the state of trade ; those of miners oscillated with special rapidity. There was an increasing resort to large-scale negotiation. Time rates were common in the building trades, piece rates in the iron industry, where a sliding scale was eventually introduced. In agriculture and coal some payment in kind remained. The actual receipts, as distinct from rates of pay, depended of course on regularity of employment and their value on the level of prices.

Long-term contracts continued, especially in the mines, though " yearly bonds " gave way gradually to shorter terms —e.g. fortnightly. Some workers were engaged on " minute " contracts, i.e. cessation of employment without notice on either side. Prosecutions, especially of agricultural workers, for leaving before the expiry of their contracts, were frequent under the old Master and Servant legislation, which provoked much trade-union agitation, and cases continued even after its modification by the Act of 1867, which abolished summary arrest, the most crying grievance in Scotland. Liability to imprisonment for breach of contract was eliminated by the Employers and Workmen Act of 1875.

Despite the Act of 1831 the persistence of truck, especially in mining and navvying, was also a subject of complaint, and of government inquiry in 1871 ; it was finally abolished in 1887. It was associated with advances of pay and the circula-

tion of local token coins ; the rise of the Co-operative movement helped to eliminate it by providing an alternative source
of supply.

Another grievance was the arrestment of wages for debt ;
some 30,000 cases a year occurred in Glasgow about 1850.
After a government inquiry, conducted by Hill Burton the
historian, a measure limiting the amount that might be
arrested was successfully promoted by George Anderson, M.P.
for Glasgow (1870). The growth of pawnbroking gives further
indication of the extent of indebtedness.

Welfare services—e.g. provision of canteens and recreation
grounds—were provided by such " benevolent employers " as
Denny the shipbuilder, the Crums and the Nelsons. Profit-
sharing schemes were introduced by the Carron Co., Robert
Duncan the Govan boilermaker and Carlylean, Brown and
Polsons, Buchanans the confectioners, Frederick Braby, a
London iron manufacturer who established the Eclipse Works
in Glasgow, and by several Hawick hosiery firms. Sir Walter
Menzies established a Workmen's Compensation Fund at his
Phoenix Tube Works, Rutherglen.

For conditions of domestic life, much material can be
gleaned from the *New Statistical Account* and from Government
Reports. Dr. A. K. Chalmers and Professor Thomas Ferguson
have surveyed factors affecting health.

Agricultural improvements provided a more adequate food
supply, and this was increasingly supplemented by imports,
e.g. of American wheat and Danish dairy produce. There
was however probably some deterioration in nutritional value,
especially in urban areas, through the substitution of milled
for whole grain, and the increased consumption of tea, spirits
and potatoes, coupled with a relative lack of milk and vegetables. The growing resort to tinned foods and poor cooking
were other factors. Adulteration and unhygienic conditions
of production, transport and sale were also prevalent, and such
" deficiency diseases " as rickets were common among children.

Water supply, especially in the larger towns, was frequently
inadequate. Provision of public wells continued till the middle
of the century ; thereafter internal piping and sanitation
became general in new construction. Factory effluvia sometimes occasioned pollution.

Some contagious diseases were virtually endemic, and the urban death-rate rose in the early decades. Mortality from smallpox was still over 10,000 per annum. Epidemics of cholera and typhus occurred from the 'thirties to the 'sixties. The average death-rate in Edinburgh and Glasgow in the 'forties was twice that of England, and a third higher than London. The infantile-mortality rate was still well over 100 at the end of the century.

The traditionally low standard of housing was intensified by the rapid growth of the towns. One-fifth of the families were housed in one room in 1861 ; 25 per cent in Glasgow in 1880. Rents were relatively high, averaging one-fourth of wages.

Intemperance was rife, due largely to the increase of whisky drinking. Glasgow was described about 1850 as " a Presbyerian Rome and modern Gomorrah ", when the " Drunken Statistics " showed that 1 in 22 were annually prosecuted, as compared with 1 in 100 in London. Gangsterism and sectarian strife were familiar in the area. Illegitimate births reached a maximum rate of over 10 per cent in the 'sixties, and were most frequent in rural districts, though there said to be largely pre-marital. The two best-known Labour leaders, Keir Hardie and Ramsay Macdonald, were both illegitimate, as were the novelists S. R. Crockett and Geo. Douglas Brown. In the light of such facts, the nostalgic evocation of high Victorian standards of morality and culture seems to be based on a myth.

A better side of Victorian life is seen in the prolific movements for amelioration of these conditions. Charity on a religious basis was influenced alike by the theocratic outlook of Dr. Chalmers and his disciples such as Dr. James Begg, and by the Evangelical doctrine of the " stewardship of wealth ", most conspicuously in the Free Church.[1] Mission churches of an institutional type in slum areas were a result. In general there was a growing reaction against laissez-faire, stimulated by such writers as Carlyle and Ruskin, whose Scottish origin perhaps augmented their influence, especially among the " intellectuals " and reformers of the 'eighties.

[1] This has been elaborated by S. Mechie in The Church and Scottish Social Development (1960).

Innumerable societies for the care of the destitute and disabled competed for the support of the financially privileged and philanthropic ; voluntary visitors engaged in "slumming". In times of special distress, e.g. the Highland famine of 1846 and the cotton " famine " of 1862, special funds were raised for relief and attempts at provision of work were made. Sabbatarian sentiment contributed to the restriction of Sunday labour and the extension of the Saturday half-holiday.

For " deprived " children, the well-known Industrial (" Ragged ") Schools were promoted in the 'forties by Sheriff William Watson of Aberdeen and Dr. Thomas Guthrie, the Free Church leader ; followed a generation later by William Quarrier's " Homes " at Bridge of Weir.

For adolescents, a Young Men's Society for Religious Improvement was founded in Glasgow by David Nasmyth in 1824, and became part of the Y.M.C.A. The Boys' Brigade also originated in Glasgow, where the first unit was organised by William A. Smith, a Free Church layman, in 1883. The Free Church was also responsible for the first Scottish " Settlement ", established by students of New College, Edinburgh, in the Pleasance in 1892.

The social havoc wrought by drunkenness evoked an active movement, at first advocating abstinence from the more potent liquors, but soon becoming " teetotal ". The Scottish Temperance League (1844) and the later Band of Hope (1870) for juveniles emphasised personal pledge-taking ; and the cause was much advanced by the campaign of the Irish Father Theobald Mathew in the 'forties. A change in the general attitude of the Churches is evident, not only in their collaboration with a Catholic priest, but in the growing vogue of total abstinence among both clergy and laity. The Permissive Bill Association (1855) advocated legal restriction on the model of the State of Maine ; the " P.B.'s " became an active pressure group within the Liberal Party. The Forbes Mackenzie Act of 1853 enacted limited hours and Sunday closing of public houses.

Advocacy of total abstinence was a feature of the Scottish Chartist movement, and bore fruit in the establishment of temperance hotels and coffee-houses, partly as an alternative to the " pub ", as a meeting-place for workers. The Swedish

" Gothenburg system " of " disinterested management " was experimented with in some mining districts in the 'nineties.

Some medical care was supplied by bodies like the Edinburgh Society for the Relief of the Destitute Sick, which utilised male visitors. The " voluntary " hospitals and dispensaries were augmented in number ; notable examples are the Crichton, Dumfries (1839), for mental cases, once proposed as the nucleus of a fifth University ; the Edinburgh Sick Children's Hospital (1860), the Western (1871) and Victoria (1889) Infirmaries in Glasgow. A District Nursing scheme was initiated by Mrs. Mary Higginbotham in Glasgow in 1875, and affiliated to the Queen's Institute of District Nursing in 1891. On occasions of serious epidemics, e.g. 1831, Local " Boards of Health " were temporarily established, on a semi-official basis, and emergency accommodation and treatment were thus provided.

As regards housing, a number of local organisations were founded to provide " Workmen's Dwellings ", of a model type by contemporary standards. Individual effort, especially by Free Church clergy, was responsible for such small schemes as those in Edinburgh, at Pilrig, stimulated by Dr. Blaikie, and at Abbeyhill, by Dr. Begg. The Kyrle Society, inspired by Ruskin, undertook management and inspection of slum properties in Glasgow. Dr. Begg interested himself also in rural housing, especially as a critic of the bothy system ; his attack on landlords evoked the charge from one of their spokesmen, Mr. Tollemache Sinclair, of using language " more suited to a freebooter than a Free Churchman ". Rev. Harry Stuart, an Angus parish minister, formed an " Association for Promoting Improvement in the Dwellings and Domestic Conditions of Agricultural Labourers ", with the support of landed proprietors.

James Simpson, the Edinburgh lawyer and educationalist, was a pioneer of public baths, to which he devoted the proceeds of a course of lectures (1844). More satisfactory provision of meals for workers was attempted by Thomas Corbett, a Glasgow business man, who set up Cooking Depots in various centres.

A Scottish Social Reform Association was founded by Begg in 1850, and was apparently connected with the " Association for the Study of Social Science " (1858–84), formed by

Brougham on the model of the British Association. This held several conferences in Scotland, at which papers on contemporary Scottish social problems were read by Begg and others, including trade-union leaders.

These varied types of philanthropic effort flourished chiefly during the mid-Victorian " Age of Plenty ". Their subsequent decline has been attributed by Mr. Carswell [1] to the preoccupation with individual salvation impressed on the churches by the Moody-Sankey Revival, but can more plausibly be associated with the relative decline of surplus wealth in the hands of the privileged classes during the Great Depression.

A second type of movement may be distinguished as that of Self-Help or Mutual Aid, attempts on the part of the under-privileged to improve their position by their own efforts.

The Trade Union movement developed rapidly about 1830, following on the legalisation of combination. Organisations were much preoccupied with political reform, and took an active part in the agitation which secured the passing of the Great Reform Bill (1832). A " United Committee of Trades Delegates " in Glasgow held demonstrations and published a periodical *The Trades' Advocate*. The somewhat conflicting influence of Owen, fostered by his disciple Alexander Campbell, led to the founding of grandiose but short-lived organisations aiming at universality, e.g. the Glasgow and West of Scotland Association for the Protection of Labour. With the collapse of the earlier 'thirties a few unions, mainly in the building trades, survived. The Glasgow Cotton Spinners' Union achieved further notoriety and virtual collapse by the disastrous strike of 1837 and subsequent trial and condemnation of its leaders on charges of violence.

There was a reversion to political action later in the decade, culminating in Chartism. Here, as Dr. L. C. Wright [2] has brought out, there was a national organisation (1839–42), which in some of its methods anticipated the modern Labour Party, and a distinctive outlook, which professed a religious and moral basis and leaned generally to the " moral force " position. The best-known Scottish figure, Dr. John Taylor of Ayr, was however a leader of the " physical force " section.

[1] *Brother Scots* (op. cit.)
[2] *Scottish Chartism* (1953)

Several " Chartist Churches " were established ; advocacy of total abstinence and sometimes of nature cure was a feature of the prolific Chartist press—e.g. the *True Scotsman.* The *Liberator*, under Taylor's editorship, had a circulation of thousands, but only a single copy is known to survive. After the fiasco of 1848 the movement merged in the Radical wing of the Liberal Party, led in Scotland by Duncan McLaren, brother-in-law of John Bright, and including former Chartist spokesmen like James Moir of Glasgow, Robert Cranston of Edinburgh and Robert Cochran of Paisley.

The growing prosperity of the mid-century encouraged a revival of trade unionism, especially in the heavy industries, reflecting their outstripping the textiles. Here organisation came chiefly through the English " Model Unions ", e.g. the A.S.E., which established branches in Scotland. Separate Scottish unions of shipwrights, blacksmiths and railwaymen were formed. These were primarily benefit societies, and adopted conciliatory tactics, though a Shorter Hours campaign was conducted with some success in the early 'seventies.

The coal-miners, whose history has recently been recounted by Page Arnot,[1] had hitherto only ephemeral local societies, sometimes controlled by employers. They were now organised on a national scale, thanks chiefly to Alexander Macdonald, who had worked in Lanarkshire pits before qualifying as a teacher ; from about 1850 he devoted himself to the cause of his former workmates. A Scottish Miners Association was formed in 1852, and extended across the Border in 1863. Macdonald was averse to strikes and to the restricted " darg ", and sought through legislation the prohibition of truck, of arrestment of wages, of deduction of offtakes, etc., the appointment of checkweighmen and safety regulations. To this end he entered Parliament in 1874 as " Lib.-Lab." member for Stafford and sat till his death in 1881. He was also active in the newly constituted Trade Union Congress. In the Great Depression his influence declined and the national organisation crumbled away ; local unions, especially in Fife, survived.

Several craft unions were active, especially in the building trades ; here there was prolonged friction between the English and Scottish carpenters ; this was also the case with rival

[1] *The Scottish Miners* (1955)

Tailors' Unions. The Scottish Typographical Association, after some years of union, recovered its independence in 1853.[1] Abortive attempts were made to organise farm workers in the 'sixties and 'seventies.[2]

Local joint action assumed the form of permanent Trades Councils, e.g. Edinburgh (1849), Glasgow (1858). These were largely concerned with municipal issues but promoted organisation in their areas. National organisation, which became permanent in the Trade Union Congress (1868), was largely stimulated by the initiative of Glasgow Trades Council, which formed the Committee for the Repeal of the Master and Servant Act (1864), a specially Scottish grievance. An apparently ephemeral attempt at a Scottish central body was made in the formation in the early 'seventies of the United Trades Confederation of Scotland.

The Great Depression occasioned a temporary decline in trade unionism, and loss of some of the gains recently achieved. The City of Glasgow Bank failure involved some unions in financial loss. The Depression as elsewhere shook the confidence of many in the existing economic system, and thus encouraged the revival of Socialist ideas. Agrarian unrest in the Highlands, perhaps encouraged by the example of the Irish Land League, and aided by the propaganda tours of Henry George, brought the land question to the front. Marxism was as yet exotic and exerted little influence. The Scottish ethical tradition was better expressed by Keir Hardie (1856–1915) who proclaimed the need of " independent working-class representation ", and, after unsuccessfully contesting a by-election in opposition to both parties, formed the Scottish Labour Party in 1888. This was a miscellaneous collection of " rebel " factions such as those mentioned ; its programme included nationalisation of the land, minerals and railways, and Home Rule for Scotland ; it was merged in the I.L.P. in 1893. A short-lived " Scottish Trades Council Labour Party " (1891), based on the Trades Councils, endorsed candidates in the 1892 election. In January 1900 a conference in Glasgow, attended by representatives of trade unions,

---

[1] Sarah Gillespie, *100 Years of Progress* (1953) is a centenary history of the Union.
[2] cf. G. Evans in *Sc. Historical Review*, Feb. 1952

Co-operative and Socialist societies, formed the Scottish Workers Parliamentary Representation Committee, ultimately absorbed in the modern Labour Party. Municipal candidates were increasingly run under varied auspices towards the close of the century.

There were also developments in the trade-union sphere, though little exactly comparable to the " New Unionism " south of the Border. The coal-miners were reorganised under the leadership of Robert Smillie in a Scottish Miners' Federation (1894), which affiliated to the Miners' Federation of Great Britain, the ultimately successful rival of the older national union founded by Macdonald. In close relationship at first, the workers in the growing shale-oil industry were organised by John Wilson of Broxburn (1886). Two unions catering for grades of iron and steel workers were formed in Lanarkshire, but soon transferred their headquarters to the north of England. The Scottish Railwaymen's Union virtually collapsed after the great strike at the end of 1890, though some of their claims were soon conceded ; most employees joined one or other of the English unions. The engineers became more militant and were involved in lock-outs in the 'nineties. Sailors and dockers were organised by the English " New " unions, as were some shop assistants and clerks. The women textile workers in Dundee gained improved conditions through a union founded and dominated by Rev. Henry Williamson, a Unitarian minister. The bakers achieved an effective national organisation. Largely in consequence of the exclusion of Trades Council representatives from the British Trade Union Congress, a Scottish Trade Union Congress was founded in 1897 ; 55 organisations affiliated, with about 40,000 members.

Friendly Societies, which enjoyed a secure legal basis from 1829, with some guarantee of actuarial soundness, were at first small-scale and local ; some were closely associated with trade unions. There was however a growth of national societies or " Orders ", such as the Oddfellows, who formed branches in Scotland. There were a few native bodies such as the Scottish Legal and the City of Glasgow Societies. In 1892 there were about 30,000 members. From the 'seventies the " mutual " societies had to meet the competition of the " industrial assurance " societies, notably the Prudential.

The Co-operative movement was prolific in the early 'thirties, when under the influence of Owen attempts at production and exchange were made, especially in the Glasgow area, and " Social Missionaries " such as Alexander Campbell and Robert Buchanan engaged in propaganda. As in England, few of the ventures in Co-operative production were successful ; some collapsed, others were converted into joint-stock companies, like the Edinburgh Co-operative Building Society, founded in 1861 by masons on strike. Building, tailoring and printing were the favourite spheres, but experiments were made, sometimes under trade-union auspices, in the 'sixties, in the coal, iron, textile and other industries ; the Ettrick Tweed Mills, Selkirk, came under the control of the S.C.W.S.

Retail stores were also common in the 'thirties, e.g. at Cambuslang, where the " dividend on purchase " is said to have been first tried, at the instance of Alexander Campbell. Few of these survived, but a fresh impetus was given by Chartism, when a few societies especially in the Borders were formed by its adherents. The real advance came with the improving economic conditions of the 'fifties and 'sixties ; St. Cuthbert's (Edinburgh) dates from 1859 and Kinning Park (Glasgow) from 1871. The Clyde area and mid-Scotland remained the stronghold. Local federal organisation was adopted in the establishment of the Glasgow Drapery and Furnishing Stores in 1886 and the United Co-operative Baking Society in 1869, for the sale of domestic goods, and the baking and retail of bread respectively.

Large-scale manufacture was undertaken in 1868 by the Scottish Co-operative Wholesale Society Ltd., which was controlled by local retail societies, and owed much to the efficiency and zeal of its first manager, James Borrowman. Factories for soap, furniture, footwear, clothing, etc. were established at Shieldhall (Glasgow) and at Grangemouth (1897) ; and flour mills were acquired in Glasgow and Leith.[1]

The Co-operative Union formed a Scottish District in 1873 ; a periodical, the *Scottish Co-operator*, was published, Men's and Women's Guilds were founded and a Convalescent Home for members established in 1893.

Another characteristic Victorian movement was that for

[1] cf. W. Maxwell, *History of Co-operation in Scotland* (1910)

Adult Education. Mechanics' Institutes flourished in the industrial areas in the middle of the century, when there were about 50, with some 12,000 members. Instruction was chiefly on scientific subjects, and the best of them evolved into Technical Colleges—Heriot-Watt, Edinburgh and Royal, Glasgow. Others declined into recreational clubs. Many had libraries of which some formed the nucleus of later public libraries. For the middle class there were "Philosophical Institutions" as in Edinburgh, and Athenaeums as in Glasgow, where also commercial courses were given. Mutual Improvement Societies were common in the small towns and villages, notably in Aberdeenshire, where a Union existed for some years. Many churches had fellowships or guilds attached to them, at which secular as well as religious topics were expounded and debated. "Soirées" with "readings" and "spelling bees", etc. catered for less-exalted intellectual tastes. The "Glasgow lecture system" was commented on, and a critic deprecated the vogue of "intellectual dram drinking". There became almost a profession of itinerant lecturers, such as Dr. Thomas Murray, Carlyle's fellow student, subsequently an Edinburgh printer and councillor ; while noted scientists and men of letters thus added to their fame and income. The "phrenological" votaries of George Combe were particularly zealous, e.g. James Simpson, the eccentric Edinburgh advocate, who formed and lectured to a "Society for the Diffusion of Moral and Economical Knowledge" (c. 1840).

Stimulated by the example at Cambridge of Professor James Stuart, a native of Fife, the Universities, particularly Glasgow and St. Andrews, undertook "Extension Courses", primarily for women, then excluded from the regular classes. St. Andrews instituted a special degree of L.L.A. in 1876, and Glasgow founded Queen Margaret College in 1883. Committees for the purpose were formed in the Universities about 1890 but were short-lived, partly because of the admission of women to ordinary courses after the Universities Act of 1889. Professor Patrick Geddes, a leader in the movement, was also a pioneer of Summer Vacation Courses.

The principal libraries were still those of the Universities and of the Advocates and Writers to the Signet. Subscription Libraries were founded in several towns from the late eighteenth century. As already noted, considerable provision of books was made by some Mechanics' Institutes ; news-rooms and reading-rooms with working-class patrons appeared in the 'forties and 'fifties, often attached to coffee-houses.

Museums and art galleries were founded and usually passed under municipal control, e.g. that of Bailie McLellan in Glasgow (1856). The National Museum of Antiquities was founded under the auspices of the Society of Antiquaries (1859) and the National Gallery came under the aegis of the Board of Trustees. The Outlook Tower, Edinburgh (1892), was another product of the versatile genius of Patrick Geddes.

There was a prolific but often ephemeral local press, sometimes *journaux d'opinion*, political or ecclesiastical, rather than newspapers. The repeal of the " Taxes on Knowledge " in the 'fifties cheapened prices and encouraged daily instead of the previous usual bi-weekly issue. Among influential organs were the *Witness* (*c*. 1840–60), especially when edited by Hugh Miller, and the *Scottish Guardian*, both Free Church organs. Peter Mackenzie issued in the 'thirties and 'forties under various titles a series of polemical " Reformers' Gazettes " ; these give a vivid if somewhat unreliable impression of the Radical politics of the day. The short-lived Chartist periodicals have already been mentioned. " National " status was attained by the *Edinburgh Courant*, the chief Tory organ discontinued in 1886 when its rival the hitherto Whig *Scotsman*, edited from 1849 to 1876 by the witty and sardonic Alexander Russell, became Unionist. The *Glasgow Herald* also circulated widely. Evening dailies such as the *Glasgow Citizen* and the *Edinburgh Evening News* had considerable popularity. In Dundee the *Advertiser* acquired a high reputation under the half-century-long direction of Sir John Leng, and met the active competition of the *Courier*, controlled from about 1880 by the Thomson family. Notable provincial papers included the *Fife Herald*, the *Peebles Advertiser*, the *Dumfries Courier* and the *Arbroath Guide*.

The older magazines were supplemented by *Tait's* (1832–1864), expressing the Radical views of its owner William Tait ; and the *North British Review* (1844–71), edited for some time by Professor W. B. Blaikie and associated with the Free Church. Of a more popular type were *Good Words*, started by

Norman Macleod in 1860 ; the *People's Journal* and the *People's Friend*, weeklies published by Lengs of Dundee ; and the *British Weekly* founded in 1886 by W. Robertson Nicoll, a Free Church minister, which, though published in London, had a large Scottish clientèle.

Chambers and Collins published cheap reprints. Though Scottish fiction did not usually reach a high literary standard, writers like " Sarah Tytler " (Henrietta Keddie), William Black and, in their earlier work, Margaret Oliphant and George Macdonald, depict Scottish social life more realistically than the end-of-century " Kailyard School " (whose nostalgia for an earlier rural life has recently been diagnosed by George Blake) of Barrie, "Ian Maclaren" and Annie S. Swan. "George Douglas " (Brown)'s equally one-sided counterblast, the *House with the Green Shutters*, appeared in 1901. The romantic tradition of Scott was ably revived in the same period by R L. Stevenson, Neil Munro and John Buchan.

Anglicising trends and the lure of London as a literary centre drew the best Scottish writers away from their native environment and themes—Macaulay, Carlyle, George Macdonald, Robert Buchanan, Barrie, Buchan and other lesser practitioners in Grub Street. Leading publishers, such as Black, Collins and Blackwood also removed their headquarters to London.

Something must finally be said about Public Action in its relation to social and economic conditions. In the central government a main feature is the extension of the franchise by successive Acts, assimilating the Scottish to the English system. There were abortive movements for Women's Suffrage, especially in the 'sixties and 'seventies, of which Duncan McLaren and Professor Calderwood were protagonists ; Bills were later introduced, one by Ferdinand Begg, a Glasgow M.P. and son of the well-known cleric. Representatives were at first in the main local gentry and magnates ; later there appeared the " carpet-bagger ", and a tendency for a party caucus to nominate and promote candidatures. English-born members (some like Macaulay and Gladstone, of Scottish descent) were increasingly elected ; conversely there was a choice of Scots by English constituencies, from the time of Joseph Hume. In the development of the Cabinet system Scots frequently attained high office, including two—not very happy—Premierships, those of Aberdeen and Rosebery.

Responsibility in Parliament for Scottish affairs normally fell to the Lord Advocate, until after considerable agitation, headed by McLaren, the Secretaryship for Scotland was restored in 1885 ; his powers were augmented by subsequent legislation. The office was at first usually held by a Scottish peer such as Dalhousie or Lothian ; a later occupant was Sir George Trevelyan, an Englishman sitting for a Scottish constituency.

With the growth of a professional civil service, following the mid-century reforms, several Scottish Departments were constituted. The Board of Supervision was set up by the Poor Law Act of 1845 ; it was merged in the Scottish Local Government Board in 1894. A separate Scottish " Committee of the Privy Council on Education " was established in 1872, and is said to have shown a " marked tendency towards assimilation of policy ", which was partially reversed after the Scotch Education Department was formed in 1883. Other *ad hoc* Departments included the General Board of Control, to administer the Lunacy Acts (1857), the Fisheries Board (1882), the Prison Commissioners (1877), when central was substituted for local responsibility ; the Crofters Commission (1886) and the Congested Districts Commission (1897).

Royal and other public Commissions and Select Committees of Parliament became frequent, and their Reports are among our main sources of information. Some may have served to shelve an issue, but at times they prepared opinion and provided knowledge for subsequent legislation. Among those of importance, the purely Scottish include the Royal Commissions on Municipal Corporations (1833–5) and on the Poor Laws (1844), and Local Reports on the Sanitary Conditions of the Labouring Population (1842) ; those with an all-British reference ; the Children's Employment Commissions of 1842 and 1864, the Commissioners on Trade Unions (1867–9), on Coal and on Truck (1871) ; the Royal Commissions on the Housing of the Working Classes (1884–5), on Depression of Trade and Industry (1883–6), on Mining Royalties (1890–1) and on Labour (1892–4).

LOCAL ADMINISTRATION : STRUCTURE AND FUNCTIONS

The development of elective local government bodies is another feature of the Victorian Age. Again, while much study, notably the monumental volumes of the Webbs, has been devoted to English local government, little has yet been published in Scotland to follow up the pioneer work of the Webbs' disciple, Mabel Atkinson (1904) ; apart from a few short popular outlines, most of the literature consists of legal expositions.

Anticipating the Report of the Commission of Municipal Corporations, three Acts were passed in 1833. The first restored the " old usage " of popular election in most of the Royal Burghs, with a Parliamentary franchise. (Women rate-payers received the vote in 1869.) The second established Councils in twelve " Parliamentary Burghs " which had been given representation in the Commons the previous year. These were mainly industrial centres of recent growth such as Greenock and Paisley ; Galashiels and Hawick were added in 1868. The third was an Adoptive Act permitting the adoption by popular vote of the system of Police Commissions, already existing in certain areas. This Act, subsequently extended (to any " populous place " with over 700 inhabitants) in 1862 led to a proliferation of small " Police Burghs ", e.g. in the suburbs of Glasgow ; well over a hundred were instituted before the process was checked by an Act of 1892. In some cases the Commission existed alongside the Burgh Council, with similarity or even identity of personnel, though difference of function. The two were merged in some cases by Private Act, e.g. Edinburgh 1856 ; and universally by an Act of 1900. Distinct rating for " police " purposes was retained for another generation. The 1892 Act extended to Burghs of Barony the provisions for popular election of the 1833 Act. Other Burghs had meantime discarded their peculiar institutions for the representative system—e.g. Falkirk. Extension of boundaries took place with the growth of population ; Edinburgh, e.g., absorbed the Canongate in 1856 and Portobello in 1900 ; Glasgow, some contiguous small burghs in 1846 and 1891.

Party politics were evident in the earlier years ; the Whigs tended to dominate. Local issues such as the Annuity Tax in Edinburgh, agitated against by dissenters from the Established Church for the maintenance of whose clergy it was levied, caused some friction ; this imposition, enforced more rigidly after 1833, was abolished in 1861.

The Convention of Burghs was consulted regarding the legislation of 1833, but showed little activity until, towards the end of the century, Parliamentary Burghs (27, 1879) and Police Burghs (58, 1895) were admitted to membership.

The ecclesiastical unit of the Parish was retained as the chief unit of civil administration, though with the growing demarcation of *quoad sacra* parishes, the identity was in some cases lost. Readjustment of parochial boundaries occasionally took place. Under the Act of 1845 Parochial Boards were established in assessed parishes to administer poor relief ; half a century later forty-six parishes remained unassessed. The Boards included representatives of ratepayers, elected on a complex basis of plural voting ; in rural parishes members of Kirk Sessions and owners of land to the annual value of £20 were *de facto* members. In the burghs representatives of the Town Council and of Kirk Sessions also had seats. Additional duties, such as the registration of births and minor health services were subsequently added, and in 1894 completely elective Parish Councils were substituted ; franchise and eligibility were extended to " qualified " women.

The parochial unit was also adopted in landward areas for education under the Act of 1872. In urban areas the burgh was the unit. Here the right to vote was accorded to all adult owners and occupiers of " lands and heritages " of £4 annual value or upwards. Voting was cumulative, thus sectarian or other groups were able to obtain representation by casting all their votes for a single candidate. Women were eligible, and a few like Flora Stevenson in Edinburgh (Chairman 1900) and Grace Paterson in Glasgow attained prominence.

The County until 1888 had no corporate body other than the Commissioners of Supply, whose status was regulated by the Annual Valuation Act of 1854. They received powers for the administration of the constabulary (1857), prisons (1860–1877) and roads (1878) ; in the last case they had to devolve their duties on a Road Board nominated by themselves and supervising District Road Boards. They were also responsible for County Assessments, which were consolidated by an Act of 1868. In 1888, following the establishment of a similar system in England, County Councils were set up. These comprised elective members from landward areas and representatives of smaller burghs within their compass. A limited women's franchise operated. These Councils, apart from some early crofters' agitation in the Highlands, attracted little interest, and their activities were limited. The landing and farming interests usually predominated.

There was a tendency to the creation of *ad hoc* bodies, producing a variety of area and function. District Lunacy Boards were set up in 1857, Road Boards in 1878. Local Licensing Courts were established by the Home Drummond Act of 1828, and given further powers regarding limitation of hours, Sunday closing and grant of off-licences by the Forbes Mackenzie Act 1853. There were numerous local Trusts, Commissions, etc. for the administration of water supplies, harbours and docks, and latterly libraries ; these usually contained representatives of Burgh Councils in the area.

At the time of burgh reform a *laissez-faire* bias prevailed. The traditional functions of the Corporation had become largely identified with the administration of the Common Good ; those of the new elective bodies were confined to minimal " police " duties. There seems to have been a relative lack of the civic pride associated with the Greek and medieval city, but there were outstanding examples of municipal statesmanship in the careers of Lord Provosts Adam Black, Duncan McLaren and William Chambers in Edinburgh, Blackie and Chisholm in Glasgow, and in the twenty years' service (1841–61) of Sir Hugh Playfair in St. Andrews, which did so much to retrieve it from its eighteenth-century decline. Later collectivist developments, due more to considerations of practical expediency than to theories of " gas and water socialism ", were illustrated in the expansion of public health services and public utilities.

(i) *Poor Relief.* With the growth of industrialism and urban life the traditional system was obsolescent, and by the 'forties about half the parishes had resorted to assessment. Controversy came to a head in the famous verbal duel between Chalmers and Alison, both Professors in Edinburgh. Chalmers, whose theocratic views were fortified by the experiment in his Glasgow parish, upheld the " voluntary system " ; Alison from his practical experience as an urban physician pleaded the necessity of rating. He was supported by the Association for an Inquiry into the Poor Law of Scotland (1840), while a Church of Scotland Report (1839) endorsed Chalmers. The latter however precipitated a decision against himself by leading the Disruption of 1843. A Government Commission of 1844 produced an inconclusive report, but the split in the Church made it obviously incapable of operating a national scheme, and the Act of 1845 provided for the semi-elective Parochial Boards already described, with rating powers and paid Inspectors of Poor. Though not obligatory, it was almost universally adopted by the end of the century. The ineligibility for relief of the able-bodied was maintained ; relief was in practice given, especially in cases of severe unemployment, as in Paisley (1849), but was finally ruled to be illegal by the House of Lords in the case of Isdale vs. Jack (1866). Institutional treatment was provided for the aged and infirm, and one of the first central grants was that given for their medical care in 1847.

(ii) *Education.* Here a similar inadequacy of the existing system became apparent ; the parish schools were educating only about one-fourth of the total pupils in the 'thirties. They were supplemented by Sessional and denominational schools, including subsequently those under Free Church auspices after the Disruption. There were some works schools like the famous one at New Lanark ; and a great variety of private schools, including those established by endowments, to some extent on English " public school " lines, such as Fettes and Glenalmond.

Public provision was gradual and tentative, commencing with grants made in 1833 and inspection in 1840. The practice of " payment by results " was introduced in 1861 and continued for about thirty years, though apparently less rigidly applied in Scotland. Complete public control was delayed by sectarian controversy, though this was not so acute as in

England. An Act of 1861 confirmed secular control in the burghs. The Argyle Commission (1864–8) reported that about 100,000 were without regular schooling. The National Education League, of which Professor Edward Caird was a leader, advocated non-sectarian education. The Act of 1872 instituted, as described, elective School Boards, whose powers included the provision of secondary and further education ; burgh schools were transferred to their control. Continuation Classes for those who had left school were initiated in 1873. Secondary Education Committees were authorised in 1892 and Higher Grade Schools commenced in 1899. The 1872 Act prescribed compulsory attendance to the age of 13, raised to 14 in 1883, though subject to considerable exemptions till 1901. Primary education was made free in 1890. Church influence remained strong, especially in rural areas, where the parish minister usually dominated the Board.

In accordance with the recommendations of successive Commissions, most of the old endowed " hospitals ", such as those of the Edinburgh Merchant Company, were converted into modern Secondary Schools. Provision for technical education was initiated through the Science and Art Department grants in 1856. Such training as was given to teachers was in Normal Colleges, which remained under the auspices of the various churches. The pioneer one, founded under David Stow in Glasgow in 1834, passed to the Free Church in 1843. The Universities remained outwith the public system, though reorganised and reformed by Acts of 1858 and 1889.

(iii) *Miscellaneous.* Libraries. Under an Adoptive Act of 1853 promoted by William Ewart, long M.P. for Dumfries, Local Authorities were empowered to establish public libraries after a poll of the electors and to levy a halfpenny rate for upkeep. Airdrie was the first to accept this (1856) ; few followed until the 'eighties when Andrew Carnegie offered endowment.

Local control of the constabulary was regulated by Acts of 1857 and 1892. A municipal fire service was pioneered by Glasgow in 1809, and developed towards the close of the century by William Paterson, who was Firemaster (1884–1906) after a varied experience as joiner, trade-union official and Factory Inspector.

(iv) *Public Health.* Temporary Local Boards of Health, sometimes called Fever Commissioners, were set up in some areas
in times of epidemic. The influence of the " sanatory idea ",
of which Chadwick was the chief exponent in England, was
retarded in Scotland by the emphasis laid by Alison and others
on destitution rather than on environmental conditions ; hence
there was considerable opposition to the short-lived central
Board of Health (1848–54). Nevertheless " environmental "
health services developed piecemeal under a series of Police
and other Acts, and legislation was consolidated in the Act of
1867, superseded by that of 1897. Edinburgh and Glasgow
initiated the appointment of Medical Officers of Health, in the
persons of Harvey Littlejohn (1862) and William Gairdner
(1863) ; the latter's successor, James B. Russell (1837–1904),
did much to build up a public service in Glasgow(1872–98)
and was author of an authoritative exposition (1895).

One of the prime aspects of a public health service is the
provision of an adequate water supply. The unsatisfactoriness
of the private companies which had entered the field early in
the century led to the establishment by Glasgow of the famous
Loch Katrine scheme (1855), which has been hailed as the
first " triumph of municipalisation ". Edinburgh after much
controversy entrusted its supplies to a Water Trust (1869).
Availability of water facilitated the general introduction of
internal pipes and the establishment of public baths, lavatories
and washhouses, as well as of public drains and sewers. Refuse
collection was undertaken by Councils, and its utilisation—
e.g. for fertilisers—subsequently developed. Following on
medieval precedent, the siting of " offensive trades " such as
abattoirs and gasworks was regulated, and an attempt made
to restrict pollution of the atmosphere by smoke. Similar
efforts to check the pollution of rivers by industrial establishments had little success. Inspection of food was initiated by
the Sale of Food and Drugs Act of 1875.

" Isolation " hospitals for sufferers from infectious diseases
were started by Glasgow in 1865, and notification of certain
such ailments was made compulsory in the 'nineties.

The first steps towards municipal responsibility for housing
were taken in the interests of public health. Common lodging-
houses required registration under an Act of 1851. From 1862

excessive overcrowding was limited by insistence on a minimum
" cubic capacity " of air space per person ; hence the
" ticketed houses " of which there were still some 20,000 in
Glasgow in 1900.

Some burghs instituted City Improvement schemes by
Private Acts. The most famous were those inspired by the
publisher Lord Provosts of Edinburgh and Glasgow, Chambers
and Blackie, in the middle 'sixties. Under the former scheme
£100,000 was spent on the purchase and clearance of slum
areas. Glasgow later undertook rebuilding as well. The
" Cross " Act of 1875 gave general permissive building powers
to Councils. Greenock, under Provost Neill (1877), was one
of the few to operate the Act. A Commission on Housing in
1884–5 revealed the unsatisfactoriness of Scottish conditions,
but no effective action followed. Building in towns was
regulated by the Dean of Guild Court where this existed, or
through powers given under Police Acts.

In the latter half of the century considerable expansion of
public parks and recreation grounds was made in the larger
towns, either by private benefactions or public acquisition.
Princes Street Gardens, originally like other open spaces in the
New Town the perquisite of local residents, were municipalised
in the 'seventies ; the Blackford and Braid Hills became public
property in 1884 and 1890 respectively. With the expansion
of the city, Glasgow secured " lungs " in the Kelvingrove,
Queen's and Alexandra Parks.

(v) *Public Utilities.* Certain services came to be recognised as
local monopolies, suitable for " municipal trading ", i.e. where
payment is made on commercial terms by users. Public
ownership of the manufacture and distribution of gas was
facilitated by the Burgh Gas Supply Act of 1876 ; that of
electricity by the Electric Lighting Act of 1882. An Act of
1870 empowered municipalities to provide local transport
services ; the operation was usually at first leased to a private
company, but on its expiry the Council sometimes undertook
direct control, as in Glasgow in 1894.

(vi) *Finance.* In the Royal Burghs, what survived of the
Common Good was at the disposal of the Councils. It consisted

chiefly in the revenue of public lands, rights in which sometimes occasioned litigation, as in the case of Lauder in the 'sixties. Local petty customs were generally abolished after an Adoptive Act of 1870, though they survived in twenty-four burghs in 1900. Profits of municipal enterprise might be added, but the amount was quite inadequate to contemporary needs, and municipalities came to rely chiefly on rates. Their involved history was expounded in detail by S. H. Turner in 1908. Originally levied as the local contribution to a national " cess ", they came to be gradually utilised for local purposes, particularly poor relief. The original Police Commissioners were given rating powers for special purposes, and separate police rates survived into the twentieth century. The usual basis of assessment was at first " means and substance ", a crude form of property tax, productive of much controversy and litigation. By the Baxter Act of 1861 " heritable property " was substituted as the usual basis and an annual valuation made. Agricultural land was partially derated in 1896. The total sum raised by rates in Scotland increased from about £1 million in 1850 to about £4 million in 1900.

Rates were supplemented by Parliamentary grants in aid of services imposed on Local Authorities by legislation. Those originally given for education (1833) and medical care of paupers (1847) were added to by a variety of special contributions, such as those of the Science and Art Department (1859) and the " whisky " money diverted to schools fortuitously in 1890. Some took the form of " percentage " or " efficiency " grants—e.g. police (1858), lunacy (1874), roads (1892)—and were designed to encourage local expenditure by guaranteeing a fixed proportion of aid. The principal example of a " block grant ", irrespective of the local expenditure, was given in the institution of the Local Taxation Account (1888) ; this introduced the " Goschen formula ", by which Scotland received eleven-eightieths of whatever was voted as a grant in aid of local services in England.

4

The Twentieth Century

THE PRE-WAR YEARS

The years 1901–14, sometimes dubbed the Edwardian Era, form an epilogue to the Victorian Age, but at the same time were the period of development of forces revealed or intensified by the War of 1914–18 and subsequently active. They were years of the growth of commercial rivalries, especially between Great Britain and Germany—a psychological and perhaps economic factor contributing to armed conflict. They witnessed the revival of the Protectionist agitation which triumphed in the 'thirties. They experienced the introduction of a policy of social reformism, pioneered by Lloyd George's insurance schemes and redistributive taxation, which has now culminated in the welfare state. They were years when the rise in the general level of prices, which has continued almost unabated, became again manifest. One result was the accentuation of industrial strife, associated with the rise of the Labour Party, at the expense of Liberalism, which gained so striking but ephemeral a triumph in 1906.

Most of the prolific social legislation of these years was common to Great Britain; but among enactments peculiar to Scotland were the Small Landholders Act of 1911, which extended to all small tenants the Crofters' Act provision of fair rent, etc., and substituted a Land Court for the Crofters' Commission; the institution in 1913 of special Medical Services for the scattered population of the Highlands and Islands; and the Scottish Temperance Act of 1913 which provided for local option by popular vote on the sale of alcoholic liquors. The Education (Scotland) Act of 1908 pooled various grants in the Education (Scotland) Fund, and made provision for the physical welfare of pupils. Andrew Carnegie founded his Trust for Scottish Universities in 1901.

Another event of considerable bearing on Scottish social history was the union of the Free and United Presbyterian Churches in 1900. The dissentient minority in the former had their claim to the properties of their church upheld by the House of Lords, reversing the verdict of the Scottish courts. The obvious inequity of the verdict was repaired by retrospective legislation (Scottish Churches Act, 1905), in terms of which a fair distribution between majority and minority was achieved.

The Scottish economy on the whole progressed, though there were years of depression. The Scottish output represented approximately one-seventh of the coal, one-third of the steel and one-fourth of the ships of Britain. Dependence on world markets was accentuated, four-fifths of tweeds, one-third of coal, two-thirds of locomotives being sold abroad. There was about 1906 a boom in company promotion ; in that year 84 were launched with nearly £4 million capital ; 71 were private, i.e. not issuing shares for public subscription.

The mining of coal expanded in the Lothians ; shipbuilding attained a record output in 1911, the Parsons turbine was introduced by Dennys in 1901, the first ocean motor-ship, the *Jutlandia*, was launched by Barclay Curles in 1912 ; Yarrows transferred their yards from the Thames to the Clyde (Scotstoun) in 1904. There was an increase in naval orders, especially to Beardmores, Browns and Fairfield ; the *Agamemnon*, then the largest dreadnought, put to sea in 1906, the same year as the largest passenger vessel, the ill-fated *Lusitania*. Lithgows of Port-Glasgow attained the leading position among shipbuilders. The Rosyth Naval Base was approved in 1903 and construction commenced in 1907 ; the Royal Naval Torpedo Factory at Greenock followed in 1909. The making of Diesel engines was introduced by the Bergius Co. ; Barclay Curle became associated with Burmeister and Wain of Copenhagen in the construction of motor-vessels. Control of Babcock and Wilcox was acquired in 1900 by Sir William Arrol and Andrew Stewart of Stewart & Lloyds, works were established in Japan in association with the great Mitsui firm in 1910. Rapidly developing engineering enterprises were established by the Harland Co. in Alloa and Cochrane & Co. in Annan, both in 1902.

In newer types of scientific industry Scotland bid fair to advance. The construction of motor-cars must however be reckoned as " Scotland's lost industry ". Of several firms established about the turn of the century the Arrol-Johnston, with works at Dumfries, Halley's Industrial Motors, Bridgeton, and the Albion Motor Co., Scotstoun, made " a notable contribution in early days " [1] and survived the First War, to which the Argyll Co., Alexandria, after vicissitudes succumbed.

The commercial success of the internal-combustion engine revived road transport. Numerous local concerns established passenger and goods services. The Scottish Motor Traction Co. (S.M.T.), of which (Sir) W. J. Thomson became general manager, commenced operations in Edinburgh in 1906 and soon defeated or absorbed rivals in the South-east ; what came to be its chief rival, and later partner, was founded by Walter Alexander at Falkirk in 1913.

The British Aluminium Co., formed in 1894, had established its first Scottish works at Foyers on Loch Ness in 1896. It was discovered that electric treatment was most effective for aluminium, and this made the company the pioneer of hydro-electric development in the Highlands through the establishment of the Loch Leven Power Co. at Kinlochleven (1904). The chemical treatment of bauxite ore, the raw material of aluminium, was undertaken at Burntisland in 1913. This industry has remained one in which " almost all manufacture in Great Britain is carried out in Scotland " (Oakley).

Tendencies to industrial combination increased. John Brown of Sheffield had acquired Clydebank shipyard in 1899 and entered into agreement in 1907 with Harland and Wolff of Belfast, who again acquired the London & Glasgow Engineering and Shipbuilding Co. in 1912. Lloyds of Birmingham, tube-makers, coalesced in 1902 with A. & J. Stewart & Menzies of Rutherglen and Coatbridge. Beardmores of Parkhead, under Sir William Beardmore, later Lord Invernairn, then the outstanding magnate on the Clyde, reunited in 1900 with Robert Napier's shipbuilding and engineering firm and entered into association with Vickers of Sheffield and Cammell Laird of Liverpool. The Fife Coal Co. absorbed several mining concerns in the county. The Scottish Iron & Steel Co.

[1] H. G. Castle, *Britain's Motor Industry* (1950)

amalgamated thirteen firms in 1912. The North British Locomotive Co. of 1903 was a fusion of four engine works. Blackwood Morton & Co., as well as combining old firms of carpet manufacturers in Kilmarnock, had subsidiaries in Yorkshire and Ulster. The absorption of most Scottish tobacco manufacturers in the Imperial Tobacco Co. in 1901 has already been noted. Nobels bought out several other makers of explosives and set up factories at Linlithgow and Waltham Abbey.

The growth of interlocking directorates and of a class of " professional " directors, chiefly accountants and solicitors rather than business men, is noteworthy. In retail trade the advance of the large producer with multiple retail branches is illustrated by the entrance of Boots " Cash Chemists " to Edinburgh about 1910, and the establishment of Birrell's confectionery in Glasgow. Patrick Thomson of Edinburgh in 1900 heralded the department store, taken over by a private company on his death in 1907. There was an increased sale of milk, and increased legal protection of its quality, which encouraged the growth of large concerns at the expense of the small dairy-farmer retailer. The production of margarine got an impetus through the transition from animal to vegetable fats as a chief source ; this fostered the vegetable-oil trade with West Africa, in which Levers became involved. Retail dairy stores formed chains such as the Maypole and the Meadow, dominated by either of the great Dutch producers Jurgens and Van den Berghs. The press was affected by the increased use of the linotype which tended to make labour redundant ; D. C. Thomson of Dundee developed popular weeklies.

Scottish overseas enterprise was largely associated with the two commodities oil and rubber, for which the expansion of road transport offered a rapidly increasing demand. The Burmah Oil Co. was promoted chiefly by David Cargill, a Glasgow East India merchant, and grew under the direction of his son Sir John. The Anglo-Persian Co., founded in 1909 to take over concessions obtained in Persia, was largely financed by the Burmah Co., and had the veteran Scots-Canadian Lord Strathcona as its first chairman. The promoters of the Trinidad Oilfields (1911) included William Fraser of the Pumpherston Co. The native Scottish shale-oil industry, now in the hands of five companies, attained its maximum output of nearly 4 million tons in 1913.

The artificial cultivation of rubber was begun in Malaya in the 1890's ; many companies were promoted with Scottish capital and estates staffed by Scottish emigrants. There was a boom in 1910 when shares tripled in value. Several finance companies were formed, some interested particularly in tea and rubber shares.

The story of the working-class movement is mainly that of two contending forces, that relying on political action and that hankering after more " direct " methods in the industrial field.

The Scottish Workers' Representation Committee set up in 1900 became the Scottish Labour Party in 1906 and was merged in the British in 1909, though a Scottish Advisory Committee and Annual Conference existed from 1913. The I.L.P. was active in propaganda ; the Fabian Society had small groups, especially in the Universities. The revival of Marxism was heralded by the secession from Ruskin College in 1908 of those who formed the Central Labour College for " independent working-class education ". John Maclean, a Glasgow teacher, held classes in Marxist economics. At the General Election of 1906 the first two Scottish Labour M.P.'s were elected—George Barnes and Alex. Wilkie ; they were joined in 1910 by Wm. Adamson, of the Fife Miners. Municipal representation increased by 1914 to 17 in Glasgow and 6 in Edinburgh. *Forward* was established in Glasgow in 1906 by Tom Johnston as an independent Socialist weekly, and the Reformers Bookstall opened there the following year.

Trends to " direct action " were encouraged by disappointment with Parliamentary achievements, by spells of unemployment on the Clyde and by the propaganda of syndicalism of which James Connolly was a spokesman. Large-scale industrial disputes affecting Scotland were rife in the years preceding the War—boiler-makers, seamen, dockers, railwaymen and miners.

Some new Scottish trade unions were established, including the Horse and Motormens in 1902, the Farm Servants, in 1913 and the Dundee Jute and Flaxworkers in 1907, after a strike ; this superseded the former union dominated by Rev. Henry Williamson. The unionisation of women and of " black-coated " workers proceeded apace, but the bodies mainly concerned — the National Federation of Women Workers, the Clerks, Shop Assistants, Postal Workers, etc.— were of English origin. A Scottish Union of Dockers became associated with the Transport Workers Union, but a breakaway from the Seamen's Union of Havelock Wilson was led by Emanuel Shinwell in 1913. The two unions of carpenters, the Associated (of Scottish origin) and the Amalgamated, ended their long rivalry by amalgamation in 1911. There were now about forty Trades Councils in Scotland.

Cultural developments included the establishment of the West of Scotland Agricultural College (1902), the Edinburgh University Settlement (1905) and the Glasgow Repertory Theatre (1909). The period was one of considerable advance in voluntary social reform, especially on the part of the churches ; the Scottish Christian Social Union was formed in 1901 and the Social Work Committee of the Church of Scotland in 1903 ; Rev. David Watson of Glasgow was active in this field.

Notable also was the increased interest in the study of Scottish history and institutions, marked by the establishment of chairs in Edinburgh in 1901 and Glasgow in 1913, and by the publication of such works as those of Andrew Lang, Hume Brown, R. S. Rait and W. L. Matheson. The Celtic element was reflected in the holding of the Pan-Celtic Congress in Edinburgh in 1907 and the first Festival of An Comunn Gaidhealich in Glasgow the same year. The Royal Commission on Ancient Monuments was set up in 1908, and the remnant of the eighteenth-century Board of Manufactures converted in 1907 into the Board of Trustees for the National Galleries. Scottish political nationalism was kept alive by the Young Scots Society, a group associated with the advanced wing of the Liberal Party.

THE FIRST WORLD WAR. 1914–18

The War was of peculiar importance to the Scottish economy, in view of its intimate dependence on the world economy which was dislocated by the war, and deteriorated further owing to the provisions of the Peace Settlement and other war consequences. Scotland's heavy industries were also over-expanded by war needs, and suffered heavily from the cessation of these demands. During the continuance of hostilities, after initial disturbance, there was increased output and productive capacity in industries providing munitions and supplies of war. Mobilisation, indiscriminate enlistment and subsequent conscription depleted labour supply.

Coal suffered loss of overseas markets, especially Germany and Russia, and export was reduced to one-fourth ; scarcity of labour was acute and productive capacity was impaired, though the use of machinery increased. Government control was instituted in 1917.

Iron and steel had difficulties in importing ore, though ultimately supplies were obtained, chiefly from Spain. Additional plant was established and equipped, and productive capacity increased. The trend to combination was encouraged ; Colvilles of Motherwell, under the management of (Sir) John Craig, extended control over collieries and became linked with Harland and Wolff.

Shipbuilding was at first concentrated on naval construction, but later, especially after submarine warfare took toll of the merchant fleet, on civilian replacement. Shipyards were controlled under the Munitions of War Act of 1915. Sir James Lithgow, the leading Clyde shipbuilder, became Director of Merchant Shipbuilding in 1917 ; and Sir Joseph (Lord) Maclay, a prominent shipowner, was appointed Minister of Shipping in December 1916. The total output for 1914–18 included over 800,000 naval tonnage and $1\frac{1}{2}$ million mercantile, besides much repair work. Rosyth dockyard was extended, and Scapa Flow (Orkney) improvised as a naval base. New firms entered shipbuilding, especially on the east coast, notably the Burntisland Shipbuilding Co., under the Ayre brothers, and Henry Robb Ltd. at Leith. Harland and Wolff acquired Cairds' yard at Greenock.

A practically new munitions industry was founded, under the control of the Ministry of Munitions set up in 1915 ; among the business men recruited to its service were the noted Clyde engineers William (Lord) Weir and Sir Frederick Lobnitz. Existing engineering works, such as the North British Locomotive Co. and Singers, were converted into factories for shells, guns, aeroplanes and tanks. " The engin-eering industry of the Clyde was virtually revolutionized by the introduction of automatic machinery and adoption of mass pro-duction " (Jeffreys). Hence the " dilution " of labour which was responsible for the acute problem to be considered later.

There is little to note regarding the textile industries, other than that jute and wool, because of their importance for war supplies, eventually came under government control, while losing their Continental markets. Scottish banking was affected by the withdrawal of gold and institution of an inconvertible note issue, including those sponsored by the Treasury. The notes of the Scottish banks were made legal tender in Great Britain for the duration of the war. Inflation as elsewhere increased the cost of living and involved social tensions.

Agriculture,[1] after a long period of relative neglect, obtained prominence in the public and official mind, as increasing difficulty of import enhanced reliance on home-produced food, while military requirements contributed to growing demand. Wheat imports declined to 40 per cent, butter and eggs to a fraction ; there was a shortage of feeding stuffs and fertilisers. Home output was eventually stimulated by guaranteed prices for grain, milk and meat, and by fixation of wages by District and National Committees, which doubled the average pay. Local Agricultural Committees supervised farming ; the Government purchased the whole wool clip from 1916 to 1918. Production of potatoes and other vegetables by spare-time effort for self-consumption was encouraged by an allotments scheme. Control of distribution of food was gradually estab-lished through a Ministry of Food ; bread was subsidised and the rationing of sugar, meat and fats introduced. The Scottish Women's Rural Institutes were inaugurated in 1917.

There was a virtual stoppage of housebuilding, which increased the already acute overcrowding, especially as munition-making attracted more workers to the Clyde. Rise of rents evoked friction, and was restricted by Acts of 1915 and subsequently. A semi-public corporation, the Scottish National Housing Co., was set up in June 1915, with

[1] Details are given in Carnegie Endowment Reports *on Clyde Valley Industries* (1924) and *Scottish Agriculture and Fisheries, Rural Scotlan dduring the War* (1926).

£1¼ million capital, and undertook building at Rosyth, where the original " tin town " was superseded by a model " garden village ". Industrial welfare was fostered by the Ministry of Munitions and a voluntary Society formed in 1918. A limited measure of control over the sale of liquor was introduced (1916) in the form of " disinterested management " in the munition areas of Gretna and the Cromarty Firth.

Officially the Trade Union and political Labour movements initially supported the War ; disputes were called off, and by the Treasury Agreement of March 1915 and the Munitions of War Act dilution of labour, compulsory arbitration, wartime relaxation of trade-union rules and control of movement and wages were accepted. Friction however developed, and the publicity given to disputes in the area earned the sobriquet of the " Red Clyde ". An underlying factor was the emergence of new techniques in engineering, hitherto almost unchanged for a century ; the propaganda of syndicalism combined with this to encourage the rise of the Shop Stewards' movement, relying on leadership from the workshop rather than from the Union's central office. Thus the body which became notorious as the Clyde Workers' Committee, under the leadership of William Gallacher, became the focus of opposition on the Clyde. It was not anti-war, but opposed payment by results and demanded " workers' control ". As the War proceeded, with deteriorating social conditions and increasing casualties, this industrial movement became associated with a policy of " peace by negotiation ", stimulated by the I.L.P. and other pacifist or near-pacifist groups. Notable incidents were the shouting down of Lloyd George (Christmas 1915) by a gathering of workers and consequent suppression of the issue of *Forward* which reported it : the deportation of Kirkwood and other stewards after a strike at Parkhead (March 1916) ; the prosecution for sedition of John Muir, editor of the *Worker*, the stewards' organ, and of John McLean, the avowed advocate of a social revolution on the lines of Russia. (Most of the " rebel " spokesmen were engineers or teachers, e.g. James Maxton). Unrest culminated after the Armistice in the semi-official strike of January–February 1919, ostensibly to secure a general forty-hour week as a palliative for the anticipated unemployment. After a riot, for their part in which Shinwell and Gallacher were imprisoned, the strike fizzled out within three weeks.

THE INTER-WAR PERIOD

This period can for many purposes be divided into four phases, that of Aftermath (1919–24), Recovery (1924–9), Crisis (1929–33), Readjustment and Armed Peace (1933–9). Though Scottish conditions must be increasingly viewed in an international setting, these distinctions are less clearly marked for Scotland where, after an initial post-war boom, a slump set in during the winter of 1920–1, and chronic depression continued till the later 'thirties. Volumes have been written to expound varied theories of its cause ; for Scotland there may be emphasised the excessive dependence on heavy industries and the permanent loss of markets, e.g. for textiles and fish in central Europe. The loss by Great Britain of economic ascendancy was peculiarly reflected in Scotland, where proportion of output to that of England diminished. There were unsuccessful attempts to buttress the basic industries by wage-cutting, " rationalisation " and derating. Increasing English control was manifest in banking, railways, retail distribution and trade unions, as the trend to combination proceeded. Especially in heavy industry the growth of " monopoly capitalism " was enhanced ; much control passed into the hands of a few men such as Sir James Lithgow, Sir Adam Nimmo and Sir John Craig. There was some improvement in the home market and in British " terms of trade " (thus lowering the cost of living) in the 'thirties ; but the expansion of new lighter consumptional industries, marked in the Midlands and the London area, had no counterpart in Scotland, which " specialised in declining industries ", and obtained only about 3 per cent of new employment. A " southward drift " was indicated in such episodes as the transfer of railway shops from centres like Inverness south of the Border, and the removal of the principal works of Stewarts and Lloyds from Lanarkshire to Corby in Northamptonshire (1934).

General trends may be illustrated from the principal industries. Coal was decontrolled from March 1921, and its story during the 'twenties was one of chronic depression and strife, culminating in the dispute which precipitated the " General Strike " of May 1926. Output fell to 15 million tons per annum ; export was further handicapped by Polish competition. The Coal Mines Act of 1930 established a Scottish District Marketing scheme, with output quotas. There was considerable improvement in the 'thirties ; output reached 30 million tons in 1938, and export improved, particularly through a Trade Agreement with Denmark. Machine-cut coal was over 75 per cent, as compared with 50 per cent in England. About 87,000 were employed, a net decline of over 7,000. The Fife Coal Co. pioneered the development of a model pit at Comrie in 1935. The leading figures in the industry, Sir Adam Nimmo, Dr. R. T. Moore and the two Carlows through their interlocking directorates largely unified its control.

The old lead-mining industry at Leadhills and Wanlockhead ceased to operate in the late 1920's. The remaining companies in the shale-oil industry amalgamated as Scottish Oils Ltd. in 1918, under the headship of William Fraser of Pumpherston, and became a subsidiary of the Anglo-Persian (from 1935 the Anglo-Iranian) of which he was a director. A preferential duty was given to home-produced oil ; refining was extended at Grangemouth.

The iron and steel industry was continuously depressed from 1921 ; many works closed, others worked to less than a third of capacity. In 1931 only 7 furnaces out of 77 were in blast. Numbers employed fell by nearly one-fourth ; the transfer of Stewart & Lloyds to Corby involved the removal of over 1,000. Combination proceeded further ; Colvilles attained dominance, controlling Smith & McLean, the Steel Co. of Scotland, the Lanarkshire Steel Co., Beardmores and James Dunlops. The Scottish Iron and Steel Co. acquired some of the interests of Wm. Baird & Co. and constituted Bairds and Scottish Steel Ltd. (1939).

Shipbuilding declined, partly owing to the fall in freights with the dislocation of international trade. A notable feature was the policy, much criticised then and since, of dismantling " redundant " yards—e.g. Dalmuir, Cairds, Old Kilpatrick— undertaken by the National Shipbuilding Security Co., financed by the Bank of England and headed by Sir James Lithgow, who in the 'thirties was the leading personality not only in shipbuilding but in heavy industry generally as a director of Beardmores, Colvilles, Fairfield, Nimmos and Dunlops. Barclay Curles came into the hands of Swan Hunter & Wigham Richardson of Newcastle · and D. & W. Henderson and A. & J. Inglis into those of Harland & Wolff. Rosyth dockyard was put on a " care and maintenance " basis. Shipbreaking firms such as Th. W. Ward of Sheffield at Inverkeithing and the Alloa Shipbreaking Co. were active ; some progress in building was made at Leith by Henry Robb Ltd. Unemployment at the peak reached 25 per cent.

In engineering much the same figure obtained ; it rarely fell below 10 per cent. The closing of railway shops reduced employment by some 8,000. Similar trends to combination are the other marked feature. G. & J. Weir became associated with the International Nickel Co. of Canada. Babcock & Wilcox, Henry Balfour & Co. (Leven) and the Harland Engineering Co. also obtained overseas associates. Allied Ironfounders Ltd., promoted by Clarence Hatry, in 1929 combined twenty-two firms in the light-castings industry, including the pioneer firm at Coalbrookdale on the Severn and several in the Falkirk area ; Rayburn cookers and Jupiter stoves became familiar among its products ; another amalgamation constituted Federated Foundries Ltd. in 1935. Frasers of Arbroath went over to textile machinery ; 95 per cent of jute machinery was made by the Dundee combine of Urquhart Lindsay & Robertson Orchar (1921).

Chemicals afforded the largest combine of all in Imperial Chemical Industries (1926), of which Sir Harry McGowan was first chairman (1926–50). This included about forty companies, among them the two former rivals in the soda branch : the United Alkali Co. (derived from Tennants) and Brunner Mond ; the British Dyestuffs Corporation, of which Scottish Dyes Ltd., headed by Sir James Morton, was a chief component ; Scottish Agricultural Industries Ltd., with nineteen artificial fertiliser factories ; Scottish Tar Distillers, Nobels and the Cassel Cyanide Co. originally of Glasgow, whose works were now removed to England.

In shipping, which reflected the decline in international trade, the same tendency is manifest in the inauguration of Coast Lines Ltd., including MacBraynes, the Burns-Laird and other local lines ; the control acquired by Cayzers of the Clan and Shire Lines ; the association of the Anchor Line with Lyles, ultimately a subsidiary of the United Molasses Co. (1935) ; and merging of the Cunard and White Star Lines.

The Scottish railways under the Act of 1921 were absorbed in the two great lines, London & North Eastern and London, Midland & Scottish. Employment fell by nearly one-half, partly owing to the competition of road transport, which conversely grew. Many small local concerns were rapidly absorbed, especially by the Scottish Motor Transport Co. and Alexanders, who came to terms in 1929, when also the railway companies acquired shares in them. Road haulage of goods expanded ; Charles Alexander of Aberdeen, e.g., established a service of night fish-lorries to England. Agitation for better communications across the Firth was temporarily appeased by the opening of a road bridge at Kincardine (1936).

The consumptional or " sheltered " industries, e.g. food-stuffs, printing, enjoyed relative stability ; about 150 new firms commenced business. Among textiles, however, jute suffered from the increased competition of Indian mills, which now had seven times as many looms as in Britain. Dundee still possessed 85 per cent of the British manufacture, and employed about 30,000 ; only one-third of output was exported, in comparison with three-fourths in 1900. Some of the leading firms, including Cox of Lochee, combined in Jute Industries Ltd. (1920) ; Low & Bonar, whose chief partner, George Bonar (d. 1935), founded the Dundee School of Economics, shared most of the rest of the trade with Cairds, under the bequest of whose head, Sir James Caird (d. 1916), the new city hall was built, after much controversy over the demolition of its " Adam " predecessor.

Linen too suffered from the cutting off of Russian flax and from Irish competition ; import from Belgium and Holland supplied the former lack. The industry in Arbroath declined catastrophically, thirteen works being closed.

In wool, Patons combined with Baldwins of Darlington in 1920 ; the brothers Paton were noted as philanthropists. In the hosiery branch, Innes Henderson & Co. developed the production of Braemar underwear, and Peter Scott & Co. that of Pesco. Export of Border tweeds fell from 80 to 50 per cent,

U.S.A. taking a fifth instead of a third. The Harris Tweed Industry grew considerably ; over 1,000 hand-looms wove yarn, chiefly machine spun in Stornoway ; the control was largely in the hands of Pringles of Hawick ; markets were found in the cities. A registered trade mark was accorded in 1934.

The boot and shoe output fell in proportion to that of Great Britain ; the small producer was increasingly eliminated by a few large manufacturers such as the S.C.W.S., the Saxone Co. of Kilmarnock and Greenlees of Glasgow ; these usually operated retail stores ; Greenlees took over those of R. and J. Dick.

House-furnishing grew largely on a hire-purchase basis. James Grant & Co., founded in Edinburgh by David Oppenheim (1877–1954) in 1923, rapidly opened nearly thirty branches.

The Inveresk Paper Co. (1922) controlled sixteen mills, and had interests in Provincial Newspapers Ltd. Other Scottish mills, including Pirie's and Annandale's, were acquired by the English combine of Wiggins Teape & Co.

In publishing, Oliver & Boyd combined with the Edinburgh booksellers Thin and John Grant.

In distilling, the pioneer combine of D.C.L. acquired Haig, Mackie and Calder with a capital of £16 million, and eventually amalgamated with Buchanan-Dewar and Walker ; thus under the long headship of William H. Ross (1862–1944) a near monopoly position was achieved. The company produced 60 per cent of Scottish whisky and 80 per cent of industrial alcohol, and established subsidiaries from the production of celluloid, plastics and penicillin. In brewing, Edinburgh had four-fifths of the Scottish output. Scottish Brewers, Ltd. (1931) was a holding company, controlling Wm. Younger and McEwan, and owning public houses and licensed hotels in England. Geo. Younger of Alloa established the Central Glass Works there.

The flour milling industry was dominated by Spillers and Rank, who each owned Scottish mills and did 80 per cent of the business ; the rest was chiefly in the hands of the S.C.W.S. Tait & Lyle (1921) held a similar monopoly in sugar, owning Fairrir's and Macfie's refineries, and plantations in Jamaica ;

they were associated with the United Molasses Co. in ship-owning. The cheap and plentiful supplies of sugar encouraged the taste for confectionery. Duncan of Edinburgh became part of Associated Chocolate Manufacturers (1930) and McColl, of British Cocoa and Chocolate Co. dominated by Cadburys (1919). Like Birrell of Glasgow they had a chain of retail shops. Keiller of Dundee were acquired in 1920 by Crosse and Blackwell.

A similar plenty of cereals encouraged the manufacture and sale of food products. Westons, of Canadian origin, were a leading component of Allied Bakeries Ltd. (1935) and manu-factured biscuits. Two Scottish firms were included in the Scribbans-Kemp combine. Mitchelhill of Craigmillar featured " Healthy Life Biscuits ". Martin, Nairn and Scott-Lyon were among new and flourishing Edinburgh firms. The old firm of Bilsland developed large-scale supply of bread to rural areas. The factory making of oatcakes was undertaken by Henderson at Restalrig and Paterson at Rutherglen.

In dairy produce, the Unilever combine of 1929, uniting Levers with the Dutch margarine firms of Jurgens and Van den Bergh, included several Scottish enterprises. The East Kilbride Dairy Farmers (1920) controlled seven companies in the Glasgow area, including Ross's and the Glasgow Dairy Co., and owned bakeries and restaurants as well as dairies. Nestlé's and the United Dairies of London owned dairies in Galloway. General Milk Products Ltd., an American firm, started manu-facture of " Carnation " Condensed Milk at Dumfries in 1935.

In fruit preserving, the English firms of Chivers and Smedley acquired fruit farms and factories in Angus and Perthshire. The Union Cold Storage Co., under Lord Vestey, combined two-thirds of the wholesale meat trade, and con-trolled many retailers, especially in Glasgow.

Linoleum was divided between Nairns, now controlled by the holding company, Michael Nairn & Greenwich Ltd. (1922), and Barry Ostlere, which became a subsidiary of another holding company, Barry & Staines Linoleum Ltd. (1930). In the dyeing industry, apart from the firms associated with I.C.I., the chief was Pullars of Perth of which control was obtained by a Lancashire firm. The old Scottish staple of calico printing came virtually to an end with the closing in 1929–30 of the works at Lennoxtown and Thornliebank by the Calico Printers Association which now held a monopoly.

In the 'thirties definite efforts were made to foster new industries, especially by the Scottish Development Council (1931), a voluntary and unofficial body, headed by Sir James Lithgow. It established the quarterly *Scotland* and engaged C. A. Oakley, of Glasgow University, to conduct a survey of industry in Scotland, published in 1937, which presented a somewhat optimistic picture of achievements and prospects. It set up a Scottish Economic Committee, which issued Reports on Light Industries, the Highlands and Islands, etc. The Empire Exhibition in Glasgow (1938), though handicapped by bad weather, did something to attract attention to Scottish manufactures.

A chief advance of the period was the development of hydro-electric power, chiefly by the Scottish Power Co. headed by George Balfour, M.P., a contractor. The Grampian scheme was launched in 1928, and the British Aluminium Co.'s station at Lochaber in 1929. In the South, the Galloway Power Co. operated from 1935. By 1937 one-third of electric power was generated from water, but at a higher cost per unit than from coal. A Bill promoted by the British Oxygen Co. to establish plant for calcium-carbide production was defeated in Parliament by a rally of varied opponents.

Metal Industries Ltd., later absorbed in the British Oxygen Co., with a capital of £4 million, was founded by Sir Donald Pollock, who from his gains became an outstanding benefactor to Edinburgh University. Commencing with salvage and shipbreaking, it established metal, electrical and engineering divisions at home and overseas.

The manufacture from cellulose by the Dreyfus process of artificial silk was introduced at Jedburgh by an English firm, the North British Rayon Co. (1928), and nearly doubled the population of the burgh through " incomers " from Glasgow and northern Ireland.

The extraction of sugar from beet, long fostered on the Continent, was undertaken by the British Sugar Corporation, which under an Act of 1925 had a government subsidy and directors. A Scottish subsidiary founded a factory at Cupar (Fife) in 1926 ; this involved three months' intensive work but liability to seasonal unemployment, alleviated by refining of Indian cane sugar. The latter however suffered from the competition of beet, and all but three of the Greenock refineries closed down.

The India Tyre & Rubber Co., an associate of Dunlops, opened a factory at Inchinnan in 1927. A London company set up a carton factory at Turnhouse in 1934. Two Scottish local airlines founded in the early 'thirties were combined in Scottish Airways in August 1937. The Blackburn Co. established an aircraft works at Dumbarton in 1937.

Television was devised by a Scottish inventor, J. L. Baird (1888–1946), but did not reach Scotland till 1952. The growing popularity of the Cinema gave scope to local enterprise in the establishment of picture houses, e.g. by James Welsh of Glasgow (the " Cosmo " and others) and Pooles of Edinburgh ; but most of the chains were controlled by Gaumont British. John Grierson acquired repute as a producer of " documentary " films.

Four of the Scottish banks passed under English control : the National acquired by Lloyds in 1918, the British Linen by Barclays in 1919, the Clydesdale (1919) and the North of Scotland (1923) by the Midland. Conversely the Royal Bank acquired Drummonds (1924) and Glyn Mills, London private bankers, and Williams Deacons of Manchester.

The Scottish banks extended their trustee and executry work, and opened savings accounts, initiated by the Commercial Bank in Dec. 1928. The Currency and Bank Notes Act of that year substituted Bank of England notes for gold as cover for the fiduciary issue. The United Dominions Trust (1925), with a Scottish Local Board, through its subsidiary, Credit for Industry, offered advances for productive enterprise. The General Accident Fire and Life Assurance Corporation, centred in Perth, continued its expansion, and controlled Motor Traders Guarantee Corporation (1923) for hire-purchase finance. With the increase in credit trading institutions of this sort developed, especially in Glasgow. Alleged abuses of hire purchase were investigated by a Scottish Committee of Inquiry, and resulted in an Act of 1932 limiting liability to forfeiture.

In retail trade pre-war trends continued in the decline of the small producer-retailer and the greater use of standard

" branded " goods ; newer features were the growth of delivery services and door sales by travelling vans, of mail orders through press advertisement and of credit trading. Here also combination was common. Great Universal Stores, controlled by Isaac Wolfson of Glaswegian birth, acquired several Glasgow soft-goods dealers. The Scottish Drapery Corporation in 1926 absorbed the leading firms in that line, including Patrick Thomson and J. & R. Allan of Edinburgh, James Daly and Pettigrew & Stephens of Glasgow, D. M. Brown of Dundee and Watt & Grant of Aberdeen. Till 1952 the majority of the ordinary shares were held by Debenhams of London. Fraser of Glasgow commenced his career of expansion by acquiring Arnott, Simpson and Muirhead. Maule of Edinburgh in 1934 passed into the hands of Binns of Sunderland. Lewis of Liverpool bought Anderson's Royal Polytechnic, Glasgow, in 1936. Montague Burton, Hope Brothers and Austin Reed, multiple tailors and outfitters, opened branches in Scotland.

Lipton was acquired by the Home & Colonial Stores and linked with Unilever. Woolworth, Marks & Spencer and Boots set up shops throughout Scotland. The Scottish Wool and Hosiery Stores, which opened over 100 new shops, Mac Fisheries and confectioners such as Birrell and McColl are other examples of the chain store. The " Eat More Fruit " campaign of the Empire Marketing Board contributed to the growth of large retail fruiterers like Malcolm Campbell of Glasgow and Rankin of Edinburgh.

The S.C.W.S. under the direction of Neil Beaton initiated a policy of opening retail stores in rural areas, by purchase of local premises or businesses, with a view to their transfer to local management of the usual type. It also acquired a linen and linoleum works at Falkland (Fife), and entered into agreement with the Swedish Co-operative (K.F.) for the manufacture of electric bulbs (British Luma, 1931).

Agriculture was affected by sharp variations in public policy. The wartime Corn Production Act was repealed in 1921. Fixation of wages, thus discarded, was in Scotland not restored until 1937, chiefly because of the official preference in the Trade Union for negotiation, by which a 54-hour week was attained in 1919 and a weekly half-holiday in 1937.

Employment fell by 9,000 to about 118,000, but remained fourth in the occupational census of 1931. The total output averaged about one-thirteenth of British agricultural production, though percentages varied considerably ; in 1934 Scottish-grown wheat constituted 6 per cent of British, barley 11, oats $36\frac{1}{2}$, potatoes 23, cattle $16\frac{1}{2}$, sheep 31, pigs $6\frac{1}{2}$. There was a prolonged world slump in grain prices, the wholesale price of wheat was almost halved in the early 'twenties. Thus government intervention was invoked and was gradually extended. Subsidies were granted for beef in 1924, wheat (1932), milk and cattle (1934,) oats and barley (1938). A " National Mark " as a token of quality was instituted on a voluntary basis in 1928, and Land Drainage assisted by an Act of 1930 which set up Catchment Boards. Under an Act of 1929 a Scottish Agricultural Securities Corporation was formed ; the leading banks supplied capital and management to make advances to farmers. Several of the Marketing Schemes of the 'thirties (bacon, potatoes, etc.) include Scotland ; in 1933 three Scottish Areas were designated for the regulated marketing of milk. The Linlithgow Commission of 1924 revealed the extent of middlemanship in farm produce. Legislation was consolidated by the Act of 1937 which fixed subsidies and standard prices.

Improvements in technique included increased mechanisation, especially in the use of tractors and milking-machines, the introduction of the ley system in pasture, and greater utilisation of artificial manures. Some progress was achieved in co-operative methods, under the aegis of the Scottish Agricultural Organisation Society, particularly in the Northeast, where a Society had 30,000 members, and in Orkney in egg production.

Much attention was given to research. The Rowett Institute in Aberdeen became famous through the Survey of Nutrition made by its director Sir John Boyd Orr (1936), which demonstrated the unsatisfactory dietetic standards of a large proportion of the community. The Macaulay Institute (1930), also in Aberdeen, founded by a Scots-Canadian, engaged in soil research. The Hannah Institute, near Ayr (1931), included dairy research as well as practical training in its activities. The Animal Genetics Department of Edinburgh

12

University also acquired repute under the direction of Professor Crew.

Land ownership frequently continued to be in the hands of large proprietors, though occupying ownership grew ; especially in the Highlands, estates were still purchased by magnates from the south, such as Lords Leverhulme, Brocket and Trent. In the immediate post-war period attempts were made to encourage the settlement on small-holdings especially of ex-servicemen. The clash between this policy and Lord Leverhulme's scheme seems to have been the main reason for the much debated failure of his efforts in Lewis and Harris. He sought to develop fishing through construction of a harbour and canning factory at Stornoway, and to establish large dairy farms. Most of his projects came to an end with the sale of the estate in 1925.[1]

A contributory cause of failure was the Depression of the Fisheries, which was chronic. There was a decline of nearly one-half in the total labour engaged, in the number of vessels in use and in the amount of catch. There was a growth of steam-trawler-owning companies at the expense of the small working owner ; notably Mac Fisheries, under Lever auspices. Similar to the experience of agriculture was government policy of the 'thirties in the initiation of marketing schemes. Some encouragement was given to the coarser types by the increasing " fish and chip " shop demand. The export of cured herrings, whose Continental markets in Germany and Russia were largely lost through the War, recovered somewhat in the latter years.

The acute shortage of housing was partly met by an expansion of the building industry. Over a quarter of a million new houses were erected, some 65,000 by private speculative builders, among whom James Miller of Edinburgh and Mactaggart and Mickel of Glasgow came to the front With the almost complete cessation of private building for letting, money for house purchase was increasingly supplied by building societies, which also offered a safe investment in times of financial uncertainty In addition to native societies such as the Scottish Amicable, societies from across the Border such as the Halifax and Huddersfield established themselves in

[1] The fullest account is in N. Nicolson's *Lord of the Isles* (1960).

Scotland. The volume of state-subsidised municipal building, to be discussed later, is an essential factor. The labour force rose to between 50,000 and 60,000. Urban expansion frequently took the rather novel form of the bungalow instead of the tenement, and occasioned controversial questions in the encroachment on farming land and the congestion and cost of transport between home and work. Brick was largely substituted for stone, and the granite industry was correspondingly depressed, as well as losing foreign markets. New techniques were introduced ; most discussed were the steel houses devised by the Weir and Atholl companies.

Social conditions were ably analysed by the late Dr. J. A. Bowie just before the War in his *Future of Scotland*. There was a net decline in population of 8 per cent between 1921 and 1931. The birth-rate fell from 23 in 1920 to 17·6 in 1937 ; infantile mortality, though falling, was still high (80). About 400,000 emigrated in the same decade ; there was a slight contrary trend in the late 'thirties. The changing " age-group composition " was illustrated by the census of 1931, which showed 11 per cent over 60 and $8\frac{1}{2}$ per cent under 5, an almost exact reversal of the position twenty years earlier.

The growth of tertiary employment was indicated by the fact that Commerce and Finance ranked as the largest group (363,000), Personal Service as third (223,000) and Transport as fifth (156,000). Mining and metallurgy took second place (280,000) and Agriculture fourth (177,000).

Unemployment, as already indicated, was high throughout, averaging between $10\frac{1}{2}$ and 27 per cent, as compared with $9\frac{1}{2}$ to 22 per cent for Great Britain as a whole. In some Highland areas it affected over 50 per cent, where forms of part-time employment came to be designated " working for stamps ". Falling price levels reduced cost of living about 10 per cent ; while social services, such as school milk supply, alleviated hardship.

As regards labour conditions, " Pre-War Practices " of trade unions were legitimated by the Act of 1919. The Forty-Eight Hour Week became usual after the Washington Convention, though this was not legally ratified for some time. Under a Mining Act a levy was introduced to provide institutes, canteens and pit-head baths in colliery areas.

The Scottish Trade Union Congress, under the able administration of William Elgar, Secretary from 1922 to 1946, acquired greater influence and prestige ; a new and more effective executive, the General Council, was formed in 1922. A Survey which it conducted in 1924 showed that only about one-third of workers eligible, or about half a million, were organised, in 227 unions, of which 90 were purely Scottish, with 200,000 members.   Attempts were made to foster organisation especially among women and juveniles, but were hampered by the chronic depression, and numbers enrolled at the end of the period differed little from those at the start.

The amalgamation of the Iron & Steel Trades (B I.S.A. K.T.A.) was completed ; the Amalgamated Society of Wood-workers in 1921 absorbed most woodworkers' unions under the leadership of Thomas Barron ;   the English and Scottish Tailors and Ironmoulders united.   The two growing " general unions ", T.G.W.U. & N.U.G.M.W., both recruited Scottish members, e.g. in the Border textiles ;   and the former absorbed two Scottish unions, the Farm Servants and the Sea Fishers. The most notable attempt at organising black-coated workers was made by the Scottish Bankers Association, which was refused recognition by the banks, and declined after a strike in 1937 proved a fiasco.

There were examples of breakaway unions, especially among the Leftish elements in coal-mining.   Dissatisfaction with a registration scheme to decasualise labour induced a secession of Glasgow dockers from the T.G.W.U. in 1932.   A National Unemployed Workers' Committee was set up and organised workless independently of trade unions, and rather in opposition to their official leadership ;   "Hunger Marches" were arranged, the most notorious being that in which the marchers camped overnight in Princes St., Edinburgh (June 1933).

Scotland shared in the prolific large-scale disputes of the early 'twenties, which culminated in the General Strike of May 1926.   One by-product was the ban imposed on trade unionism by much of the press, to which the response was a rather ineffective boycott.

The National Guild movement had repercussions in the short-lived Glasgow Building Guild under John Winning, which took contracts for municipal housing, and the longer-lived Tailoring and Clerks Guilds in that city.

After the General Strike the official trade-union policy tended to collaboration, against the sharp opposition of a " Minority Movement ", and clashes were chronic at meetings of the Scottish Trade Union Congress.

In the political sphere, the " Coupon " election of December 1918 made the Labour Party the official opposition ; seven Scottish representatives were returned, of whom William Adamson assumed temporary leadership ; the outstanding figure was William Graham, whose premature death in 1932 cut short an already distinguished career. The Communist Party of Great Britain formed in 1920 obtained a solitary success in the election of J. T. Walton Newbold for Motherwell for the Parliament of 1922–3. Splinter fractions were headed by John McLean (d. Nov. 1923) and Guy Aldred. Considerable municipal gains were made, especially at the Glasgow " General Election " of 1920 when 44 members were returned. The Parliamentary elections of 1922 and 1923 showed an increase of Scottish Labour M.P.'s to 30 and 34 respectively ; but the " red letter " election of 1924 reduced the total to 26, after the first Labour Government, which had a Scottish Premier in Ramsay Macdonald and three Cabinet Ministers in Haldane, Adamson and Wheatley.

The divisions and collapse of the Liberal Party transferred almost en bloc its former working-class support to the Labour Party, in many cases probably without any substantial change of outlook ; some prominent local leaders such as Rev. James Barr and E. Rosslyn Mitchell changed their allegiance. The religious-ethical strain characteristic of Scottish Socialism and the impact of unemployment, which branded itself deeply on the minds of many, were other factors.

The 1929 election gave Scotland 36 Labour representatives, and the participation in the second Labour Government of Wm. Graham and Tom Johnston. In the " Save the Pound " election two years later representation fell to 7. The split in the movement through the secession of the Macdonaldites was slight in Scotland ; more serious was the disaffiliation of the I.L.P., the main propagandist element, under James Maxton ; for some time it retained a small group of M.P.'s. Its place, after a short-lived Scottish Socialist Party, was in some respects taken by the organisation of Divisional Labour Parties on an individual-member basis ; a separation between these and Trades Councils was agreed on by the Scottish Trade Union Congress and the Scottish Council of the Labour Party in 1938. The General Election of 1935 showed recovery to 22 seats, plus 3 I.L.P.

Glasgow City Council was captured in 1934, and Dundee soon after. Short-lived Labour organs were started in Edinburgh and Dundee ; the ablest of the Labour press was the monthly *Scottish Farm Servant* (1922–31).

Adult education grew. The Workers' Educational Association formed a Scottish Council, with a full-time secretary, and arranged special schemes for trade unions associated with the Workers' Educational Trade Union Committee. The Scottish Education Department gave " recognition " to adult education by Regulations of 1934. University Extra-Mural Committees were set up in Glasgow and Edinburgh, but control and finance remained largely with Local Education Authorities. The Scottish Labour College, standing for " independent working-class education ", was in constant rivalry, though with a rightward trend, under the guidance of Arthur Woodburn. The British Institute of Adult Education was formed, thanks largely to Lord Haldane, as a co-ordinating body, and held annual Scottish conferences. Newbattle Abbey, the gift of Lord Lothian, was opened as an adult college in 1937.

Civic-minded women, having gained the franchise, turned their attention to municipal affairs ; local Women Citizens' Associations in the cities, and Townswomen's Guilds, chiefly in the Borders, were active in promoting reforms. Women's Rural Institutes grew rapidly in the countryside. Both public and voluntary organisation was devoted to the Welfare of Youth ; by e.g. the National Council of Juvenile Organisations (1921) and the Scottish Association of Boys' Clubs (1927).

Public Action. Increase of government intervention, fostered by war conditions, was a feature of the period, here as elsewhere. Advances were made in social legislation ; as most of this was common to Great Britain, the integration of English and Scottish social conditions was furthered. The exceptional seriousness of unemployment in Scotland enforced the legalisation at long last of able-bodied relief, by an Act of 1921. A Maternity Services Act of 1937 was also peculiar to Scotland. A general effect of the augmented social services was to transfer much of the financial burden from local to national resources.

Another result of the protracted depression was the demarcation of Special Areas in 1934, for which a Commissioner was appointed with some financial facilities to stimulate recovery. The chief expedient was the establishment of Industrial Estates, where factories, transport and power were provided as inducements to industrialists. The first was opened at Hillington, between Glasgow and Paisley, in 1938, and by the outbreak of war about ninety firms had become tenants of this and three other estates in the West. The Scottish Special Areas Housing Association was also set up in 1934 and built workers' hostels and school camps.

Housing was the other pressing social problem, and here there were fluctuations of Government policy. Rent Restriction was continued, and modified by various Acts. The famous Clydebank Case (Kerr vs. Bryde), where the tenant's defence was undertaken by the local M.P., David Kirkwood ("The Tenants' K.C."), demonstrated the illegality of a common procedure in raising rental without due notice. The Scottish Labour Housing Association and local Tenants' Defence Associations pressed demands on the authorities. State-subsidised building to provide " homes for heroes " was an immediate post-war measure (Addison Scheme), making provision by Local Authorities compulsory to the extent of a penny rate. The high cost of the scheme led to its restriction in 1923, a decision reversed by the Wheatley Act of 1925. An Act of 1932 gave Scotland preferential terms as regards grant in aid. In the 'thirties effort was concentrated on Slum Clearance and on the Housing of Rural Workers : an Act of 1926 gave assistance to landowners for reconditioning. About two-thirds of inter-war building of houses was by Local Authorities. A Survey in 1935–6 showed that nearly one-fourth still lived in " overcrowded " conditions, as compared with 4 per cent in England.

Town Planning was encouraged by Acts culminating in that of 1932, which extended its scope to rural areas.

Dunfermline was the first to adopt a statutory plan (1920), and Aberdeen was a pioneer of planned development in its Kincorth scheme. An Act of 1935 restricted " ribbon building " along main roads.

By the Scottish Education Act (1918), a Local Education Authority for each County and for the four " Counties of Cities ", elected by Proportional Representation, was substituted for the School Boards. Provision was made for the transfer to its control, under certain guarantees, of the remaining denominational schools, chiefly Roman Catholic ; for the supply of school meals and books, and for the award of University Bursaries. The operation of a further provision for the raising of the school-leaving age to fifteen was deferred throughout this period. An Advisory Council to the Secretary of State was established. More adequate salary scales and superannuation were ensured to teachers, on the recommendation of the Craik Committee. The supply of milk in schools was developed in the late 'thirties after the institution of the Marketing Board.

Much more drastic changes were effected by the Local Government Act of 1929. The prime incentive or pretext was financial. As one of the expedients for encouraging economic recovery, derating, hitherto applied to agricultural land, was extended to premises used for industry and transport. To compensate Local Authorities a General Exchequer Contribution was granted, based on a complex " weighted " formula which gave preference to " depressed areas ". A variety of " percentage " grants were merged in a general " block grant ". Administration was concentrated in County Councils, 31 in number ; the parish was abolished as an administrative unit, the burghs " demoted ", and the ten-year-old Local Education Authorities eliminated. Burghs were now distinguished as " Large " (23) and " Small " (173), a population of 20,000 being taken as the dividing line. Both were to appoint representatives to County Councils in respect of functions now transferred ; only very minor powers were retained by the Small Burghs. In the larger counties partly elective District Councils (199) were set up, with very limited responsibilities. Functions in general were concentrated in the County Councils and four " Counties of Cities " ; Statutory Committees for

Education and other major activities were to be formed. In large measure the " Break Up of the Poor Law ", as advocated by the Webbs, was achieved ; institutions were to be managed, and relief given by Public Assistance Committees of the Councils ; the age-long responsibility of the Parish was transferred to the County. Thus a unit, with only forty years' history as an elective body, superseded the much older burgh and parish, and the nineteenth-century trend to multiplication of areas and dispersion of functions on *ad hoc* bodies was sharply reversed by this revolutionary enactment.

Minor features of local government history included the extension of boundaries by Edinburgh and Glasgow (1920), the former absorbing Leith, the latter Govan and other satellite burghs ; both involved " general elections " for the new Councils. Attempts to form municipal banks, notably at Kirkintilloch and Motherwell, on the model of war-time Birmingham, were frustrated by a clause in the Companies Act of 1929 ; several " Enabling Bills " giving discretionary powers to Local Authorities for such experiments in municipalisation were defeated in Parliament. The first Local Veto polls under the Act of 1913 were held in 1920 ; " No License " was carried only in a few localities, including Wick and Kilsyth.

The Universities in general were affected by the establishment of a Scottish Universities Entrance Board in 1918 and of the University Grants Committee (1919), through which quinquennial allocations from the Treasury were administered. The curricula were expanded, more varied options were made available ; and in some cases the new degrees of Bachelor of Commerce (B.Com.) and Doctor of Philosophy (Ph.D.)—for approved research—were instituted.

Central Administration was also modified. In 1919 the Scottish Board of Health assumed the duties of the former Local Government Board, Scottish Insurance Commissioners and Highlands & Islands Medical Board. In 1928 the Secretary for Scotland was raised to the rank of a Secretary of State and an Under-Secretary added. Two reorganisations of the main Departments took place. In 1928 the rather nominal " Boards " were abolished. Following on the " Gilmour " Committee, the Scottish services were grouped in the four Departments of Home, Agriculture, Education and Health, and headquarters were transferred from Dover House, White-hall, to St. Andrews House, Edinburgh, on the site of the old Calton Jail, completed just before the outbreak of war in 1939.

Under the Ministry of Transport, an all-British Depart-ment, roads were classified, and in 1936 the administration of main " trunk " roads was transferred from local care to that of the Ministry. By an Act of 1930 Area Traffic Com-missioners, including two for Scotland, were appointed to regulate services and fares of road vehicles.

Some brief reference may be made to cultural topics. The growth of the combine was also evident in the sphere of the press, where the " Kemsley Group " and Provincial News-papers Ltd. acquired control of noted Scottish newspapers. The *Daily Express, Daily Mail* and *Daily Herald* had widely circulated Scottish editions. The Thomson-Leng firm of Dundee were publishers of the combined daily *Advertiser and Courier*, of the popular weeklies, the *People's Friend, People's Journal* and *Sunday Post*, and exploited a new line in the " Dundee School " of boys' " Comics ". They were notori-ously hostile to trade unionism and took a strong line in refusing all recognition, as was the case with the press generally, after the strike of 1926.

Among more literary journals, the *Scots Observer*, edited by William Power, put up a struggle for existence from 1926 to 1929 ; the *Scots Magazine* was revived in 1925 ; the *Scottish Historical Review* succumbed in 1928. The Scottish Develop-ment Council issued *Scotland* as its quarterly organ from 1934, and the S.M.T. from 1938 an illustrated monthly mainly concerned with travel.

Special Scottish broadcasting programmes were instituted by the B.B.C., under the successive direction of D. Cleghorn Thomson and Rev. Melville Dinwiddie. The rise of amateur drama was a notable feature, and was fostered by the annual competitive festival of the Scottish Community Drama Associa-tion. The Scottish National Players (Glasgow) from 1921 to 1934 made a gallant effort to produce plays by Scottish authors on Scottish themes. Their productions included the first works of " James Bridie " (O. H. Mavor) who in the 'thirties put Scottish drama definitely " on the map ".

The Advocates' Library in Edinburgh was handed over by

the Faculty as a National Library in 1925, to be administered by a Board of Trustees. The erection of new buildings was financed by Sir Robert Grant ; owing to protracted dispute as to a site, building was about to commence adjoining Parliament House only when the outbreak of war suspended action.

The Scottish National Trust was formed in 1931 for the protection of historic buildings and places of natural beauty. Miss Isobel Grant, noted as a historian, founded Am Fasgadh as a Folk Museum, first in Iona and later at Kingussie. The first Scottish National Park of nearly 60,000 acres was constituted in Argyll in 1936.

In the sphere of recreation, notable features were the growth of " hiking " and cycling, which ensured the success of the Scottish Youth Hostels Association, formed in 1931 by Dr Alan Fothergill, which had 64 hostels and nearly 20,000 members by 1939. Organised travel was encouraged by such bodies as the Y.M.C.A., Holiday Fellowship and Workers Travel Association, which established Guest Houses in Scotland, sometimes in Victorian mansions such as Bonskeid and Dollarberg.

In the ecclesiastical sphere, the outstanding event was the union of the United Free Church, apart from a small " Continuing " minority, under the leadership of Rev. James Barr, with the Church of Scotland in 1929. The way had been cleared by the passing in 1921 of the Church of Scotland Act, which seemed to most to concede adequate autonomy. Following upon the labours of a Committee under Lord Haldane, the Church of Scotland (Property and Endowments) Act (1925) settled the financial basis. The teind was made a " standard charge " on land, and stipends were fixed in money ; administration was given to a Board of General Trustees of the Church.

The War, with its later slogan of " self-determination ", gave an impetus to Scottish nationalism. The Scottish Home Rule Association was revived, with much Liberal and Labour support, and several self-government Bills were unsuccessfully introduced. Dissatisfaction with these efforts led to the formation of " ginger groups " and culminated in the establishment of the National Party of Scotland, under the veteran Cunninghame Graham, in April 1928 with a demand for Dominion

Status. In 1934 this united with a more moderate group as the Scottish National Party, and adopted a policy of independent Parliamentary and municipal candidatures.

THE SECOND WORLD WAR. 1939-45

The Second World War differed from the first in that it was anticipated and prepared for, hence there was almost from the first a comprehensive organisation and control of economic resources. Here only points specially affecting Scotland need be noted. The device of Regional Civil Commissioners, as emergency administrators in case of crisis, with rather unspecified powers, brought Thomas Johnston to office in 1939-41, until his appointment to the Secretaryship of State in the Churchill ministry. His tenure of office made an unusually strong and lasting impact on Scottish affairs. At his instance there were established an advisory Scottish Council of State, comprising ex-Secretaries (1941) ; and a Scottish Council on Industry (1942), representative of Local Authorities, business, trade unions and the Development Council.

The menace of air raids induced the initial division of Scotland into sending, receiving and neutral areas for evacuation purposes, but this soon broke down in practice. The shifting of population often evoked social strains and friction, and together with the requisitioning of buildings, dislocated social services, especially education. The raising of the leaving age, which was at last to have been effected in session 1939-40, was once more postponed. Some " Emergency Hospitals " were established under State auspices ; as the expected air-raid casualties did not materialise to any extent, they came to be used for the treatment of industrial workers.

The main economic effect was the renewed stimulus to the munition and supply industries, particularly shipbuilding. Scotland however obtained a relatively small percentage of the new war industry ; the Rolls-Royce aircraft factory and an explosives works at Bishopston were the chief exceptions. Hence there was transfer of labour under the provisions for civil conscription, e.g. of 13,000 girls to the Midlands. The Clyde ports, proving less liable to raiding than those farther south, became important for naval and mercantile shipping, food storage and mails ; new harbours were established at Faslane on Gareloch and Cairnryan in Wigtonshire. Prestwick and Renfrew airports were developed.

The War also encouraged hydro-electric power development, and overrode previous disputes. Following on the Report of the Cooper Committee (1941–2), under the Lord President of the Court of Session, the Act of 1943 established the North of Scotland Hydro-Electric Board as a public corporation for construction of stations and distribution of power.

Agricultural output, especially of cereals and potatoes, was stepped up, in view of the cutting down of import. Two and a half million acres were under tillage in 1944, an increase of 600,000 ; the wheat crop was doubled. County Executive Committees were empowered to enforce good standards of farming ; sheep and cattle rearing was subsidised. The number of tractors doubled ; there was an increase of about one-fourth in employment, partly through the Women's Land Army, later supplemented by prisoners of war.

Afforestation also was promoted. The Forestry Commission was reorganised, and the Secretary of State made answerable for it to Parliament ; Crown Lands in Scotland were put under his aegis. About $2\frac{1}{2}$ million acres were now available and about 150,000 employed.

Social conditions were influenced by virtually full employment, including much woman labour. Despite shortages, food standards were relatively well maintained, thanks to an efficient rationing and " Points " system, and to the new appreciation of nutritional values. Milk priority schemes were introduced ; National Restaurants and Industrial Canteens established. Supplies were on the whole more plentiful than in some overcrowded parts of the South.

There was a partial suspension of housebuilding, and the labour force was reduced to 60 per cent ; but altogether about 36,000 were erected. Scotland suffered comparatively little from " enemy action " ; about 7,000 dwellings were destroyed, mainly in the Clydeside raids of spring 1941. Town and Country Planning Acts extended control over the whole country.

The working-class organisations, influenced by anti-Fascist

sentiment and especially by the treatment of the movement in Nazi Germany, gave active support to the war effort throughout ; the initial opposition of the extreme Left was reversed after U.S.S.R. entered the war as an ally. The only political opposition to the war-time truce came from a few independent candidatures sponsored by the I.L.P., the new Commonwealth group, and the more militant section of the Scottish Nationalists, who split over war policy ; the election for Motherwell of Dr. Robert McIntyre shortly before the armistice was their sole electoral success.

Trade-union membership grew from under 400,000 to over 600,000. The movement lost some of its best-known leaders through the deaths of Smillie (Miners), Barron (Building Trades), Syme (Juteworkers), Walker (Ironworkers) and Hunter (Bakers). *The Edinburgh Clarion*, started unofficially by West Edinburgh Labour Party, for a year or two made a lively addition to the Labour press.

The divergence of outlook among Nationalists culminated in the foundation in 1942 of Scottish Convention, headed by John McCormick, making a non-party appeal and seeking a measure of devolution. The London Scots Self-Government Committee, largely Labour in composition, issued in 1942 a composite booklet, *The New Scotland*, outlining a similar policy in the economic and political spheres.

5

Scotland since the Second World War

(c. 1945-61)

CONTEMPORARY material for the future economic historian has multiplied in the last decade. Since 1947 a Government Report on " Industry and Employment in Scotland " has been issued every spring. Further factual and statistical detail is to be found in the annual Review published by the Clydesdale and North of Scotland Bank, in periodical supplements issued by *The Scotsman* and the *Glasgow Herald* and in the Reports of the Scottish Council. Two authoritative composite volumes, *Scottish Industry* (1953), edited by Oakley, and *The Scottish Economy* (1956), edited by Cairncross, cover much of the field. John Gollan's *Scottish Prospect* is more sketchy, and critical from a " Leftish " standpoint. The *Third Statistical Account*, launched in 1951, will when complete give a detailed picture of social life comparable to those of its predecessors of a century and a century and a half ago.

Probably the outstanding feature of the first decade, demanding priority of mention, is, in contrast with the years following the First World War, the maintenance and extension of public ownership and control. The triumph of the Labour Party at the Election of 1945, and its subsequent tenure of office, is immediately responsible, but probably the underlying influence was not so much a widespread acceptance of collectivist theory as the large degree of transformation of the economy by war conditions, involving an almost irreversible intervention by the State. In Scotland particularly the bitter memory of the Great Depression of the inter-war years was strong in encouraging the continuance of public action, while to many the growth of combination seemed to offer only a choice between public and private monopoly.

The measures of " nationalisation ", on a " public corporation " pattern, require notice here only in respect of particularly Scottish features.   An Aberdonian, Lord Catto, was appropriately retained as first Governor of the nationalised Bank of England, now virtually the " Bank of Great Britain " ; its notes permanently substituted gold as " cover " for Scottish notes, and also amounted to about half of those in circulation in Scotland ; the Scottish note issue constituted about 6 per cent of the British.

The Coal Mines Act centralised control in the National Coal Board, but a Scottish Divisional Board was set up under Lord Balfour.   Of 314 mines in Scotland, owned by 62 companies, 213 were taken over ; the remaining small units were worked privately under licence from the Board.

Transport control was similarly centralised ; a nominee Transport Users' Advisory Committee for Scotland was set up. All Scottish railway services were unified, and in 1955 a Scottish Area Board of British Railways was established.   Canals were brought under the Ministry of Transport, and the Monkland Canal was closed in 1950.   The partial denationalisation of road transport in 1953 added to the complexity.   Traffic Commissioners were retained and a Scottish Transport Advisory Committee set up.   Passenger road transport was largely unified in the Scottish Omnibus Group, based on the S.M.T. ; purely local services continued to be operated by municipalities.

The same applied to their Gas and Electricity Departments. In the former case, larger autonomy than in other nationalised enterprise was assigned to the Scottish Area Board.   In the latter the North of Scotland Hydro-Electric Board " retained financial autonomy and independence " ; the rest of Scotland comprised two Area Boards subordinate to the British Electrical Authority, until in 1954 a South of Scotland Board was constituted, on a par with that of the North.

Civil Aviation was put in the hands of the British Overseas Air Corporation (1950) ; a Scottish Advisory Committee was active under the Chairmanship of Sir Patrick Dollan.

In the Iron and Steel Act of November 1949 the operative

units were maintained, so that when the measure was repealed these were able largely to resume possession (1953), though subject to considerable State control through an Iron and Steel Board.

In the establishment of the Welfare State the Social services were in general identical for England and Scotland, but administrative differences necessitated a special Scottish National Health Services Act (1946). This set up five nominee Regional Boards for hospital services ; assigned the administration of Domiciliary and Clinic Services and of the prospective Health Centres (of which the first was opened at Sighthill, Edinburgh, in 1953) to major Local Authorities ; General Practitioner Services to local Executives with municipal and professional representation.

The National Assistance Act of 1945 finally made " poor relief " a national rather than a local responsibility. Local Authorities were left the care of " deprived " children, in accordance with the proposals of the Children's Act of 1948, and the provision of accommodation for the homeless aged and infirm.

The Education (Scotland) Act (1945), formally superseded by a Consolidating Act next year, though less thorough-going than the English measure, extended the powers of the Secretary of State to make regulations ; all L.E.A.'s had to submit for his approval schemes for primary, secondary and " Further " education ; stress was laid on the latter, for which co-operation with voluntary agencies and encouragement of informal and recreational activities were approved. Compulsory attendance to the age of 15 was at long last brought into effect in 1947, and a scheme of Junior Colleges providing part-time education to the age of 18 was adumbrated but deferred. Community Centres were fostered, and the Scottish (Youth) leadership Training Association set up temporarily by the Education Department to train workers for this and similar service. Newbattle Abbey, after utilisation for the Forces, was reopened in 1950 with state grants as an Adult College under the Wardenship of Edwin Muir, poet and literary critic.

Town and Country Planning was made obligatory and universal by the Act of 1947, under which Local Authorities had to make surveys and submit development plans within

13

three years ; an extension had to be allowed in many cases, 34 out of 57 were to hand by 1955. Regional Advisory Committees, e.g. for the Clyde and the Borders, were formed in some cases. The renewed attempt under the Act to secure public enjoyment of the " unearned increment " of land value under the name of Development Charges was reversed in 1952. A Scottish Act of 1954 permitted the conversion into feus of long leases, of which many were then due to expire.

Under the Distribution of Industry Act (1945) considerable industrial districts were demarcated as " Development Areas ", in which assistance was to be given to the attraction of industry ; the Inverness district was added in 1949. Subsequently a demand arose for a modification of policy in the interests of the neglected areas from which enterprise was thought to be diverted. This feeling was voiced by the Select Committee on Estimates (Jan. 1956). The Cairncross Committee on Local Industrial Development (1952) also put a case for the fostering of enterprise in other than congested localities.

The inter-war device of Industrial Estates was expanded ; in 1954 there were 17 estates, employing over 60,000, chiefly in lighter industries ; of 365 tenants about 200 were Scots, 100 English, the rest mainly from U.S.A. and Canada. It was estimated that nearly one-half of new enterprises had been located on the estates.

Under the New Towns Act of 1946 the establishment of East Kilbride, hitherto a residential village, was sanctioned. A Corporation was set up in 1947 under Sir Patrick Dollan, and it was made a centre of Research. Glenrothes in Fife followed ; it was intended to cater primarily for the anticipated transfer of coal-miners from the West ; it was not in a Development area, and languished from lack of other industrial opportunities. Cumbernauld was envisaged as another satellite to Glasgow, and a Development Corporation was appointed in Jan. 1956.

Scottish housing legislation continued subsidisation. Private building was restricted until 1952. Labour supply was considerably raised, and training schemes instituted. New " non-traditional " types of building—e.g. concrete—were introduced ; many municipal schemes were of the " pre-fabricated " professedly temporary type. Over 150,000 houses were built in the first five post-war years ; in the 'fifties annual output ran to 30,000 to 40,000, of which less than 10 per cent were privately built. The Scottish Special Housing Association contributed about one-fifth of the public programme.

Some powers were withdrawn from Local Authorities, they were submitted increasingly to central control, and there was a tendency towards regionalism in the inauguration of larger areas for water, police and fire services (1946–7) by the constitution of joint authorities in several contiguous areas. The labours of the Jeffrey Committee, appointed in 1937, bore fruit in the Consolidating Acts of 1947–8 which repealed 26 Acts and amended about 150 relating to local government. The Representation of the People Act (1945) assimilated the municipal to the Parliamentary franchise ; in 1948–9 provision was made for proxy and absentee voting at local elections, and allowances for expenses and loss of income incurred by Councillors owing to public duties were extended. The Act of 1947 also substituted for the General Exchequer Contribution " Equalisation Grants ", proportioned to rateable value per head of population. Alleged inequity to Scotland because of its different rating system and generally higher rateable values was examined by a special Committee in 1955, which recommended higher government grants. The second Sorn Committee (1953) proposed the abolition of owners' rates, and this was implemented by legislation (1956). Drastic reassessment of property values was effected in 1960. Rates in 1953–4 were estimated at a total of nearly £50 million, with an average of 19/- in the pound ; rate expenditure increased nearly two-thirds since 1939 and rateable value only one-fifth. Some relaxation of control in minor matters was recommended by a Local Government Man Power Committee of 1950–2.

As regards national government, some concession to the agitation for devolution was intimated in a White Paper of 1948. The Scottish Grand Committee of the Commons was given power to consider Scottish Bills in principle as well as in detail, and Scottish Estimates were referred to it for consideration. The Scottish Office in 1950 issued a *Handbook on Scottish Administration*. The Catto Committee on Scottish Financial and Trade Statistics produced inconclusive material on the disputed question of the financial relations of England and Scotland, and extent of self-sufficiency of the latter. The Royal Commission appointed in 1952 accumulated much evidence ; the sole positive result was the transfer of the regulation of Transport from the Ministry of that name to the Secretary of State.

Apart from the direct effects of government intervention, industrial trends were influenced by the chronic " unfavourable " balance of trade, commonly called " the dollar gap " ; hence the emphasis laid on increasing exports, though this was cut across by the " rearmament " measures of the early 'fifties and later curtailment of credit. Production increased nearly 20 per cent in 1948–53, and an approximation was made to " full employment ", though it was asserted by experts that Scottish industry remained more " vulnerable " than English, and was inadequately diversified. An eastward trend, reversing the process of two centuries earlier, became manifest, as coal-mines in the Clyde area became exhausted and shipbuilding grew in Forth ports. The rapid expansion of Grangemouth with its docks and chemical works is a chief example. The introduction of new scientific industries and the still further growth of combination, especially with English enterprises, and the introduction of American capital and expertise are other notable features.

These and other trends may be illustrated in more detail. The expansion of hydro-electric power schemes, especially in the Highlands, continued and supplied power to industry as well as for domestic use. Their potentialities as a factor facilitating the deconcentration of industry were much canvassed.

A target of 30 million tons a year was set up for coal output, but the maximum reached in any one year was less than 25 million. Output suffered from inadequate labour supply, absenteeism and stoppages. About 85 per cent of coal was now machine-cut and over two-thirds mechanically conveyed. Recruitment and training schemes were fostered, and organisation of transfer from the declining pits of the West to the new ventures in Fife and the Lothians was attempted. Numbers employed were between 80,000 and 90,000. An eleven-day fortnight was adopted in 1947. Export was raised to about $1\frac{1}{2}$ million tons per annum. Up to 1 million tons a year was produced by open-cast mining which for some years extended considerably. An extensive programme of new sinkings and reconstruction schemes gave promise of long-term improvements.

The oil industry was monopolised by Scottish Oils, a subsidiary of the British Petroleum Co. (formerly known as Anglo-Persian). The production of oil from local shale, though enjoying a 50 per cent preferential duty over imported oils, declined ; several pits and works were closed and employment fell to less than 3,000. The refining of imported oil increased considerably, especially at Grangemouth ; a depot was opened at Kirkcudbright in 1956. With the growth of road transport, the growing displacement in municipal transport of the electric tram by the petrol bus and the utilisation of oil for power by industry, demand continuously expanded.

Experiments were made in the utilisation of peat as industrial fuel. The lead-mines of Lanarkshire, long closed, were taken over by the Siamese Tin Syndicate in 1952 and plant established with a view to redevelopment. The long-extinct kelp industry was revived on a small scale to provide supplies for chemical products. The wealth of Scotland in lesser minerals was explored, and was publicised by Dr. Archie Lamont and Mr. R. H. S. Robertson. The working of diatomite and barytes was undertaken.

The denationalised iron and steel industry was virtually dominated by Colvilles, managed for many years by Sir John Craig until he retired in 1956. Much reconditioning and modernisation of plant was undertaken. The industry was handicapped by shortage of supply ; there was considerable export demand.

Shipbuilding developed in Leith and Burntisland as well as on the Clyde. Output was curtailed by inadequate supplies of steel, but attained 40 per cent of British. Foreign competition grew in the 'fifties.

Engineering achieved special importance as the chief export industry. Besides traditional products such as textile and agricultural machinery and locomotives, there was an expansion of lighter types—motor vehicles, cycles, aircraft, office and refrigeration machinery, clocks and watches, etc. Some small-scale local ventures were pioneered, notably by J. H. Rollo in Highland villages.

Textiles underwent some vicissitudes, partly owing to the high cost of raw materials. Considerable technical improvements were introduced, especially in jute. The growth of markets for Harris tweeds, despite the handicap of purchase tax, was a feature of the woollen industry ; similar ventures were made in other rural areas, and the popularity of knitwear stimulated the Border manufacture. The rayon factory at Jedburgh closed down in the summer of 1956.

Whisky, another pillar of the export trade, achieved a record output of nearly 40 million gallons in 1954–5, of which over 15 million went overseas, largely to U.S.A. and Canada.

Among the newer scientific industries, reference may be made to the manufacture of concrete in Lanarkshire, of nylons and ardil fibre, of asbestos, plastics and electronics. The first atomic energy station was inaugurated at Dounreay in Caithness in 1954.

Inadequate supply of capital for new enterprise was sometimes deplored. Industrial finance companies however developed, especially in Glasgow, and there were several Scottish Investment Trusts and Fixed Unit Trusts. Between 1950 and 1955 about 3,750 limited companies were floated, with a total capital of £126 million. These were mainly private companies with capital of less than £5,000. There was a growth of holding companies, investing in real estate as well as industry.

The Co-operative movement continued to invest surplus capital in buying enterprises, e.g. a jute factory and an aerated-water works ; it specialised in the acquisition of hotels and restaurants and in holiday services. Some marketing schemes were launched in the Highlands. A few local amalgamations took place, but fusion of the S.C.W.S. with the (English) C.W.S. was rejected. There were about 200 retail societies with 1¼ million members and £24 million share capital.

In transport the chief features were the development of air services and ports, and the expansion of road transport. The consequent need of road improvements and of road bridges over the Forth and Tay and of a Clyde tunnel produced much agitation but little result until the end of the decade.

Tourism was fostered, largely because of its dollar-earning

capacities. Non-Scottish visitors were reckoned as about one-half of holidaymakers ; one-tenth came from overseas, bringing in £40 million to £50 million per annum. Organised coach tours were popular. The Scottish Tourist Board, a voluntary body, was formed in December 1945 under the chairmanship of Thomas Johnston, who retired from political life at the end of the War. Scarcity of staffs and limitation of hours imposed by the Catering Board under the Act of 1943 handicapped hotels and restaurants and encouraged the vogue of the self-service snack bar.

In agriculture total output increased considerably, attaining in the early 'fifties over 50 per cent above the pre-war figure. Tillage declined slightly from the war-time maximum ; livestock and dairy farming expanded ; cattle were reared for milk rather than beef. The Agriculture (Scotland) Act of 1948 continued control, including Agricultural Executives (whose disciplinary powers were abolished in 1958) and Wage Regulation. Price and market guarantees were retained, and their administration was, on the demise of the Ministry of Food in 1955, transferred to the Secretary of State. Yet another was added to the list of Agricultural Holdings Acts in 1949 ; this gave L.A.'s power to acquire land for the purpose. Shortage of labour was only temporarily and slightly relieved by the use of European " displaced persons " ; the employment of school children for the potato harvest continued, and was the subject of sharp controversy because of alleged injury to their education. Public assistance was given for drainage and reclamation. Long-term loans were available through Scottish Agricultural Securities Corporation. Co-operative schemes developed, e.g. in the Orkneys and the Western Isles.

Afforestation was further pursued. An Act of 1945 established a Scottish Committee of the Forestry Commission and transferred acquisition of land to the Secretary of State. The Commission held over 1 million acres, and added to its properties, e.g. the Glenlivet estate (Banff) of 120,000 acres, against some opposition on aesthetic and agricultural grounds. Over $10\frac{1}{2}$ million trees were planted between 1939 and 1953. Private landowners undertook " dedication " agreements to engage in planting ; by 1955, 272 such schemes were in operation, covering over 200,000 acres.

In the fisheries the policy of organised marketing was continued by Acts of 1950 and 1953, and grants were given for replacement of obsolete vessels, etc. The herring fishery was helped by a scheme for the conversion of surplus catch to oil and meal, operated from 1948 by the Herring Industry Board, with a government subsidy. Oil began to supersede steam as motive power for trawlers. Large-scale combines grew. Disputes with Norway and Iceland over " territorial waters " attracted much attention ; the Hague Court in 1951 decided in favour of Norwegian claims.

Turning to some economic trends of the period, several Scottish firms, especially in engineering, established or acquired overseas subsidiaries ; e.g. William Baird & Co., deprived by nationalisation of much of their original interests, invested in West African mining. Conversely, there was a growth of American investment and enterprise in Scotland, particularly in the newer types of industry in industrial estates—e.g. Edisons, Hoovers, Remington-Rand. Investment Trusts which had formerly held much capital in America had passed into American hands during the two wars ; the process was virtually completed when the Matador Land and Cattle Co. of Dundee was taken over by a New York firm in 1950. The International Nickel Co. and Massey-Harris, producers of tractors, were among the large American concerns which established factories in Scotland. Perhaps the most spectacular instance was the purchase of the leading Edinburgh paper, *The Scotsman*, for generations a family organ, by a Canadian magnate, who also became interested in Commercial Television.

The progress of English enterprise and investment in Scotland continued rapidly. Among English firms which undertook productive activities in Scotland were Rolls-Royce, the India Tyre and Rubber Co., Salt of Saltaire (woollens), Summers of Glossop (cottons), Hector Powe (clothiers) and Boots Pure Drug Co.

Among acquisitions of Scottish businesses may be mentioned that of the Albion Motor Co., the only Scottish survivor in the industry, by the Leyland Co. ; of the old Edinburgh family enterprises of Gibson (grocers) by Littlewood, Allan (boot-makers) by Jones of Northampton, Saxone by Lilley and Skinner, Darling and other outfitters by Great Universal

Stores (dominated by the financier Isaac Wolfson) ; of the remaining independent tobacco manufacturers, Dobie of Paisley and Thomson & Porteous of Edinburgh by Godfrey Phillips ; of Arrol's Brewery (Alloa & Glasgow) by Ind Coope & Allsops, and of the main Edinburgh firms by Northern Breweries. Greater notoriety was given to the acquisition of the Scottish Motor Traction Co. (1956), after a contest with Hugh Fraser, the Glasgow Drapery magnate, by another financier, Clore of Sears Holdings ; and to the transfer of the independent Socialist weekly *Forward* to a company associated with " Transport House " (1956).

Some firms located in Scotland extended their control within its bounds and even beyond. The House of Fraser, under the direction of Hugh Fraser, bought up several firms in Glasgow and elsewhere, acquired from Debenhams two-thirds of the Ordinary shares in the Scottish Drapery Corporation and the whole capital of Binns, and thus obtained a large degree of monopoly in the retail drapery trade. Blackwood Morton and Sons, carpet manufacturers of Kilmarnock, and Donaldsons Textiles Ltd., Alloa, had subsidiaries in England and overseas. The D.C.L., sometimes in association with the British Petroleum Co., expanded its concern with various branches of the chemical industry and in rayon and plastics. The I.C.I., whose successive chairmen were Scots, was also linked with the great oil companies in activities at Grangemouth and elsewhere, and reckoned ninety-five subsidiaries. Darling & Co., before being merged in Great Universal Stores, had entered the book trade by controlling Robert Grant & Son and Wm. Brown of Edinburgh. John Menzies & Co. absorbed leading booksellers in Edinburgh and Dundee. The Scottish Mercantile Investment Co. unified the leading shipyards of Burntisland and Aberdeen.

The device of the interlocking directorate gave much industrial power and prestige to men like Lord Bilsland, Sir William Wallace and two ex-Lord Provosts of Edinburgh, Sir William Y. Darling and Sir Andrew Murray.

Social conditions were marked by a growth of population and a tendency to rising birth-rate. The continued ravages of tuberculosis, and the apparent increase of cancer and thrombosis, were the chief menaces to health and longevity.

Relatively full employment was maintained, though often felt to be somewhat precarious, and the validity of the Keynesian techniques of fiscal control was not seriously tested. Unemployment figures ranged higher than in England, and some degree of " concealed unemployment " was suspected, through the uneconomic distribution of labour in some industries, and the continuance of conscription, which levied a toll of nearly 20,000 a year though averaging only 60 per cent of those registered.

The official policy of collaboration was largely maintained by trade unions ; until 1956, when serious friction developed in the heavy industries, most of the disputes, particularly numerous in coal and road transport, were small-scale and unofficial. The non-recognition of trade unionism by the Thomson-Leng press provoked conflict and litigation in 1952.

Trade-union membership grew in numbers to nearly 900,000. Nearly half of these were in the four cities ; the metal working, building and distributive trades were those most effectively organised.

Among social aspects may be noted the growth of voluntary associations, and of Community Centres ; many of the former were federated in the Scottish Council of Social Service (1943). The Iona Community, under Dr. George Macleod, became an active social force and attained recognition by the Church of Scotland.

The Highland Folk Museum established by Dr. Isabel Grant was taken under the trusteeship of the Scottish Universities in 1954 ; and a Lowland equivalent was formed at Forfar in 1953 by Lady Maitland, later transferred to Glamis. There was considerable expansion of National Parks, the fourth, in the Loch Vennachar area, being constituted in 1954 ; several areas were declared Nature Reserves.

The Glasgow Citizens' Theatre, founded in 1943, largely at the instance of James Bridie, received financial aid from the Corporation, and was able to obtain larger premises ; it specialised in Scottish plays. The Wilson Barrett Co. from 1940 to 1955 provided repertory seasons in Edinburgh and Glasgow. In Edinburgh the Little Theatre provided a home for amateur companies until 1961, and the Gateway, under the auspices of the Church of Scotland, a small repertory company as well. Local repertory theatres arose with varying success in several towns, notably Perth, Dundee and St. Andrews. The annual Edinburgh Festival was inaugurated in 1947 and proved a commercial success in the attraction of visitors. The " Fringe " which developed around it did more for Scottish culture than the official programme with its cosmopolitan bias ; the revival of the *Satire of the Three Estates* was the exception. Local festivals and pageants—e.g. Arbroath, Musselburgh—were frequent, especially during the " Festival of Britain " year (1951). A festival theatre was started at Pitlochry to cater for summer visitors to the Highlands. The Scottish Community Drama Association continued to flourish.

The Saltire Society and the Stair Society promoted interest in Scottish literature, art and law. The Edinburgh University School of Scottish Studies was formed in 1950 and concentrated on linguistic research. The *Scottish Historical Review* was revived in 1947 under the editorship of Professor Croft Dickinson. The Scottish Economic Society was refounded with a quarterly *Scottish Economic Journal* (1954).

The Scottish Nationalist movement was encouraged by reaction against centralised control, particularly of nationalised enterprise, and by neglect of such Scottish interests as the projected Forth Road Bridge. Scottish Convention held several national assemblies and promoted the signing of a Covenant demanding devolution (1949). The Scottish National Party continued to fight elections national and local, with occasional success in the latter. There were a few splinter groups such as Scottish National Congress.

The special problems of the Highlands evoked much consideration. An Advisory Highland Panel was set up in 1947. The crofting system was again investigated, and on the Report of the Taylor Commission (1954) legislative action was taken, modifying conditions of tenure, and giving executive powers to a new Crofters' Commission.

EPILOGUE

THE REPORT of the Toothill Committee (November 1961), appointed in 1959 by the Scottish Council, gives a useful survey of the Scottish economy at the beginning of the 'sixties, and affords a convenient stopping-point. Its eighty-one recommendations include the establishment of a new Department to co-ordinate government activities in Scotland,[1] encouragement of industrial expansion on a regional basis rather than in Development Areas, improved transport and industrial training and technical education.

The story of the past few years has in the main been in sharp contrast with the full employment and rising output of the Affluent Age in other parts of Britain. The shale-mining industry has virtually come to an end. Coal-mines have been closed, especially in Lanarkshire, the life even of some of the more modern ventures in the East has been rendered precarious. While some modernisation has taken place in the construction of marshalling yards and the introduction of diesel services and the electrification of Glasgow local lines, closure of branch lines and minor stations has severely curtailed transport of passengers and goods, and much larger " cuts ", especially in the North, are threatened. The Forth and Clyde Canal has been closed to traffic. The motor bus has almost entirely superseded the electric tram for municipal services and the train for local and rural services, thus making Scotland increasingly dependent on imported sources of power. To cope with increased road transport, the Forth Bridge and the Clyde tunnel are belatedly under construction.

Shipbuilding again yields ground to foreign competition. Textiles suffer from tariff and other restrictions in overseas markets as well as from heavy cost of imported materials. The old dyeing industry of the Vale of Leven has been extinguished. The relative decline of conventional arms has enforced the closure of munition works, docks, etc.—e.g. Greenock, Dalmuir,

[1] A Scottish Development Department was set up in April 1962 as part of a reorganisation of Scottish central administration.

Irvine and Cairnryan, for which the much disputed Polaris station in the Holy Loch and N.A.T.O. bases elsewhere afford meagre economic compensation.

Most of the " new " industries are of extraneous origin, and as subsidiaries are liable to supersession, as has already occurred in some cases, notably the rayon factory at Jedburgh. The most important large-scale enterprise in the motor industry (the B.M.C. factory at Bathgate) is an example of the " durable consumers' goods " type, for which demand is notoriously fluctuating, and in this case may already be reaching its peak.

Under the Local Employment Act (1960) financial stimulus for new industries has been more widely extended, to include most industrial areas in Scotland ; some sixty applications have been approved, grants to Scotland constituting over one-half the total sum.

More " New Towns " are planned, mainly under private auspices, in Fife and in the Glasgow area, but the experience of those already in operation is not encouraging. Grange-mouth remains almost the sole example of a " boom " town, rapidly expanding. The proliferation of estate companies, some emerging from industrial concerns—e.g. Argyll Securities —supplanting the private landlord, has increased the costs of building in grandiose redevelopment schemes. Glasgow Corporation, in addition to large-scale rebuilding within its own bounds, has promoted schemes for transfer of " surplus " population and even factories to other burghs as far afield as Haddington.

The " take-over bid " proceeds apace, and several old and famous Scottish firms have been merged in new financial holding companies. The prospective effects of entry into the European Common Market are much debated, and may well affect different industries in varied fashion. Agriculturalists are particularly concerned about probable reduction of State support.

Labour unrest has been intensified, partly by claims to maintain " differentials " in wage rates under conditions of inflation, partly by demarcation disputes resulting from the introduction of new techniques ; the menace of reduced employment through closures of mines and railways has stimulated the chronically militant outlook of trade unionists in these industries.

Thus the post-war years have witnessed an apparent diminution of Scotland's already attenuated economic identity, and at the same time a growing consciousness of distinctive national features.

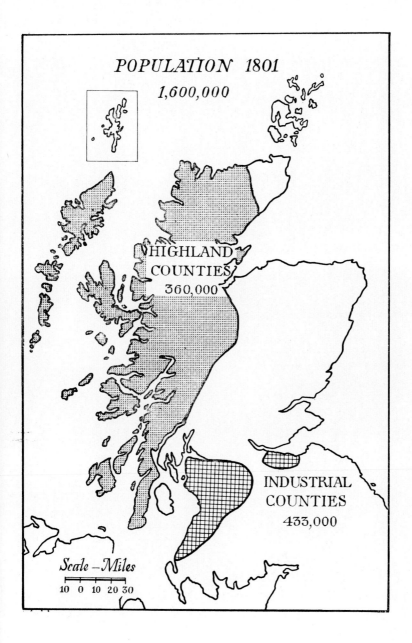

POPULATION 1801
1,600,000

HIGHLAND
COUNTIES
360,000

INDUSTRIAL
COUNTIES
433,000

Scale – Miles
10 0 10 20 30

INDUSTRIES & OCCUPATIONS

CHIEF CENTRES

VICTORIAN ERA

Crofting

Crofting

Sheep

Fishing

Cattle

Paper

Granite

Sheep

Linen

Crofting

Jute

Distilling

Coal, Linoleum

Iron, Steel,
Shipbuilding. Shale

Brewing

Coal, Paper

Sugar, Engineering.

Coal, Iron, Carpets.

Tweeds

Dairy

Lead

Sheep

Hosiery

Farming

Scale — Miles

10 0 10 20 30

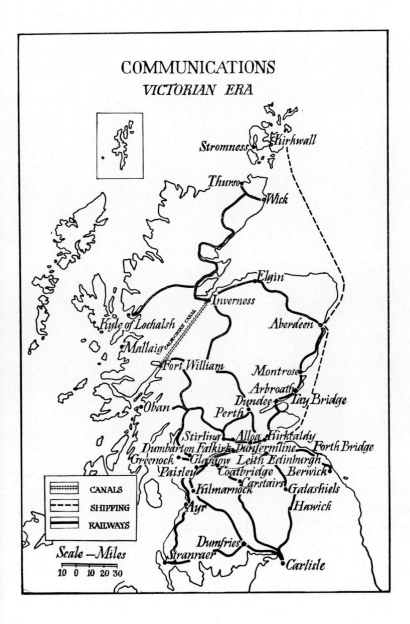

COMMUNICATIONS
VICTORIAN ERA

Stromness • Kirkwall

Thurso • Wick

Elgin

Inverness

Kyle of Lochalsh • Aberdeen

Mallaig

Fort William

Montrose

Arbroath

Oban • Dundee • Tay Bridge

Perth

Stirling • Alloa • Kirkcaldy

Dumbarton • Falkirk • Dunfermline • Forth Bridge

Greenock • Glasgow • Leith • Edinburgh

Paisley • Coatbridge • Berwick

Carstairs

Kilmarnock • Galashiels

Ayr • Hawick

Dumfries

Stranraer • Carlisle

CANALS
SHIPPING
RAILWAYS

Scale — Miles
10 0 10 20 30

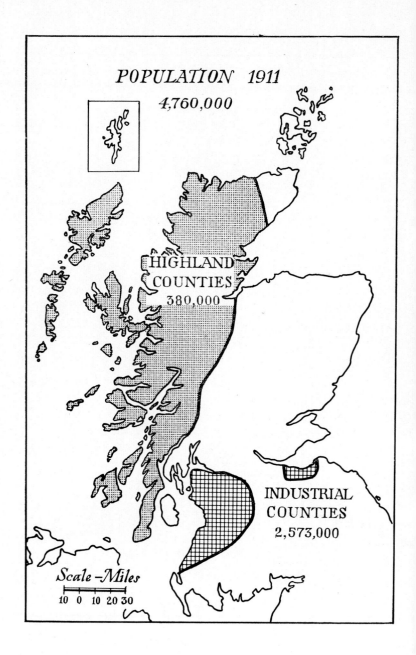

POPULATION 1911
4,760,000

HIGHLAND
COUNTIES
380,000

INDUSTRIAL
COUNTIES
2,573,000

Scale –Miles
10 0 10 20 30

BIBLIOGRAPHY

Full annotated bibliographies of Scottish economic history are contained in my articles in the *Economic History Review*, Vol. III, No. 1 (Jan. 1931), and Vol. IV, 2nd. ser., No. 3 (1952), the latter covering works published during the intervening twenty years. A third article, comprising works published in the last decade, awaits publication. P. D. Hancock's *Bibliography of Works Relating to Scotland, 1916–50* (2 vols. 1959–60) includes many economic items. Here only some of the most important works utilised in this study are cited.

The only works on the whole economic history of Scotland, *The Social & Industrial History of Scotland*, by J. Mackinnon (2 v. 1920–1), and I. F. Grant's *Economic History of Scotland* (1934) have been supplemented on many points by subsequent study of the last two and a half centuries. The latest general history of modern Scotland, *Scotland from 1603*, by G. S. Pryde (1962), gives much attention to the economic aspects.

I. THE EARLY EIGHTEENTH CENTURY

H. G. Graham's *Social Life of Scotland in the Eighteenth Century* is a classic ; it is in some respects superseded by J. E. Handley's *Scottish Farming in the Eighteenth Century* (1953) and Marjorie Plant's *Domestic Life of Scotland in the Eighteenth Century* (1952). Professor H. Hamilton's long-expected survey of the century was published while this was in the press. Dr. I. F. Grant has illustrated Highland life in her *Everyday Life on a Highland Farm* (1924) and *Highland Folkways* (1961) ; the *Drove Roads*, by A. R. B. Haldane (1952), deals particularly with the growth of the cattle trade.

The most modern treatment of the economic aspects of the Union of 1707 is in G. S. Pryde's *Treaty of Union* (1950) and A. M. Carstairs' article in the *Scottish Journal of Political Economy* (Feb. 1955).

II. THE PERIOD OF REVOLUTION

The Old Statistical Account, edited by Sir John Sinclair (21 v. 1790–5), is the indispensable source for later eighteenth-century Scotland.   For agriculture it is supplemented by various County Reports and *Sinclair's General Report* (1814).   Rosalind Mitchison's *Agricultural Sir John* (1962), a definitive biography of Sinclair, depicts his varied contributions to Scottish economic development.   Among contemporary writings, J. Anderson's *Observations on National Industry* (1777), D. Loch's *Essays on the Trade of Scotland* (3 v. 1773), J. Naismith's *Thoughts on Industry in Scotland* (1790), R. Heron's *Journey Through the Western Counties* (2 v. 1793) and R. Forsyth's *Beauties of Scotland* (5 v. 1805–8) contain useful material.   A thorough treatment of the situation in the Highlands is afforded by Malcolm Gray's *Highland Economy* (1957) ; and some chapters of J. A. Symon's *Scottish Farming* (1959) deal with the agricultural revolution in the Lowlands.

H. Hamilton's *Industrial Revolution in Scotland* (1932) is still the standard work on industrial change.   D. F. Macdonald's *Scotland's Shifting Population 1750–1850* (1937) also more slightly outlines industrial development.   The most important studies of particular industries are A. J. Warden's *History of the Linen Trade* (1864), J. U. Nef's *Rise of British Coal Industry* (1932), Vol. I, Part 1, A. & N. Clow's *The Chemical Revolution* (1952) and R. H. Campbell's *Carron Company* (1961).

H. W. Dickinson's *James Watt* (1936) and L. C. T. Rolt's *Thomas Telford* (1958) are valuable biographies of leading engineers ; A. R. B. Haldane's *New Ways Through the Glens* (1961) is also largely devoted to the latter.   A. W. Kerr's *History of Banking in Scotland* (1884, revised by F. H. Allan 1926) and W. Graham's *One Pound Note in Scotland* (1886) are standard works on banking ;   histories of the chief banks have also appeared.

III. THE VICTORIAN AGE

D. Bremner's, *The Industries of Scotland* (1869), gives a unique presentation of their growth and condition in the mid-Victorian era.   My *Economic Developments in Victorian Scotland* (1937) gives the results of research on several aspects of the period, and includes a classified list of sources. The brilliant work of L. Saunders, *Scottish Democracy 1815–40* (1950), presents the social structure at the beginning of the era. Recently published works give histories of industries such as sugar and distilling, and a large number, of varied quality, those of individual firms and companies. A few recent local histories —e.g. *The Second City (Glasgow)* by Oakley (1946), *Dunfermline* and *Port-Glasgow*—are serviceable.

T. Johnston's polemical *History of the Working Classes in Scotland* (1920) was a pioneer effort to depict social conditions. These are carefully analysed in T. Ferguson's *Dawn of Scottish Social Welfare* (1948) and *Scottish Social Welfare 1864–1914* (1958). Elizabeth S. Haldane's *Scotland of our Fathers* (1933) is a slighter sketch. R. M. W. Cowan's *Newspaper in Scotland 1815–60* (1946) illustrates many aspects of social development. The Poor Law has been extensively studied ; probably the most satisfactory treatment is in W. Smart's *Memorandum*, included in the *Report of the Poor Law Commission* (1909).

The New Statistical Account (15 v. 1845) is for the mid-nineteenth century as invaluable as the Old for half a century earlier. It is supplemented by numerous local records, especially for the Glasgow area ; and by *Reports of Government Commissions*, e.g. those on *Municipal Corporations* (1835), *Sanitary Conditions of the Labouring Population* (1842), *Poor Law* (1845), *Coal* (1871), *Crofters* (1883). The structure and functions of Local Government are delineated in Mabel Atkinson's *Local Government in Scotland* (1904), S. H. Turner's *History of Local Taxation in Scotland* (1908) and W. M. Mackenzie's *Scottish Burghs* (1949). The growth of the working-class movement is summarised in my booklet *Labour in Scotland* (1949) ; there are a few works dealing with individual trade unions—e.g. coal-miners, printers, horse- and motor-men ; and a study of *Scottish Chartism*, by L. C. Wright (1953).

IV. TWENTIETH CENTURY

Reference may be made to the *Industrial Survey of South West Scotland* (1932), C. A. Oakley's *Scottish Industry Today* (1937) and *Scottish Industry* (1953), J. A. Bowie's *Future of Scotland*

(1939), *The Scottish Economy* (1954) edited by A. K. Cairncross ; the annual *Government Reports on Scottish Industry and Employment since 1948*, the annual *Survey of Economic Conditions in Scotland* issued by the Clydesdale and North of Scotland Bank, the *Toothill Report of the Scottish Council* (1961), and the volumes of the *Third Statistical Account* so far published.

INDEX